Malcolm MacColl

The Sultan and the Powers

Malcolm MacColl

The Sultan and the Powers

ISBN/EAN: 9783743331891

Manufactured in Europe, USA, Canada, Australia, Japa

Cover: Foto ©ninafisch / pixelio.de

Manufactured and distributed by brebook publishing software (www.brebook.com)

Malcolm MacColl

The Sultan and the Powers

THE SULTAN
AND THE POWERS

BY THE REV.

MALCOLM MacCOLL, M.A.

CANON OF RIPON

'Curse ye Meroz, said the angel of the Lord, curse ye bitterly the inhabitants thereof; because they came not to the help of the Lord, to the help of the Lord against the mighty.'—JUDGES v. 23.

> 'They are slaves who fear to speak
> For the fallen and the weak:
> They are slaves who will not choose
> Hatred, scoffing, and abuse,
> Rather than in silence shrink
> From the truth they needs must think:
> They are slaves who dare not be
> In the right with two or three.
> — LOWELL

LONGMANS, GREEN, AND CO.
LONDON, NEW YORK, AND BOMBAY
1896

All rights reserved

DEDICATED

TO

HIS GRACE THE DUKE OF WESTMINSTER, K.G.

My dear Duke of Westminster,

I take the liberty of dedicating this volume to your Grace as a small token of the admiration and gratitude which I feel for all that you have done for the suffering Christians in the Turkish Empire. When my dear friend, the late Dr. Liddon, and myself returned from South-Eastern Europe in the end of the year 1876, and felt the need of some visible proof of British sympathy for the suffering Christians, your Grace gladly accepted the presidency of an influential committee formed to assist the Russian and other sick and wounded in the war of liberation. And when the massacres in Armenia could no longer be concealed you disregarded your own convenience and, I fear, your health, and readily agreed to become President of the Grosvenor House Committee, which has for its object to aid, in every way open to it, the Armenians and other Christians suffering under Turkish misrule. Under the shadow of the Grosvenor House Committee the Armenian Relief Fund—so admirably organised by its indefatigable Honorary Secretary and Treasurer, Mr. Atkin—has saved the lives of thousands of starving Armenians; and thousands more are still dependent on it for their lives.

Dedication

But while the Grosvenor House Committee has left to the Armenian Relief Fund the management—which it has so well executed—of relieving distress, there is need of another work, that of enlightening the public on the facts of the Eastern question, and the present volume is intended as a small contribution towards that end. As Honorary Secretary, jointly with Mr. Atkin, of the Grosvenor House Committee, I shall deem it an honour as well as a pleasure to be allowed to dedicate the volume to your Grace.

I remain, dear Duke of Westminster, with sincere gratitude and respect,

Yours very truly,

MALCOLM MacCOLL.

MEMBERS' MANSIONS, VICTORIA STREET, S.W.:
November 19, 1896.

PREFACE

The first half of this volume consists of signed articles, revised and enlarged, which I contributed to the *Daily Chronicle* in the end of September and the first half of October. I received numerous letters from all parts of the country, as did also the Editor of the *Daily Chronicle*, urging that they should be republished. On re-reading them for that purpose, I saw that a good deal more was needed to elucidate the subject, and the result is the present volume.

I have tried to be fair all round, and have striven to obey the precept: 'Nothing extenuate, nor set down aught in malice.' It would have been more agreeable to me to praise instead of blaming men whom I admire, and from whom I have received undeserved kindnesses; and I can only plead—*si parva licet componere magnis*—Aristotle's excuse for criticising his great master's doctrine of Ideas. 'Where the interests of truth are actually at stake it is a duty to sacrifice in its defence the most valuable private possession, including precious friendships. Both are alike dear to us; but it is a religious duty to prefer truth.'

In political matters I have generally found myself hitherto in sympathy with the Liberal party. A careful study of the Armenian question has convinced me that the late Government mismanaged it from the beginning, and I have said so, and given my reasons. One of the evils of party Government is the too common tendency to condone in one's political friends what one would condemn, perhaps denounce, in one's political opponents. It seems to me, on the contrary, that one ought to be more severe on the delinquencies of one's own party than on those of the opposite party. First, because one has a right to expect more from it; next, because the exposure of its faults should serve it as a warning in the future. What I have condemned in a Liberal Government I should have condemned in a Conservative Government, and I am not going to belie my convictions in the interest of any party. It is the helpless Armenians, after all, whom I am anxious to help—next to my zeal for the honour of my own country—and I care little for the convenience of any party in comparison, if so be that I succeed ever so little in my endeavour. Politicians and parties will find it easy to survive my criticism; but myriads of innocent Armenians will not survive this winter unless Europe can be roused immediately to the imperative duty of staying the hand of the assassin. He is still busy at his work. The crowds of Armenians whom he has driven from the sight of Europe into the recesses of Anatolia, and the other crowds in Armenia whom he has robbed of their all, are already, according to the latest accounts, 'dying like flies' from cold and starvation; while the children are carried off by the Turks to be brought up as Muslims, in order to recruit the decaying race of their oppressors. The boys will be brought up for service in the Turkish Army, while the girls, on reaching the age of puberty, will be sold as slaves into those unspeakable hotbeds of vice—the harems of dissolute Turks.

And Christian Europe looks on with less concern than on an outbreak of rinderpest among some of its cattle! 'Shall I not visit for these things, saith the Lord? And shall not My soul be avenged on such a nation as this?' And the Sovereigns of Christendom hold familiar intercourse with, and treat as an equal, this man whom their own Ambassadors have twice branded as a wholesale murderer. It may be that the God, whom Christian Europe appears to have practically disowned in this matter, will yet punish the Great Powers by that very scourge, the dread of which has benumbed their consciences and paralysed their strength—a great European war. A little disinterestedness now, and a little common sense and courage, would prevent that dire calamity, the bare possibility of which makes them tremble like chickens at the shadow of a passing bird in the air? This very dread of war is indeed the most damning proof of the selfishness of the Great Powers; for what can cause a great war but the selfishness of the Powers themselves— their greed to grasp what does not belong to any of them; like a band of brigands watching some booty which they dare not seize for fear of quarrelling among themselves over its distribution? It is the most ignoble spectacle that the history of Europe affords. God can afford to be patient, for He has an eternity to work in; but we, creatures of a day, must work in our own way, however humble, until 'this tyranny be overpast.'

There is one Power which, even at this late hour, could save the Armenians without trouble. It is Russia. I have endeavoured to do her justice in this volume, and I received the thanks of the late Tsar for defending Russia in the troubles of 1876-78. Is Russia going to allow the Armenians to be exterminated when one stern word from her would stay the hand of the murderer? England prevented her from saving them eighteen years ago. Is she going to prevent England from saving them now? Would that be a revenge worthy of her great traditions as Protector of the Christians of the East? I will not believe it. England has abjured the past, and will give Russia a free hand now.

CONTENTS

CHAPTER I

CAN NOTHING BE DONE?

Impossibility of stopping agitation on the Armenian Question.—Parallel of the Bulgarian agitation.—Political officials and wirepullers then out of touch with the feeling of the country.—Probably the same now.—What caused the agitation of 1876-78 to become a party organisation.—Mischief caused by Mr. Forster's speech in October 1876 paralleled by Lord Rosebery's speech in Edinburgh on October 9, 1896.—Mistakes made by Lord Rosebery's Government in its management of the Armenian Question.—State of affairs as to Armenia when Lord Salisbury's Government was formed 1–13

CHAPTER II

WHAT ENGLAND CAN DO

Coercion the only effective weapon.—Argument from alleged combination against Britain.—Our treaty rights not likely to be contested by other Powers.—Improbability of war against England.—Russia and Constantinople.—Proposed settlement in 1867.—German and Austrian Press playing a game of chess 14–24

CHAPTER III

MUSULMANS DESIRE EUROPEAN CONTROL

Both Liberals and Tories are to blame: therefore let bygones be bygones, and let there be a fresh start on non-party lines.—Ottoman Empire moribund.—Deposition of the Sultan.—Chronic condition of the Christians of Turkey.—The Sultan not Khalif.—European control desired by Musulman population, provided religion is respected.—Threats of massacre unreal, and not to be regarded.—Put Turkey in commission.—Public opinion abroad.—Withdrawal of British Ambassador 25–38

CHAPTER IV

TIMID COUNSELS

Russia under obligations to Lord Salisbury.—Policy for public meetings.—Advice of Sir Charles Dilke and Lord Rosebery.—Prince Lobanoff's declaration misunderstood.—A material guarantee.—No danger of European war.—'Toujours de l'Audace.'—Duty of Liberals.—Conservatives should welcome the agitation.—Mr. Gladstone's intervention.—Continued inaction impossible . . . 39–49

CHAPTER V

POLICY OF AUSTRIA

War not the object of the agitation, but assurance to the Government that they may rely on the support of the whole nation in any effective steps which they may take for protecting the Armenians.—Press of Vienna.—Count Goluchowski on the massacres.—The Sultan branded as a murderer by the Powers.—Apathy of the Powers encouraged by Austria, backed by Germany.—Lord Salisbury on Austria's policy 50–57

CHAPTER VI

LORD SALISBURY'S RECORD

Mr. Gladstone's resolution and speech (1858) in favour of the union of the Danubian Principalities supported by Lord Salisbury, and opposed by Mr. Disraeli and Lord Palmerston.—Concert of Europe baffled by Roumania.—Lord Salisbury on the Eastern Question in 1877-78.—Lord Salisbury and coercion.—Lord Salisbury's policy: How his policy was defeated.—Lord Beaconsfield's policy in 1877: How it was defeated.—Lord Salisbury and Russia 58–72

CHAPTER VII

LORD SALISBURY AND PRINCE BISMARCK

Instances of separate action by Lord Salisbury and Mr. Gladstone.—Different kinds of separate action.—The division of Bulgaria.—Reunion of divided Bulgaria.—A secret of diplomacy.—Proposed naval demonstration in 1895: Why it did not take place.—England's greatest enemy.—Motives of his enmity 73–83

CHAPTER VIII

PRECEDENTS FOR SEPARATE ACTION

Lord Beaconsfield's plot against Russia in 1877: Its rashness and immorality.—A Russian precedent for separate

action.—European approval of separate action in 1877.—
Separate action defined.—Involves no danger of war.—
Austrian and German designs 84–96

CHAPTER IX

BRITAIN'S TRADITIONAL POLICY

Admission of Turkey into the comity of European nations
in 1856 a blunder and a crime.—Appeal to history.—
Representative British statesmen on Turkey.—Lord
Palmerston on coercion.—Reforms in Turkey impossible without coercion.—Turkish Ministers in 1877 on
coercion 97–108

CHAPTER X

THE NEW POLICY AND ITS CAUSES

Pitt's policy towards Russia.—The triumvirate who
plotted the Crimean War.—Story of Sir Stratford
Canning.—'Massacre of Sinope.'—Anglo-French affront
to Russia.—Unpopularity of the Aberdeen Cabinet.—The
Queen and Prince Consort on Turkey.—Palmerston's
intrigue.—The Prince Consort slandered.—Prince
Consort the first proposer of the 'bag and baggage'
policy.—His policy defeated by Palmerston.—A new
departure initiated by Lord Derby.—Its real author was
Lord Beaconsfield.—Lord Derby's political defects.—
Lord Beaconsfield's ideals 109–126

CHAPTER XI

POLICY OF TSAR NICHOLAS

Russia's desire for a good understanding with England.—
Visit of Nicholas to England.—Nesselrode's Memorandum.—Nicholas on the 'Sick Man.'—Russia and
Constantinople.—England's blunder.—Napoleon the
prime author of the Crimean War.—His reasons.—
France and England should acknowledge their mistake 127–137

CHAPTER XII

ISLÂM AS A RULING SYSTEM

The Turkish Government is a strict theocracy.—Consequent disabilities of Christians.—Mohammedan belief
as to the Koran.—Koran *plus* the traditions constitutes
the immutable sacred law of Turkey.—Disabilities of
Christians.—Taxation of Christians.—A sophism refuted.
—Limit of religious toleration.—Christians cannot be

citizens.—Sultan and India.—The Sultan not Khalif.—Qualifications of Khalif.—Ibn Khaldun on the Khalifat.—Origin of qualification for the Khalifat.—The Khalifat elective.—Indian Musulmans and Turkey.—Extinction of the Khalifat.—Rise of the Ulema to power.—Why coercion of the Sultan is necessary.—Lord Stratford de Redcliffe's error.—Apostasy a capital offence in Turkey.—British ignorance of Turkish law.—Crusade against Islâm repudiated.—Musulman rule inhuman 138–162

CHAPTER XIII

MR. GLADSTONE'S LIVERPOOL SPEECH

Feeling in Ireland on Armenia.—Origin of the agitation.—Consultation with Mr. Gladstone.—Misrepresentation of Mr. Gladstone's speech.—Chief points of his speech . 163–175

CHAPTER XIV

LORD ROSEBERY'S EDINBURGH SPEECH

The speech a surprise.—Author's feeling towards Lord Rosebery.—Effect of Lord Rosebery's speech.—Lord Rosebery on Mr. Gladstone.—Lord Rosebery himself in favour of separate action.—His indictment against the Concert of Europe.—Gospel of material interests *versus* the Gospel of Humanity.—Sir H. Elliot's despatch in 1877.—What are British interests?—Lord Rosebery's change of mind requires explanation 176–191

CHAPTER XV

POLICY OF SEPARATE ACTION CONSIDERED

Lord Rosebery's idea of separate action.—Prerogative of the Sheikh-ul-Islâm.—The Sultan not a free man.—Separate action various.—Interdiction of separate action a dangerous precedent.—Examples of separate action.—Withdrawal of British Ambassador.—Continued diplomatic intercourse may be mischievous.—Sultan's triumph and character.—Suppression of Consular reports.—Lord Rosebery's unfairness to Mr. Gladstone.—Why did Lord Rosebery resign? . . 192–206

CHAPTER XVI

ALLEGED COMBINATION AGAINST ENGLAND

Lord Rosebery's reasons examined.—Language of diplomacy.—Prince Lobanoff interprets himself.—The 'Twenty Floddens' appeal 207–216

CHAPTER XVII

A BAD BEGINNING IN BRITISH POLICY

Sultan begins to organise massacres.—A Turkish 'monster' rewarded by the Sultan.—How to deal with the Sultan.—The Turkish Commission.—Sultan's insult to the British Government: How it was rescued.—Mr. Shipley's report.—The Scheme of Reforms indirect cause of massacres.—Lord Rosebery on the Scheme of Reforms.—Initial mistake.—Why Russia objected.—Separate action suggested by British Government.—Two offers of coöperation by Russia repelled.—Explanation of Prince Lobanoff's policy.—Lord Salisbury's plan.—Paper reforms useless.—'Turkey never changes.'—The clergy and the Eastern Question.—Evils of red-tape diplomacy 217–247

CHAPTER XVIII

THE ARGUMENT OF MASSACRE

The argument of massacre a stale one, and always refuted by events.—Key of the Eastern Question.—A Sultan's 'royal word' tested by facts.—Religious toleration as understood in Turkey.—Various illustrations.—Crescentade by the Sultan.—His triumph over the Concert of Europe.—Selfishness of the Concert.—Austria and the Duke of Wellington 248–268

CHAPTER XIX

CYPRUS AND EGYPT

A good understanding between England and Russia and France desirable.—Vitality of political delusions.—Examples.—Russian invasion of India a superstition.—No motive for such invasion.—Alarming increase of Indian population.—No cause of antagonism with Russia. — The future of Cyprus. — The Porte an organised brigandage.—Anglo-French lien on Cyprus.—British occupation of Egypt paralleled by French occupation of Tunis.—Certain relapse of Egypt under Islamic rule.—What solution will France offer?—Dongola Expedition defended 269–283

CHAPTER XX

CONCLUDING OBSERVATIONS

Duke of Argyll's explanation of the cause of the Crimean War questioned.—*Status quo ante* Crimean War.—Russia's statement of her case.—No new claims made by Russia.—Protectorate exercised by France and England as well as by Russia.—Protectorate by the Concert of Europe tested by results.—Concert of Europe at Dulcigno.—Lord Salisbury on the Concert of Europe. —Inaccurate charge against Mr. Gladstone regarding the Concert of Europe.—An *amende* due to Russia.— Mischief of guaranteeing the *status quo*.—Sultan's power of mischief augmented by the Crimean War.—A forgotten factor in the case.—Nations ruined from within.— A warning by Burke.—Ominous symptoms of decadence.—Conscription not needed to enable England to do her duty.—Military occupation unnecessary.—European control the one need.—Providence needs coöperation of human wills.—True source of national strength.— Critical moments in a nation's life 284-308

Errata.

Page xi, line 22, *for* chess *read* bluff
„ 214, „ 9, *for* from *read* with
„ 220, „ 22, *for* massacres *read* massacre
„ 251, „ 17, *insert* the *before* human
„ 279, „ 7, *for* as *read* than
„ 298, last line, *for* concerns *read* concern

THE SULTAN AND THE POWERS.

CHAPTER I.

CAN NOTHING BE DONE?

THE one or two organs in the Press, which deprecate any agitation against the continued irresponsible rule of the Sultan and his parasites, are doing a bad service to the Government. They might as well try to stop the inflow of the rising tide. Perhaps I may venture to say that I am in a better position than most men to express an opinion on that subject. In conjunction with my lamented friend, Dr. Liddon, I got together an influential but non-partisan committee in 1876, of which the Duke of Westminster was president and the late Marquis of Bath vice-president. We established auxiliary committees all over Great Britain, and I was thus, as honorary secretary of the central committee, put in touch with a series of political nerve-centres outside the range of ordinary politicians. I had piles of letters from country clergymen and quiet squires, who, in sending contributions to the Russian Sick and Wounded Fund, assured me that they longed for the day when they could show their disapproval of Lord Beaconsfield's policy by voting for the first time in their lives against a Tory Government. Very few people on either side of politics had any idea of the disaster that was in store for Lord Beaconsfield's Government. Mr. Gladstone divined it with that magnetic insight which is quicker than reason in placing a leader of men *en rapport* with a great and free people, and acted on his belief while some leading Liberals, judging from parliamentary majorities and the talk of the clubs, thought that Mr. Gladstone was ruining the Liberal party. On the eve of the Midlothian campaign the Liberal whip, Mr. Adam, asked me what I thought of the prospects of the General Election. 'I give the Liberals,' I said, 'a majority of sixty for a minimum and 100 for a maximum.' He thought me almost crazy. 'The utmost I hope for,' he said, 'is to reduce the Government majority to about twenty.' Never, I venture to think, was a great majority more gratuitously thrown away than Lord Beaconsfield's majority in that memorable campaign. The agitation of 1876-77 sprang up spontaneously, like the present agitation. Indeed, it is impossible in a free, self-governed country like ours to get up an agitation on any subject in which the people are not profoundly interested.

At the beginning of the Bulgarian agitation there was no difference between Liberals and Tories. They attended meetings side by side to denounce the massacres perpetrated, or sanctioned, by the present Sultan, who began his novitiate of infamy in Bulgaria. In the early stages of that agitation it received the approval of such distinguished members of Lord Beaconsfield's Government as Lord Salisbury, Lord Cross, the late Lord Carnarvon, and the late Lord Iddesleigh, then Leader of the House of Commons. On September 20, 1876, Lord Beaconsfield made a speech at Aylesbury which fell upon the country like a bolt from the blue. Admitting that 'it would be affectation for him to pretend that he was backed by the country,' he went on to denounce the agitation, and appealed to the British public on the ground of British interests against such 'sublime sentiments' as were uttered at public meetings. The superb courage of that speech must extort the admiration even of the strongest opponents of Lord Beaconsfield's policy. But it set the heather on fire, and stimulated to fever heat an agitation which eventually overwhelmed Lord Beaconsfield, who, with all his ability, did not understand the passion of mingled pity and indignation which sometimes makes a great people dare almost anything in putting down such horrors as those perpetrated by the Sultan and his instruments.

Lord Beaconsfield's speech only stimulated the agitation. Liberals and Conservatives still continued to attend public meetings together. The speech that did the mischief was that delivered by Mr. Forster on his return from Constantinople in October 1876. I travelled home with him from Vienna, and we had much talk on the Eastern question. He expressed himself strongly against Mr. Gladstone's policy, not at all because he feared that it would lead to war, but because he believed that the Bulgarians were not fit for self-government. Centuries of Turkish oppression, he thought, had so cowed and unmanned them that they would not be able to stand up and hold their own against even the small Musulman minority who would still remain among them if Mr. Gladstone's policy of getting rid of the Turkish administration and giving the Bulgarians autonomy were carried out. 'The Musulmans,' he said—I remember the phrase—' would chaw them up in no time.' I ventured to suggest that the air of freedom had a wonderfully invigorating effect, and might be trusted to endow the Bulgarians with manly courage as soon as they had fairly breathed it. And I quoted the opinion of Lord Strangford and other competent authorities. But I could make no impression. Servitude, Mr. Forster thought, was in the blood of the Bulgarians, and it would take a new generation to profit by the autonomy which Mr. Gladstone claimed for them. He spoke in this sense at a great meeting after his return to England, and ended by expressing his confidence in Lord Derby in preference to Mr. Gladstone. The speech had the same effect as Lord Rosebery's, but to a more mischievous degree; for Lord Salisbury's policy now is very different from Lord Derby's in 1876. Mr. Forster's speech encouraged the Sultan to resist all proposals for reform in the provinces which, in Mr. Gladstone's words, he 'had desolated and defiled.' It encouraged Lord Derby in his *laissez-faire* policy. It encouraged the pro-Turkish party to organise an agitation in favour of Turkey, and thus caused a division in the national protest against Turkish misrule.

But it is a great mistake to suppose that there was any reaction in the national mind. On the contrary, the determination to carry out Mr. Gladstone's policy increased in volume, till it returned him to power in 1880 with a majority considerably over 100. The reaction caused by Mr. Forster's speech never penetrated below the surface of national feeling. It influenced, as Lord Rosebery's speech has influenced, the clubs, some journalists and political wire-pullers, and what is called society. Mr. Delane hurried back from Scotland and altered the policy of the *Times*, which had hitherto on the whole supported Mr. Gladstone. Other journals followed suit, and the Jingoes were encouraged to come to the front and organise a counter demonstration. But to cite this as a reaction on the part of the country is a gross error, as the verdict of the constituencies proved when they had an opportunity of recording it.

Similarly, Lord Rosebery's speech — well meant, I have no doubt, like Mr. Forster's—has only intensified the feeling of the country at large in favour of the policy of Mr. Gladstone's Liverpool speech—namely, to give Lord Salisbury a free hand without imposing upon him any of the restrictions with which Lord Rosebery would fetter his discretion. Perhaps I may venture to give two incidental proofs of this. I received the report of Lord Rosebery's speech in the country on the evening of the Saturday after it was delivered. I was engaged to speak at a large meeting in Harrogate on the following Monday, and I determined to test the feeling of the meeting by replying to Lord Rosebery's speech point by point. The Town Hall was crammed with an audience which the Mayor, who was in the chair, estimated at 1,800. I was told that the majority consisted of Liberals. In my dissection of Lord Rosebery's speech I carried the entire audience with me, except one person in the body of the hall and a gentleman on the platform, who, in language courteous and friendly to me, asked the chairman—a strong Radical—to rule me out of order in criticising Lord Rosebery's speech. The chairman refused, with approving cheers from the audience. I proceeded with my speech, and received a unanimous vote of thanks at the close of the meeting. The following Thursday I addressed, with a similar result, a large meeting at Warminster, presided over by Lord Bath. There was one small difference. At Warminster there was not a single dissentient voice, and, when I sat down, the leading Nonconformist minister in the place, an earnest Radical, thinking that my criticism of Lord Rosebery's speech was too gentle, got up and denounced it in vigorous language, amidst the cheers of the audience.

Mr. Forster saw cause to change his opinion. He adopted Mr. Gladstone's policy; and when he returned from a second visit to Bulgaria a few years later he expressed his admiration of the results of the policy which he had himself condemned in 1876, and expressed his surprise that anyone should ever have doubted the fitness of the Bulgarians for freedom; forgetting that he was himself the coryphæus of those sceptics.

The channels of information which served me then serve me now as honorary secretary of the Grosvenor House Committee. We have sources of information with which official politicians are not in touch. The agitation is genuine and spontaneous. It is quite impossible to stop it; the attempt would only stimulate it. But it is possible to guide it. It is not hostile to the

Government, nor need it become hostile. Lord Salisbury is not held responsible for the present situation. His difficulties are recognised, and there is every wish to avoid saying or doing anything which might tend to render his difficult task more difficult still. I did all I could against Lord Beaconsfield's Government in the agitation of 1875-77, and for that very reason I feel all the more bound to do Lord Salisbury justice now. What is his record in this Armenian business? Let us remember that he did not start with a clean slate. He did not originate, he inherited a policy. And what was that policy? My firm conviction is that if the Government of Lord Rosebery had grasped the nettle immediately after they got authentic information of the Sassun massacres they could have settled this matter in friendly co-operation with Russia. Russia was at that time in a most amiable mood towards England. The outburst of British sympathy with the Russian nation in connection with the pathetic circumstances of the late Tsar's death, coupled with the charm of manner and tact of the Prince of Wales on that sad occasion, made a deep impression on the Russian mind.

If the Liberal Government had utilised that favourable moment, I believe it might have come to terms with Russia without the intervention of any other Power. It might have conciliated the *amour propre* of Russia by admitting the failure of the Cyprus Convention and inviting Russia to move troops into Armenia, while the British fleet, if necessary, would occupy Smyrna or some other place agreed upon by the two Powers. The mere threat of such combination would have brought the abject coward of Yildiz Kiosk to his knees. But what happened? Lord Rosebery's Government recommended, even pressed, the Sultan to appoint a purely Turkish Commission of Inquiry. What did they expect a Sultan's Commission to do? Did they really think that its inquiry would be an honest one? Did they not know that the hell of Turkish misrule is paved with the lying reports of Turkish Commissions, whose aim is always to acquit the guilty and damn the innocent? Of course the Sultan wasted weeks over the preliminaries of that Commission, and months over the tragical farce of its inquiry. And meanwhile the Armenians were being harried out of home and honour and life, while the British fleet, cruising off the coast of Asia Minor, instead of menacing the Sultan, was exchanging hospitalities with Turkish pashas. And all this folly did not pass without a solemn warning from Russia, as the following extract from a despatch from the British Ambassador at St. Petersburg will show:—

'His Excellency (Prince Lobanoff) replied that he had never entertained much hope of a satisfactory result [from the Turkish Commission], and he doubted whether the perpetrators of the Sassun massacres would be brought to justice. In his opinion, however, the most important question to be considered was what was to be done when the Commission had finished its labours; and he sincerely hoped that some practical suggestion would be made.'

That was a straightforward invitation to the British Government to come to terms with Russia in regard to Armenia. What was the response? A rebuff of silence. Was not that calculated to raise the suspicion of Russia? But Prince Lobanoff made another attempt to come to terms with England. Russia was seriously alarmed by the sudden collapse of China, and the equally sudden apparition of Japan as a power of the first class. It was not Austria, or Germany, or even France that Russia then invited to co-operate with her in the far East; it was England, with the implied promise of co-operating with England in pacifying Armenia. Again, Russia's offer of co-operation was repelled, with the result that France and Germany were invited to occupy the place which England had refused; that Armenia was ruined; and that Japan got much worse terms than she would have got had we accepted Russia's offer of partnership.

That was the commencement of the isolation of England. Then followed the abortive scheme of reforms, which the Sultan treated with such contempt that for three weeks he would not take the trouble to say whether he approved of it, or even read it. Why was that insolence endured? And the scheme itself? It was not worth the paper on which it was written, as I showed at the time. 'The scheme of reforms,' said the Italian Ambassador in a despatch to his Government—which refused to have anything to do either with the Turkish Commission or with the scheme of reforms—'would be useless.' And he gave excellent reasons for his opinion. Prince Lobanoff described it with perfect accuracy as 'unworkable.' But useless as it was even in its original form, it was made ridiculous by the surrender of the one tolerable thing in it— namely, that a High Commissioner should be appointed for a term of years, subject to the approval of the Powers. This provision would have been of little value so long as the High Commissioner was to be a Musulman and an ordinary subject of the Sultan. 'And this proposal was abandoned,' said the Italian ambassador, 'for the sake of keeping up the *entente* with France and Russia, who recognised the inutility of the scheme.'

Such was the state of affairs when Lord Salisbury took office. His knowledge of Turkish administration showed him at once the fatal flaw in the scheme of reforms—namely, the lack of European control. And he sought to remedy it by the insertion of an effective surveillance, but was naturally met by the objection that he was proposing to upset the scheme of his predecessor. This perfectly futile scheme was at last accepted by the Sultan; in other words, Lord Salisbury carried out the policy of his predecessor at the Foreign Office. Austria and Germany, who had previously refused Lord Kimberley's invitation to coöperate, now insisted on having their fingers in the pie, and the 'Concert of Europe' followed. I have no doubt that when Lord Salisbury uttered his menacing warning to the Sultan there was a scheme of coercion in the air. How it fell through is one of the secrets of diplomacy for the present.

But meanwhile let us face the facts. There is at this moment, I believe, a combination of three Powers—Austria, Russia, and Germany—to resist any action that might imperil the stability of the Turkish Empire; and I suppose that Russia would be likely to carry France. Such then is the plain fact that we have to face. It will not do to talk airily about bombarding Constantinople and hanging the Sultan. That is not practical politics. Can nothing then be done? I believe that something may be done. The resources of British diplomacy are not yet exhausted, nor is England the effete and impotent Power that our continental critics love to paint her. What I have to say further must, however, be reserved for another chapter. It is no use beating the air in public meetings. We must aim at something definite and practicable. Meanwhile do not let us exaggerate the importance of the combination to which I have referred. It aims at upholding the territorial *status quo* in Turkey. It does not follow that it would oppose action which virtually would have the same aim by coercing the Sultan into such conduct as is most likely to prolong the existence of the Ottoman Empire.

CHAPTER II.

WHAT ENGLAND CAN DO.

I SHOULD like to preface the observations which follow with an expression of my opinion that Lord Rosebery's own views and feelings on the Armenian question were much sounder than the deplorable policy pursued by his Government. What occult influence overcame his own better judgment I know not. Why did his Government persistently, almost rudely, refuse to publish its own Consuls' reports from Armenia, thus forcing enterprising journalists to ferret out and publish horrors of which the Government had evidence locked up in the pigeon-holes of the Foreign Office? Lord Beaconsfield's Government at least published the facts, even in the darkest days of the Bulgarian agitation, except in one instance, where Lord Derby suppressed some Consular reports and a despatch from Sir Henry Elliot charging the Sultan with allowing his officials in Bosnia to perpetrate 'horrors,' including impalements, which, says the Consul's report, ' are matters of almost daily occurrence here.' Why did Lord Rosebery's Government almost force the Sultan to appoint a Turkish Commission to inquire into the truth of the reports sent by British Consuls from Armenia? Did they think the Sultan's creatures more trustworthy than their own Consuls? And why, after wasting six months of precious time, did their protracted deliberations result in the elaboration of a scheme of reforms for Armenia which was, in plain language, an imposture? A Liberal Government will be in office some day again, and may possibly have to deal with some other phase of the Eastern question. Let it take warning from the disastrous failure of the last Liberal Government, and understand that the only rational policy is prompt coercion. No Sultan has ever yielded, or ever will yield, or ever can yield, to any other argument in the case of reforms which would violate the unchangeable theocratic law of the Turkish Empire by putting the non-Musulman subjects of the Sultan on a footing of equality with the Musulmans. Do nothing, or use the only effective argument—coercion. Let the Powers, or any one of them, with the acquiescence of the rest, or even of a majority, formulate a plan, offer it to the Sultan with a plain intimation that its rejection will be followed by coercion, and success is certain. But mere argument, 'representations,' 'admonitions'—anything short of 'Do it or I'll make you'—might just as well be addressed to the unhearing winds. Any reform which lacks European control is of necessity an imposture, and no Sultan will accept European control without coercion. Therefore I repeat my formula: Leave it all alone, or use the only effective weapon.

Let us now see whether anything really effective can be done to prevent the Sultan from carrying out his policy of exterminating the Armenians. According to my information, which I believe to be good, Prince Lobanoff and Count Goluchowski at their recent interview in Vienna mutually pledged each other to uphold the Turkish Empire to the best of their ability, but without making any provision for safeguarding the rights of the Sultan's Christian subjects. Germany has joined this combination to hand over some millions of Christians for an indefinite time to the tender mercies of Ottoman thraldom. I believe that France has not joined yet, and I trust that she will refuse to fix so dark a stain on her historical escutcheon. But let us include her in the pro-Turkish league, for the sake of argument. Italy, which has behaved right nobly all through the Armenian troubles, has nothing to do with the fatal policy of leaving things alone, and she would certainly sympathise with any action on behalf of the Armenians by England; but I will not assume her active co-operation. What, then, could England do alone to put an end to the pandemonium to which the arch-criminal of Yildiz Kiosk has reduced his empire? There are various alternatives, and I will begin with the most formidable and drastic. We have a treaty with the Sultan which gives us, I believe, a right to insist on reforms in his Asiatic possessions. In the Cyprus Convention England acquired 'a right to insist on satisfactory arrangements' for reforms as 'an indispensable part' of the Convention. In a despatch from M. Waddington to the French Ambassador in London, dated July 21, 1878, the French Government admitted that by the Cyprus Convention England had 'acquired a right to intervene henceforth actively in the administration of all the territories of Asia subject to Ottoman jurisdiction.' I am not aware that any other Power has protested against or disputed the right which France has thus so explicitly admitted. The right was tacitly allowed by the Berlin Congress, to which the Cyprus Convention was made known, though not formally communicated.

We have thus unquestionably a separate treaty right 'to insist' on the Sultan carrying out his engagements under the Cyprus Convention. But Great Britain has an additional right, in common with the other Powers, in the 61st Article of the Treaty of Berlin. On June 11, 1880, an Identic Note was presented to the Sultan by the Ambassadors of the Great Powers, calling his attention to the fact that he had done 'nothing' to fulfil his obligations. The British

Note was signed by Mr. Goschen as special Ambassador for England, and contains the following words :—' Her Majesty's Government, therefore, as one of the signatory Powers of the Treaty of Berlin, must demand the complete and immediate execution of Article 61 of that treaty,' &c. In this document, then, the six Powers claim, unitedly and severally, the right to enforce on the Sultan the fulfilment of his obligations.

England has thus a twofold legal right to coerce the Sultan, and to adopt any measures for that purpose which do not touch the rights of any other Power. Let us suppose, then, that England calls upon the Sultan to accept, for his Asiatic provinces, such European control as may suffice to guard the rights of the Christians, giving Russia singly, or in union with the other Powers, liberty to settle the character of the control, with an intimation to the Sultan that, on his refusal, the British Fleet will occupy some Turkish port as a material guarantee. Can any one doubt that the Sultan would yield at once? Mr. Goschen will not doubt it, for by a similar action he compelled the speedy submission of the Sultan in 1880, though Germany, Austria, and France refused to sanction it. Is it conceivable that any of the Powers would make war on England in a case where she had the right so distinctly on her side, and in a cause which appeals so strongly to the conscience of civilised mankind, and from which she would reap no material advantage? I cannot believe it. But let me assume for the sake of argument that the three Northern Powers would refuse to sanction the action of England. (I exclude France, for she has publicly admitted the right of England to intervene single-handed, as I have shown.) Look at the risk to them of conduct equally insane and inane. Is there the least likelihood that the three Northern Powers would translate their refusal to sanction into a declaration of war, after the British Government had given them satisfactory assurances that this country had no private or selfish objects, but, on the contrary, aimed at the same end as themselves, though with a better promise of success than the impotent policy which has hitherto prevailed? That any of the Powers, still less all of them, should meet so reasonable a proposal with an immediate declaration of war is a vagary more befitting the phantasms of political mythology than the sober reflections of rational statesmen. The nightmare which lies upon them all is the premature (for them) dissolution of the Turkish Empire. England could bring the rotten structure down about their ears in a week. And where would they be then? At each other's throats, with England quietly looking on. When that day of Armageddon comes, the Powers which now amuse themselves by jeers at England's isolation will need all their fleets and armies to settle their own quarrels instead of combining in fraternal union against England. The possession of the Holy Places in Palestine will test to the quick the Franco-Russian alliance. Germany, too, has of late years been acquiring large pecuniary interests in Asia Minor and Syria, and both Russia and France will have to reckon with her when the scramble has begun for the Sick Man's possessions. Then there is Constantinople, on which both Russia and Austria have their eyes. It is Bismarck's policy which still dominates the German Foreign Office, and one of the cardinal points of that policy is to make of Austria a great Slav Power, with Constantinople for her capital, as a counterpoise to Russia; the German population of Austria being annexed to the German Empire. The claims have also to be considered of Greece, Servia, Roumania, and Bulgaria, with their considerable forces; while Italy has not relinquished her idea of an 'Italia Irredenta.'

And the three Northern Powers are to run the risk of all this cataclysm, which would be the inevitable result of trying, *vi et armis*, to prevent England from enforcing single-handed—without any risk to the territorial *status quo*—the fulfilment, from which she would derive no benefit, of a treaty to which they have all affixed their signatures! That is what their Press tells us. It is all brag and bluster. See how Lord Salisbury's refusal the other day to sanction the blockade of Crete, instead of combining the European Concert against him, forced them to adopt his policy, which they would now fain claim as their own.* So it would be in Asiatic Turkey. Is France going to join in a war against England in order to aggrandise Germany? Or Germany, in order to strengthen France? Or Austria and Russia, in order to precipitate between them a race for the possession of Constantinople? There is not one of the Powers which are now supposed to have combined against England, which would not gladly purchase the alliance of England with a heavy bribe. But instead of wanting bribes England has more to offer than any other Power. The possession of Constantinople, for instance, has come to be recognised as a matter of no consequence to British interests. If Russia were to turn her back on Austria's cruel policy and revert to her old *rôle* of protecting the Christians of Turkey, I do not believe that it would be possible to get up a single public meeting in this country to protest against

---

* Since this was written the Russian Press has changed its tone, and its leading organs advocate a friendly understanding with England. What is still more remarkable, the *Novosti* and *Bishevoi Viedomost* have both declared that 'the granting of autonomy to Crete is solely due to England, whilst the conduct of her statesmen towards the Sultan compares very favourably with that of the Emperor William or of Count Goluchowski, who desire Crete to be crushed out of political existence.' This confirms what I have said elsewhere, namely, that the great sinner in this matter has been Austria, with Germany at her back. It is also a decisive testimony to the signal success of 'separate action' by Lord Salisbury.

Russia's possession of Constantinople; if (which I doubt) she desires it. Hitherto we have been wasting blood and treasure to pull the chestnuts out of the fire for Germany and Austria, and they have thus very cleverly got us to push Russia away from Constantinople towards our Indian frontier. If Russia is to be kept out of Constantinople, it is the interest of Germany and Austria, not ours, to keep her out. An Austrian journal, which is really the property of the Turkish Government, has been trying of late to inflame Russia against England, by accusing us of aiming at the possession of Constantinople under a mask of zeal on behalf of the Armenians. Very good. Let the matter be brought to the test. Let Lord Salisbury propose to the Powers a self-denying ordinance pledging themselves not to acquire a rood of Turkish territory in any measure which they may agree to enforce on the Sultan for the amelioration of his Christian subjects. We shall then see which of the Powers are most sincere in their professions of disinterestedness in this matter.

One of the most extraordinary facts connected with this question is the almost preternatural stupidity of the Powers, who think that they are likely to prolong the existence of the Turkish Empire by allowing the criminal maniac at Yildiz Kiosk to pursue the conduct which is most likely to bring about the very catastrophe, the mere shadow of which seems to have upset their mental equilibrium. Surely it requires very little intelligence to see that the most likely way to prolong the framework of the Turkish Empire is to compel the Sultan to make life tolerable for his subjects. And this has hitherto been the policy of the Great Powers. Let me give an example from each of the Powers who are most interested in preventing the sudden disruption of Turkey—Austria and Russia. In 1867 Count Beust, then Prime Minister of Austria, declared that Austria wished to encourage among the Christian population of Turkey 'a wider development of their privileges, and to promote the establishment of a system of autonomy, *to be limited only by a tie of vassalage.* This, moreover, would be the surest means of making lasting peace between the Sultan and the Rayahs.' In a subsequent despatch Count Beust proposed 'a medical consultation' of the Great Powers 'on the condition of the Sick Man and the distribution of his territory'; suggesting the necessity of 'heroic remedies,' beginning with the annexation of Crete to Greece. In that year Prince Gortchakoff advocated the same policy, and expressed his opinion that 'the only possible escape open to the Powers from the course of expedience and palliatives, which up to the present had but served to increase the difficulties,' was to promote 'the gradual development of autonomous States' among the Christian population of Turkey. The French Government cordially supported Count Beust's policy, while England alone opposed it. This is the very policy which Russia and Austria have now, it is said, combined to prevent by force of arms. I cannot believe that Russia is partner in a scheme which would imply the policy not of statesmen but of lunatics.

So much for my first suggestion as to what I consider feasible in this crisis. I believe that the anti-English Press of Germany and Austria is playing a game of bluff. England has, in other days, stood alone against a world in arms, and she is not now going to cringe and cower before the swashbucklers of the Continental Press, who would soon begin to sing another tune if England took them at their word. I have hope that Lord Salisbury will be able to bring the other Powers to reason on the Armenian as he did on the Cretan question. But everything depends on his being backed up loyally by the country. His record on the Eastern question is but little understood. I hope to find time to give a summary of it later, as well as to suggest some additional means of suppressing the homicidal amusements of Abdul Hamid.

CHAPTER III.

MUSULMANS DESIRE EUROPEAN CONTROL.

I TRUST that in all meetings on this subject no attempt will be made in resolutions or otherwise to dictate any specific policy to the Government. The choice of effective means must be left to the Government, and if the meetings are to do good instead of harm, their aim must be to show foreign nations that Lord Salisbury will have the whole country, without distinction of party, at his back in putting an end to the inhuman orgies in which the contemptible miscreant of Yildiz Kiosk has been allowed too long to indulge. Let there be no criticisms or recriminations about the past. Let bygones be bygones henceforth on all sides. Both parties—*i.e.* the whole nation—are grievously to blame for the insane endeavour for half a century to protect a moribund and foul tyranny against the inevitable Nemesis of its own incurable vices. The Ottoman Empire has now arrived at that pass so tersely described by the Roman historian. It can no longer endure either its vices or their remedies. It can no more be vitalised into a new lease of life than could the mesmerised semi-defunct corpse in Edgar Poe's hideous tale. Not all Germany's horses nor all Austria's men can put Humpty-Dumpty on the wall again; and if they are wise in their own interests they will join England in helping to provide a bloodless euthanasia in lieu of a violent dissolution for the most infamous despotism which Providence has ever permitted to afflict mankind. How to provide that euthanasia is the subject of our present discussion. I have suggested one method, which still seems to me the best. Propose a self-denying ordinance to the other Powers, and convince Russia especially that England has no *arrière-pensée* in this matter, and I believe the Northern Powers will find their interest in acting with Lord Salisbury instead of against him in saving the political framework of the Turkish Empire for some years to come. And let the remedy include not Armenia only, but all the disturbed regions of the Turkish Empire. Let Governors be appointed under the control of the Powers, with force enough to keep order, and of course with due regard to the circumstances of each place.

It would probably be best to let Russia administer Armenia under the nominal rule of the Sultan, as we administer native States in India—*i.e.* under the supervision of a Political Resident. Similar provision might be made for Macedonia, and I believe the Musulmans themselves, outside the official class who batten and fatten on corruption, would welcome such a relief from the intolerable yoke of Abdul Hamid. I doubt whether a hundred Musulmans can be found outside the walls of Yildiz Kiosk who would not rejoice at the deposition of the Sultan, or at the extraction of his claws and fangs. He is detested throughout his empire, over which he has spread a network of espionage which has crushed out all freedom of speech, and almost of thought. In Constantinople and the neighbourhood he is hated and loathed by Christians and Musulmans alike. The Turks are at least a brave race, and they feel humiliated in having over them a wretched coward who trembles at his own shadow. Moreover, they do not believe that he is a Turk at all. The general belief among Musulmans and Christians in Constantinople is that Abdul Hamid is the son of an Armenian menial in Abdul Medjid's service by an Armenian slave girl in that Sultan's harem. Among the Musulmans he is known, *sotto voce*, as 'the Armenian Bastard.' Doubtless this has reached his ears, and it probably accounts in part for his policy of extermination against the Armenians, in the hope of clearing himself in the eyes of his Musulman subjects from any suspicion of favouring his own race. A proposal to depose him would therefore be hailed with satisfaction by the Musulmans, not only on account of his cruel despotism, but also because they believe that he has no legitimate right to the throne.

But apart from the personal aspect of the matter, I believe that the Musulmans would welcome European control, provided they were assured that it would not interfere with their property or religion. The recent massacres have not been the result of local fanaticism; they have all been organised at Yildiz Kiosk. Indeed, all the great massacres in Turkey have been the work of the Government, never of the local population. When you have a dominant caste over a subject race, with no arms and practically no rights, the subject race is sure to be oppressed. Nevertheless, the Christians and Muslims in Turkey would manage to find a rough sort of *modus vivendi* if only the central Government and its host of corrupt and rapacious police and officials would leave them alone. The Government is the *fons et origo malorum*. All suffer from it; but of course the Christians suffer much more than the Musulmans. For, in addition to their being by law unarmed and practically outlaws, they have to pay all the taxes paid by the Musulmans and many more besides; the most cruel tax of all being the 'hospitality tax,' which obliges every Christian subject of the Sultan to provide three days' gratuitous board and lodging for every Musulman official and traveller who demands it. Christian households are hardly ever free from these unwelcome guests, who constantly (though the law does not sanction this) order the men out of the house at nightfall, leaving the women at the mercy of the guests. Our Consular reports are full of harrowing details of this horrible custom. Do journalists who write indignant articles against 'Armenian desperadoes' know the provocation those men have? The *Times's* Special Commissioner in Armenia two years ago declared, after careful inquiry, that in a certain district which he named he believed every woman had thus been outraged before she was married. And what is true of Armenia now was true of Bulgaria down to the day of its liberation, and is true of all the Christian population still subject to the Sultan's rule. It is one of the horrors of Turkish rule of which outsiders hear but seldom, for it is one which the victims naturally desire to conceal. But it overshadows and embitters the daily life of the Christians; and I own that to my mind the chronic condition of these dumb, helpless victims of Turkish brutality is more horrible even than the massacres which have lately drenched the streets of Constantinople with blood. It is not the Musulman rural peasantry who commit these horrors, but the ruffianly police (who live on the Christian inhabitants), and the troops—the irregular troops especially—and the travelling dervishes, and the unclean brood of officials generally who get no pay and live on bribery and extortion, having the Christian population absolutely at their mercy. Behold the hell to which Governments who profess lip allegiance to the Virgin's Son have doomed, for their own fancied interests, millions of their fellow Christians! On that infernal policy England at last has turned her back for ever, and no cry of ' British interests ' will ever again tempt her to raise a little finger to save the Ottoman Empire from its righteous doom. As if British interests could be served in the long run by an alliance with Sodom and Gomorrah!

The present Sultan on his accession sought to find compensation for the abridgment of his temporal power by trying to extend his assumed spiritual influence as Khalif. Now, the truth is that he has no more right to the title of Khalif than I have, and he is not acknowledged as such in any Musulman country out of Turkey, or even there except by the Turks. The Arabs repudiate with scorn the spiritual claims of the Sultan, for it is a cardinal article of the creed of Islâm that the Khalif must be an Arab of the tribe of Mohammed. It may suit hybrid Muslims like Mr. Justice Ameer Ali to magnify their office by saluting the Sultan as Khalif; but this only proves insincerity or ignorance. Nor is this a mere academic question, for this Sultan, in his usurped character of Khalif, has for years been sending preachers of sedition all over India, and promoting a Crescentade against Christianity throughout his own dominions. In this way he has doubtless succeeded in rousing in parts of Turkey the dormant spirit of fanaticism against the Christians. Fortunately, however, he has neutralised the mischief by the hatred which he has inspired against himself. On the whole, then, the feeling of the unofficial Musulmans of Turkey is now what it was when Abdul Hamid ascended the throne. And what was that?

The first thing Lord Salisbury did when he reached Constantinople in 1877 was to send two competent agents, Consul Calvert and Captain (now Sir John) Ardagh, to different parts of European Turkey to find out the feelings of the Musulman population in regard to European control. The result is published in a Blue Book, from which I make a few extracts. Writing from Bulgaria, Consul Calvert says:—

I have now seen all the local Beys or Turkish landowners. They every one comment strongly on the wretched state to which the population at large has been reduced through Ottoman misgovernment, which has caused the discontent that has brought the country to its present pass. One Bey, without any leading on my part, volunteered confidentially his opinion on the subject as follows:—'The best remedy,' he said, 'for these evils would be for the Foreign Powers to insist on the association of an experienced European in the administration of the province, with power to control all abuses.' He made this remark as an original idea of his own, and apparently in ignorance that anything of the sort had been projected by the Western

Powers. ... On my inquiring whether the Musulman population would not view with jealousy reforms carried out under foreign auspices, he energetically exclaimed:—'Every man of us would bless the Powers if they would undertake so good a work.' I sounded the other Beys by asking in a casual manner:—'Supposing now the friendly Powers were to put pressure on the Porte with regard to administrative reforms, how would it be viewed by you Musulmans?' They one and all energetically replied with the same formula. One Bey even laughed outright at my simplicity in putting such a question. Another remarked:—'Our religion teaches us to appreciate good from whatever quarter it may come. It is enough that it is good. Should the Powers give us prosperity and quiet, we would all of us put up prayers for them.' There is among Muslims a greater uniformity of character and ideas than is the case with Europeans, and there is no doubt that sentiments similar to these would be found to prevail throughout Turkey.

Consul Calvert adds that even if it were otherwise—

The power of the central Government is absolute and complete over the Musulman population. ... I believe every Consul in Turkey would be able to confirm the statement that there cannot be a more hollow plea than that which the Porte finds it convenient to put forward, of its inability to control the Muslim population. The Musulmans have concentrated their opinion that all the excesses, massacres, and other mischief are due to the central Government in the popular proverb, 'The fish rots from the head.'

Captain Ardagh bore similar testimony. A short extract from his report will suffice. He asked the Beys 'their views as regards the superintendence of reforms':—

All but one considered that the appointment of foreign Commissioners, selected by the guaranteeing Powers, would be acceptable; and several expressed a strong opinion that the presence of such officials in the general and local administration would be an unmixed benefit. . . . With the exception of the one I have mentioned, all the other Turkish gentlemen agreed in saying that, whatever other measures were proposed by the Conference, and agreed to by the Porte, if promulgated *bonâ fide*, would be received without opposition by the Musulman population, provided only that religion was not interfered with.*

The reason given for his opinion by the single dissentient is remarkable. I quote Captain Ardagh :—

This opinion is rather to be interpreted that the Porte and the official class, in the event of the Conference [of Constantinople] extorting an involuntary consent to measures to which they are at heart opposed, would create an antagonistic feeling among the lower classes, in order to throw difficulties in the way of rendering such measures practically operative, and would foment, or at least be at little pains to repress, any disturbances which might arise. . . . Without such provocation there is strong reason to believe that the lower part of the urban and rural population would accept without a murmur any changes likely to be proposed. There is little or no probability of any outbreak on the part of the Mohammedan population of internal origin, and disturbances are only to be apprehended from the action of exterior influences, namely, of the central Government.

* *Turkey*, No. 2 (1877), pp. 170-3.

The Porte tried in vain to prevent Anglo-French intervention in Syria in 1860 by conjuring up a terrible vision of Turkish fanaticism in the event of foreign interference in the internal affairs of Turkey. It was, like all similar threats, a *brutum fulmen*. The answer of M. Thouvenel, the Foreign Minister, is worth quoting :—

M. Thouvenel [French Foreign Minister] observed that he could not admit the reasoning that because a Turkish Minister was apprehensive that if a foreign force should be landed in Syria there would be disturbances at Constantinople, the Great Powers were on that account to desist from a measure that had appeared to them necessary for the future tranquillity of that country. If such reasoning were once to be admitted, it would be put forward on every occasion when an abuse was to be corrected in Turkey.*

I could produce abundant evidence from other sources to show the ignorance or disingenuousness of the German official Press in urging that the Musulman population of Turkey would rise against any scheme of European reforms and control; and I can, moreover, bear personal testimony from my own visits to different parts of the Ottoman Empire in Europe, Asia, and Africa, that the Musulman population would eagerly accept European control on being assured that their religion and property would be respected. They are, on the whole, a submissive and patient people, and easily governed when not

* Correspondence on the Affairs of Syria (1860–61), p. 14.

stimulated to the commission of outrages by the authorities.

If, therefore, the Powers who are so anxious to put off indefinitely the dissolution of the Ottoman Empire would only depose Abdul Hamid, and put his dominions in commission under some *roi fainéant*, who would reign but not rule, they would be much more likely to achieve their purpose than by the imbecile policy of 'supporting the *status quo*.' You don't stop the progress of dry-rot in a building by supporting the *status quo*, but by putting an end to it. Is it really come to this, that there is not a single statesman worthy of the name in all the Continental Cabinets of the 'Concert of Europe'? Are they all smitten with judicial blindness, like the Syrian army which was led by the prophet into the capital of its enemy with open eyes and closed minds? But their folly is Lord Salisbury's opportunity. He understands the Eastern question in all its bearings better than most of them, and he showed at Constantinople in 1877 that he held the key of its solution—namely, European control in friendly co-operation with Russia. If he had been loyally supported at home he would have succeeded. He failed because he was the victim of underhand intrigues and of a vacillation not his own. It is an interesting story, but must be reserved for another article. Mr. Frederick Greenwood has just been lifting a corner of the veil. I will lift another corner. Meanwhile Lord Salisbury has more than one string to his bow in giving check to the stupid diplomacy of his Continental opponents. I have suggested one which would, I believe, be speedily successful. It is easy to practise the goose-step in line; but it is a different matter when the awkward squad begins to run forward. It is easy to form a combination to stand in line watching the *status quo*. The first proposal to attack England for attempting to discharge a duty to which she is pledged by treaty, and which the other Powers have flagrantly neglected, would dissolve the combination. After all, there is still a Christendom, and Christendom would cry shame on such portentous wickedness. Besides, these potentates would have to reckon even with some of their own people. Let it be considered that under a despotism the ruler is, on an occasion which appeals to the moral sense of mankind, more amenable to public opinion than a constitutional Sovereign. Under an autocracy there is no barrier between the monarch and the multitude. Let Lord Salisbury offer the Powers their choice of co-operating with him in coercing the Sultan, accompanying his offer with a self-denying ordinance by which they would mutually pledge themselves to abstain from taking individual advantage of the issue; or of acquiescing in his acting alone in coercing the Sultan into submission to the will of Europe. I venture to say that not a single Power would dare to oppose him for very shame, to say nothing of the certainty of their immediately beginning to quarrel among themselves if they did. Lord Salisbury's literary skill would enable him so to expound the whole situation that it would simply be impossible for his opponents to make out a case for interfering with him. And, after all, even despots will not dare to go to war nowadays without at least a plausible case.

Another alternative is to withdraw the British Ambassador from Constantinople, and give the Turkish Ambassador his passport, leaving the British residents and British interests under the protection of Italy or France. The Powers could not quarrel with that, yet it would make them reflect and the Sultan tremble. There is nothing a coward dreads so much as the possibilities of the unknown. There are so many things which England can do against Turkey without moving a regiment or an ironclad. A breach of diplomatic intercourse with this red-handed murderer would cause a ferment throughout his Empire. It might lead to a rebellion in Arabia or a rising in Macedonia. The Sultan knows that. Austria knows it too. It is all very well for the hireling Press of Austria and Germany to hurl defiance at England — defiance, however, which has a comic quaver in its tone; but the moment Lord Salisbury formulated his case and offered his terms, this Press, which is largely the property of financial gamblers, would show its impotence and would then begin to claim, as in Crete, the credit of what it did its best to defeat. But everything depends on the nation showing a united front, and this again can only be done by Conservatives and Liberals appearing side by side at meetings which cannot be prevented, but may be made of the greatest service to the Government.

CHAPTER IV.

TIMID COUNSELS.

It seems to be thought in some quarters in this country—Madame Novikoff has done her best to propagate the same view in Russia and France— that Lord Salisbury's record on the Eastern question has placed him in a peculiarly disadvantageous position for coming to an agreement with Russia at this moment. I hope in a following chapter to prove, on the contrary, that Russia is under deep obligations to Lord Salisbury. But let me begin by explaining as clearly as I can the policy which I venture to recommend for public meetings and elsewhere. It is to assure Lord Salisbury that he has the whole nation at his back in any measure which he may take for the effectual protection of the Armenians, and for delivering England from all further complicity in the policy of futile remonstrance and criminal inaction, which has already sacrificed the lives of some 100,000 innocent men, women, and children, massacred in cold blood; and will, probably, if persevered in, result in a general massacre of Christians all over Turkey. If the

Concert of the Powers agree to act with Lord Salisbury in putting an end without delay to a state of things which has already covered Christendom with infamy, well and good. If not, then perish the Concert of the Powers! At this moment shiploads of Armenians are being deported before the eyes of the Ambassadors to be drowned at sea or massacred in some obscure corner of Anatolia. And the Ambassadors do nothing to stay the hand of the assassin. And then we are told, forsooth! by some weak-kneed and invertebrate politicians that England must only bewail her impotence and sit wringing her feeble hands in the Concert of Europe. Can she not at least leave the Concert, shaking the dust of her garments against its guilty complicity in the stupendous crimes of a red-handed murderer, whose continued impunity emboldens him to meditate and organise further excesses? Time was when the slave and the oppressed plucked up hope from the ashes of despair wherever the flag of England was seen waving. Is this great nation, with its glorious history, fallen so low that it has no longer the courage to defend with its own right arm its own honour and treaty obligations, without stooping, 'in bondman's key with bated breath and whisp'ring humbleness,' to ask leave of some foreign potentate?

I am not surprised that such advice should be given by Sir Charles Dilke. Her Majesty's Government, it seems, refused to shape their naval policy by his sage advice, and so 'the weakness' of the strongest fleet that ever sailed the seas has now reduced England to impotence! If Sir Charles Dilke had commanded the British fleet at Trafalgar he would have counted the enemy's ships through his telescope, and, finding them to outnumber his own, would have run away. Whenever Nelson saw the enemy's ships he made for them without counting the odds, and beat them. I have followed the various phases of the Eastern question with at least as much care as Sir Charles Dilke, and I do not hesitate to say that 'his remembrance of the fickleness of public opinion' on the Bulgarian question is only a reminiscence of his own fickleness. Then as now he veered about with the superficial eddies that babbled over the shallows of public opinion, but was never in touch with the nation's pulse, and has thus remained ignorant to this hour of the outburst of sympathy for the oppressed which went on increasing in volume till it achieved its purpose. There was no fickleness and no reaction, as I have already shown.

But I am more than surprised that the leader of the Liberal party should follow Sir Charles Dilke's example. Lord Rosebery 'is not prepared to assume the position of the Executive, and to attempt to direct the Government of the country.' Yet he does not hesitate to lay down a policy for the Government as a condition of his support, but which imposes no sort of responsibility on himself. 'Separate action,' on the part of England, 'would involve a European war.' Why? Because of 'the declaration of Russia, in August 1895, that she would oppose separate action on the part of any Powers.' But the circumstances of August 1895 are not the circumstances of September 1896. Much has happened since then which may well modify the policy of Russia. Moreover, Russia never made the declaration which Lord Rosebery's lapse of memory has imputed to her. In answer to the British Ambassador's inquiry whether Russia would be willing to employ force against the Sultan, Prince Lobanoff replied that 'the employment of force was personally repugnant to the Emperor.' And being pressed to say what Russia thought as to the employment of force by other Powers, Lobanoff said 'that the employment of force by any one of the Powers would be equally distasteful to the Russian Government.' That is a very different thing from saying that Russia 'would oppose' the employment of force by any of the Powers. There might then have been some lingering hope that the Sultan might be made to see the peril of further massacres, and agree to a *modus vivendi* for the Armenians. There is no such hope now. I do not believe that Russia would oppose coercion in the present dangerous crisis, when a spark may fire the magazine, if she were convinced that England desires no individual benefit, and is willing to come to a friendly understanding with the Tsar. What is suggested is that England should propose coercion to the other Powers, or to one of them acting as the mandatory of the rest, not by a declaration of war against the Sultan, but by a method well known to diplomacy, the method of a material guarantee —that is, the temporary occupation of a portion of the Sultan's territory. It is a method which all nations have used at various times. England has used it quite lately. Russia used it before the Crimean war with the assent of England; and Germany used it against Turkey not many years ago. I do not suppose that any one would dispute England's right by international law to adopt that mode of proceeding in forcing the Sultan to fulfil his obligations to Europe under the terms of Article 61 of the Treaty of Berlin, and to England in addition by the Convention of Cyprus. Certainly Russia cannot dispute it, for she has agreed to it already in a less aggravated case than the present. When the Sultan, in 1880, insolently refused to surrender to Greece and Montenegro the territories which he had agreed to give up in the Treaty of Berlin, Mr. Gladstone assembled contingents from the fleets of the Powers at Dulcigno. And when the Sultan still refused, he determined to seize Smyrna, thereby intercepting, for the time being, the largest part of the Sultan's revenues

Austria, Germany, and France refused their consent. Russia acquiesced. But before the answer of Italy was received the Sultan got wind of Mr. Gladstone's intentions, and hastened to avert the blow by unconditional submission to Mr. Goschen, then British Ambassador at the Porte.

Let Russia be convinced of England's disinterestedness, as she easily can, and I do not believe that she will go back on her own precedent. But let us assume the worst—namely, a declaration by the other Powers that they would resist by force England's temporary occupation of some Turkish port. Where is the danger of Lord Rosebery's 'European war'? No one says that Lord Salisbury should in that case take the risk of a war against Russia, Austria, Germany, and France. But he could warn them of the consequences of their short-sighted selfishness, throw on them the responsibility of whatever might happen, break off diplomatic intercourse with the Sultan, and quietly await the result. This Lord Salisbury, with his literary skill, and with the damning array of facts at his command, could do in a despatch that would brand his opponents with an infamy which they would not dare to face. Where is the danger of European war there? Would not Lord Salisbury's hands be immensely strengthened if Europe saw that he had the British nation, like one man, at his back in any measure which he may adopt, however vigorous, leaving him meanwhile to choose out of several alternatives the policy which he considers most efficacious?

What the nation will not stand is any further continuance of the policy of pothering and peddling which the other Powers, with the noble exception of Italy, seem to regard as the *ne plus ultra* of statesmanship. I can understand Liberals—if there be such, who are willing 'to give up to party what was meant for mankind'— trying to dissuade Lord Salisbury from a policy which would undoubtedly secure for him a great diplomatic victory and place him at a bound at the head of European statesmanship. What I cannot understand is Conservative newspapers falling into the snare. I remember a speech by Lord Salisbury some sixteen years ago in which he barbed an argument in favour of a bold policy with Danton's famous phrase: *Il nous faut de l'audace, et encore de l'audace, et toujours de l'audace*; and I think too well of his knowledge and political sagacity to believe that he agrees with those who would persuade him that pusillanimity is the most successful weapon in the armoury of diplomacy. To proclaim upon the housetops that England will never risk war in defence of her duty and honour is to invite aggression and disaster.

One thing, however, cannot be made known too soon. Lord Rosebery's policy is not the policy of Mr. Gladstone. The late leader of the

Liberal party has the courage of his convictions, and is not afraid to say before the world that he will support Lord Salisbury in coercing the Sultan, leaving to him the choice of such effective measures as may seem to him best for effecting his purpose. That assurance is much more likely to strengthen Lord Salisbury's hands than counsels of timidity and dishonouring lamentations over England's inability 'to go forward alone' in defence of her just rights. England was never better able than she is now 'to go forward alone' where duty calls her; and none know that better than her Continental traducers. The crisis is a testing one for English Liberals. In my humble judgment their interest, not less than their duty, should make them support Lord Salisbury, without 'ifs' or 'buts' as to the means he may use, however extreme, provided only that they are effectual. To tell him that they will support him only on condition of his doing nothing beyond dancing attendance on the Concert of Europe is to paralyse his hands instead of strengthening them. And, above all, let the support be hearty and without reservation. Foreign statesmen are sharp enough to see the difference between such support and that so felicitously described by Pope :—

> Damn with faint praise, assent with civil leer,
> And without sneering teach the rest to sneer;
> Willing to wound, and yet afraid to strike;
> Just hint a fault, and hesitate dislike.

And now a word as to the attitude of the Conservative party towards the agitation. Let them oppose it and they will inevitably make it a party question, and put a powerful party weapon in the hands of their opponents. Let them remember 1876. In the early stage of that agitation it was supported quite as earnestly by the Tory party as by the Liberals; nay, more: some members of Lord Beaconsfield's Government took part in it. The leader of the House of Commons (Sir Stafford Northcote), Lord Cross, and Lord Carnarvon are names which occur to me at once. Lord Carnarvon said:—

> I rejoice to believe that the heart of my countrymen beat so soundly as it did when such a tale of horror was unfolded. I rejoice that there was neither delay nor hesitation in the expression of that feeling; and, so far from weakening the hands of the Government I believe that, if rightly understood at home and abroad, nothing could more strengthen the hands of my noble friend the Foreign Secretary than the burst of indignation which has gone through the length and breadth of the land.

Wise words! And Lord (then Mr.) Cross and Sir Stafford Northcote spoke out quite as strongly. In the initial stages of his wonderful campaign Mr. Gladstone was an honoured guest at leading Conservative houses—Mr. Arthur Balfour's for example, and the Duke of Northumberland's. I don't remember whether Lord Salisbury spoke on the subject at the time; but in the end of September

1876 a great meeting was held in the Guildhall, under the presidency of a Tory Lord Mayor, one of the leading speakers being the Right Hon. J. G. Hubbard, one of the Conservative Members for the City. Lord Salisbury was invited to attend, and, while pleading his official position as Minister for India to excuse his absence, he expressed his hearty sympathy with the agitation. His son has just expressed his sympathy with the present agitation in language as strong as Mr. Gladstone's, and his hope that other countries will imitate it. Conservatives have everything to gain, and nothing to lose, by participating in the agitation; and I would especially implore the Conservative Press to welcome Mr. Gladstone's intervention in a friendly spirit. He has been most reluctant to emerge from his privacy, and one of his reasons for hesitancy has been his anxiety to say nothing that could in the least embarrass Lord Salisbury or wear the appearance of forcing a policy on him. The condition of the political atmosphere is at this moment very electrical, and an attack on Mr. Gladstone from the Ministerial side would be pretty certain to cause an explosion. Let there be hearty co-operation now, and let the keynote be a resolution to support Lord Salisbury in his righteous endeavours to obtain reparation and protection for the Armenians without prescribing for him any specific method of procedure.

Let him have a free hand whether he shall act with or without the Concert of Europe. I see no reason, however, why speakers should not express their own individual opinions on alternative plans.

The one thing which meetings will not tolerate is a recommendation to sit with folded arms and do nothing. That, I am sure, is not the policy of Lord Salisbury. I do not doubt at all that he feels as keenly as any of us the pain and shame of the callousness of the other Powers, and that he is doing his best to realise in action the universal desire of the country. The agitation is intended to reinforce his diplomacy, and will unquestionably do so.

I shall presently show that Lord Salisbury is peculiarly well qualified at this moment to settle the Armenian question—qualified by his ability, his comprehensive knowledge of the subject, his genuine sympathy with the Christian population of Turkey, and—not least—by his antecedents.

CHAPTER V.

POLICY OF AUSTRIA.

BEFORE I enter on the interesting subject of Lord Salisbury's record on the Eastern question I must make one more effort to make plain, as I understand it—and I have more than average means of knowing—the aim and purport of the agitation. There is no desire to dictate any policy to Lord Salisbury. Nobody urges him to make war or do anything in particular. But the country wishes foreign Powers to know that if Lord Salisbury, in despair of persuading the other Powers to secure reparation and justice for the Armenians, decides to act alone, he will have the whole nation behind him. It is the worst possible policy to tell foreign Powers that in no case will Great Britain act alone. It is just the way to paralyse Lord Salisbury's diplomacy and to encourage the Sultan to go on with his massacres. And it is not true. The country will act if Lord Salisbury think it necessary; and Lord Salisbury himself cannot possibly tell whether circumstances may not arise any day which might force him to act alone. As we have no desire to force his hand, still less have we any wish to fetter his discretion. Let him have a free hand to act with or without the other Powers in carrying out the policy of the nation, which is doubtless his own—namely, to deliver England from all complicity in the tacit assent of the other Powers to the Sultan's deliberate purpose to exterminate the Armenians. The agitation has already compelled the Press of Vienna to change its tone of menace and bluster towards this country to one of supplication. But there is no indication of any change of policy. The *Standard*—to whose ability and honourable conduct in this matter I wish to pay my small tribute of gratitude—gratefully accepts the following passage in a Vienna paper as 'English policy in a nut-shell':—'So long as the present Government is at the head of affairs in England, abhorrence of Turkish rule, though well-founded enough, will not be allowed to conjure up the spectre of European war.' I am sure the *Standard* does not realise the hideous significance of that passage. Let it read it again in the light of the following facts. On the 13th of last December the British Ambassador at Constantinople informed Lord Salisbury by telegraph that—

A moderate estimate put the loss of life at 30,000. The survivors are in a state of absolute destitution, and in many places they are forced to become Musulmans. The charge against Armenians of having been the first to offer provocation cannot be sustained. Non-Armenian Christians were spared, and the comparatively few Turks who fell were killed in self-defence.

Four days later the British Ambassador at Vienna handed a copy of this telegram to Count Goluchowski, and begged him to read it carefully.

Count Goluchowski did so, and observed that the description is doubtless true enough, and very impressive; but that, as he had already stated, there is nothing to be done but to wait and see if the Sultan will be able to carry out his promises and restore order. Every kind of admonition had been given to him, and his Excellency did not see what more could be said to him than has already been repeatedly urged. Intervention of any other kind must inevitably result in the further disaggregation of the Ottoman Empire. But, if Count Goluchowski rightly understands the situation, this is the last thing that the Powers desire. . . . He must therefore maintain that, lamentable as the condition of affairs in Anatolia undoubtedly is, there is nothing whatever to be done but to give the Sultan the opportunity of doing what he has engaged to do. The prospect is not a hopeful one.

A fortnight later the Austrian Minister received news of more horrors, and again unbosomed himself to the British Ambassador.

His Excellency went on to deplore that, beyond making representations [to the Sultan] the Powers can do nothing for the Armenians, of whom several thousands may be computed to have perished by violence; while the rigours of winter, bringing famine, want of shelter and warmth—in fact, destitution in its most appalling shape—might be calculated to destroy many more before the return of spring.

This foreboding has been but too well fulfilled. Sir Philip Currie's 'moderate estimate' of 30,000 massacred in cold blood does not come down farther than the end of October, embraces only a limited area, and takes no account of those who perished from cold and starvation. Massacres have taken place since then in many other places, and a moderate estimate of the total number of victims, including deaths from exposure and starvation, down to now is 200,000. Count Goluchowski was prepared for all this and more. Let me continue my quotation from the Blue-Book:—

In presence of this heartrending prospect it is intelligible that numbers of humane people are revolted at the idea that Europe is powerless, and, regardless of consequences, would wish that action should be taken by some, or even by one of the Powers, to put a stop to the extermination of the miserable Armenians. But practical statesmen are bound to consider the situation from another standpoint.*

Which means, in plain language, that Austria covets Macedonia, Salonica, and Constantinople, if England will be good enough to help her, and therefore is willing—very sorrowfully, of course, but with philosophic equanimity—to watch the gradual 'extermination of the

* See *Turkey*, No. 2 (1896), pp. 210, 252-3, 290.

miserable Armenians,' with every circumstance of revolting cruelty, rather than run the smallest risk of losing one morsel of her coveted prize. The Austrian Minister frankly admits that 'admonitions' and 'representations' addressed to the Sultan are absolutely useless, and he knows that the Sultan is himself the arch-criminal. For it was the Austrian Ambassador who, after consultation with his colleagues, went in person as their accredited representative to the Sultan on November 18, 1895, and delivered the following stern message on behalf of the six Great Powers :—

> The only means of restoring confidence is to put a stop to the massacres, *which we are convinced the Sultan can do if he is sincere in his profession*; that an inquiry should be held as to the participation of soldiers in the outrages, and the guilty be punished; that the orders recently sent to the Valis and military commanders should be published, *and assurances given that previous orders* [to commit massacres] *have been cancelled*; that a Hatt should be issued by the Sultan ordering his subjects to obey his wishes.*

That is, the Sultan hypocritically assured the Ambassadors of his fatherly affection for the Armenians while he was deliberately ordering his soldiers and encouraging the rabble to massacre them. That was nearly a year ago, and the Sultan has gone on systematically to this very hour with his work of 'exterminating the miserable Armenians.' And the masters of

* *Turkey*, No. 2 (1896), p. 160.

some 15,000,000 drilled soldiers, and navies such as the world has never seen before, look quietly on, and call heaven and earth to witness that they are 'powerless' to prevent this monster in human form from pursuing his career of bloodshed! And the Austrian Government calmly believes that the British people and their statesmen may be trusted 'to lend their co-operation' to the consummation of this hellish plot! Was ever such insult offered to the British nation before?

I will not insult the *Standard* by asking whether it regards this as 'English policy in a nut-shell'; and to suppose that it could excite any other feeling than loathing in Lord Salisbury's breast would be not to insult him merely, but to accuse him of repudiating the whole of his record on the Eastern question, as I shall show conclusively in my next chapter, for I find it impossible to compress my evidence within the limits of this. What I am trying to do now is to show cause for believing that the great sinner in the tragedy that is being enacted in Turkey is Austria, backed by Germany, rather than Russia—Austria, which has ever pursued a huckster's policy, and has never in all her history struck a blow or spent a shilling in any cause or interest but her own. Russia, as I have shown, offered on two occasions to work amicably with England in pacifying Armenia, and suspected some underhand schemes against her from the rebuffs which she received. Then there was much foolish talk in this country about forming an autonomous Armenian State under an Austrian governor—a proposal most offensive to Russia. There were also paper schemes of partition of the Turkish Empire—by amateur and unauthorised theorists, 'tis true. But all this alarmed Russia and increased her suspicion of England.

Austria, on the other hand, has been playing a sordidly selfish game all through. I shall have more to say on that subject later; but I must give one piece of evidence here which seems to show that Austria, more than Russia, has been opposed to the coercion of the Sultan. In a despatch from Lord Salisbury to Sir E. Monson, on November 13, 1895, the Prime Minister relates a conversation which he had the previous day with the Austrian Ambassador, who had called at the Foreign Office to ask what Lord Salisbury proposed to do in the event, which the Ambassador feared, of 'an outburst of Musulman fanaticism' in Constantinople. 'What remedy had' Lord Salisbury 'to suggest?' Here is Lord Salisbury's answer:—

I asked him whether he contemplated acting through the Sultan, or in despite of the Sultan. He replied that of course his Government only contemplated acting through the Sultan. I said that if the mere impression ever gained ground that so conservative a Government as Austria was prepared to act *with the unanimous concurrence of the Powers, but without the assent of the Sultan,* that assent would not then be difficult to obtain.*

Is it not a legitimate inference, from the words which I have marked by italics, that at that time Austria was the only member of the European Concert who opposed coercion of the Sultan?

* See *Turkey*, No. 2 (1896), p. 126.

CHAPTER VI.

LORD SALISBURY'S RECORD.

ON May 4, 1858—Lord Derby being Prime Minister and Mr. Disraeli leader of the House of Commons—Mr. Gladstone initiated a great debate on the union of the two Principalities—then under Turkish rule—which now constitute the kingdom of Roumania. The question of their union came before the Congress of Paris in 1856, and the Plenipotentiaries of France and England strongly supported it, and had influence enough to get their policy thus recorded in the twenty-eighth Article of the Treaty of Paris:—

His Majesty the Sultan promises to convoke immediately in each of the two Provinces a divan *ad hoc*, composed in such a manner as to represent most closely the interests of all classes of society. These divans shall be called upon to express the wishes of the people in regard to the definite organisation of the Principalities.

Austria and Turkey—*Arcades ambo* as foes of freedom—opposed the union; and, when an appeal was made to the people of Moldavia, stifled the popular will by the grossest intimidation. England urged the quashing of the elections and a fresh appeal to the people, and, of course, Austria and Turkey opposed, but in vain. In the second election the people of both Principalities voted unanimously in favour of the union. Still Austria and Turkey opposed, and there was thus a second Congress of Paris to adjudicate upon the matter. While the Congress was sitting Mr. Gladstone moved in the House of Commons a resolution in favour of the union. His most eloquent speech is well worth reading now for its far-seeing statesmanship. Suggesting that 'the Mohammedan Power in Europe could not be permanently maintained,' he advised the endowment of its Christian population with practical self-government under the protection of the Powers, yet leaving them under the rule of the Porte, and thus maintaining as long as possible 'the territorial integrity of Turkey,' to prevent a scramble, possibly leading to a great war, on the part of ambitious neighbours. He was not surprised that Austria should join Turkey in opposing the union of the Danubian Principalities.

I will not undertake to say that it is convenient to Austria to have freedom in conjunction with prosperity close by her threshold; but that is her fault, not mine.

Mr. Gladstone was supported, in a generous and powerful speech, by Lord John Russell, and fiercely opposed by the Government and, in a violent speech, by Lord Palmerston, who affirmed that the Principalities did not wish for union. It was all a factitious excitement got up for sinister purposes by 'foreign agency.' Carry out Mr. Gladstone's policy, and 'Russia would in a moment overspread' Roumania, which would thus become a scene of confusion and intrigue, and, like Poland, 'be absorbed by Russia, or divided between her and Austria.' And, above all, Mr. Gladstone's policy would be fatal to 'the independence and integrity of the Turkish Empire.' Three years previously Lord Palmerston said that his own policy was 'to emancipate the Principalities from foreign interference, and to tie them more closely to the Sultan.'

The debate was remarkable, not only for the eloquence of the veteran orators of the House, but for a brilliant speech in support of Mr. Gladstone by a young Member on the Conservative benches.

The House must consider maturely (he said) what would be the fate of those Principalities if the motion of his Right Honourable friend should be rejected. . . . The probability was that if the strong assistance of Europe were given in favour of the claims of Turkey, the Principalities would be handed over for the present to Turkey, the most oppressive and rapacious of all governments. As long as Turkey lasted they would be subjected to her rule; and when Turkey fell, as she ultimately must do, they would become a prey to some other Powers who would divide her remains between them. He trusted that the House of Commons would show themselves on this occasion to be the supporters of freedom. They had made many efforts and had talked a great deal about propagating the principles which they professed, and of spreading the institutions which they revered, in other countries. . . . There was now an opportunity, which might never recur, of supporting those principles which we revered, of establishing those institutions to which we owed our own happiness, and of securing the freedom and welfare of thousands of our fellow-creatures. That opportunity had been afforded in consequence of a pledge given by ourselves, and if it should be neglected and thrown away the responsibility would fall upon us, and all would feel that it had been lost by our betrayal and our falsehood.

The name of the young orator was Lord Robert Cecil, now Marquis of Salisbury. The speech made a great impression on the House, and was deeply resented by Mr. Disraeli, who devoted a considerable part of his own speech to the task of neutralising that impression. The following extract from Mr. Disraeli's speech shows how angry he was at this display of independence by one of his own party :—

If the views expressed by the noble Lord the Member for Stamford are sound, then you are justified in supporting the Address to the Crown. If, indeed, the fall of Turkey is to be looked on as a realised fact, . . . then you would be justified in ratifying the sentiments of the noble Lord the Member for Stamford. But, as I believe the opinions of the noble Lord are raw and crude opinions, as I believe they are not the opinions of any one who has sufficiently thought on the subject on which he has spoken with so much authority, I must decline to follow his example. But that such opinions should be in any degree sanctioned by the right hon. gentleman the Member for the University (Mr. Gladstone) is to me matter of deep astonishment.

It was a thoroughly pro-Turkish and anti-Russian speech, ridiculing the idea 'of raising up in the Danubian Principalities a fantastic kingdom, and of establishing in those countries what indeed would be but the phantom of independence.' By the coalition of Palmerstonians and Mr. Disraeli's followers, Mr. Gladstone's motion was defeated by a majority of 292 against 114. The bugbear of 'a European war' was then also raised by Lord Palmerston and Mr. Disraeli to frighten a timorous Parliament from fulfilling a national pledge and discharging a national duty. Read in the light of events, how prescient and statesmanlike are the speeches of Mr. Gladstone, Lord John Russell, and Lord Robert Cecil! And what political rubbish are the speeches of Lord Palmerston and Mr. Disraeli! But the vote of the House of Commons was a triumph for Austria and Turkey—on paper. The Congress of Paris, under the influence of the British Government, riveted the yoke of the Sultan on the necks of the people of Roumania. Nevertheless, the speeches of the champions of freedom in Parliament encouraged the Roumanians to take their destiny into their own hands, and by the device of electing the same Prince for both Principalities they defeated the scheme of selfish statesmen and cemented their own union. The statesmen looked on baffled and helpless, for brave as they were in a policy of inaction, their courage oozed out at the tips of their fingers when it became a matter of moving forward to undo the plucky manœuvre of little Roumania. Yet timid politicians now assure us, with bated breath and trembling limbs, that a Concert of Powers would join in a war against mighty England if she determine to vindicate her honour and treaty rights in any legitimate way which would not encroach on or imperil the rights of others. The bond which binds the opponents of England in a policy of doing nothing to stay the reign of terror and massacre in Turkey is a rope of sand, which would fall to pieces the moment any of them proposed to move to the attack. Timid Austria, which now declares that the six mightiest States in the world are 'powerless' to prevent the miserable poltroon of Yildiz Kiosk from exterminating the Armenians in his dominions, would, forsooth, rush madly into a war with Britain—a war which would be much more likely to destroy the Turkish Empire than isolated action on the part of any Great Power. Will sensible men face the problem which separate action on the part of England would mean to Austria? What Austria dreads is the downfall of Turkey before she is ready to grasp as much of the spoil as she covets. But the continued disorganisation of Turkey is exceedingly likely to precipitate that catastrophe. England says, in effect:—'I am willing to join you in maintaining the Turkish Empire for the present—but on one condition, namely, that security for life, religion, property, and honour shall be guaranteed to the Christian subjects of the Sultan. You have admitted that mere diplomatic intervention is useless without force. But if the Powers unanimously demand the Sultan's submission to their wishes, with the alternative of force to compel him, the Sultan will yield at once. If, however, you object to this, I am entitled by treaty rights to coerce the Sultan, and I can do it with my fleet without the smallest risk of war. I will, at the same time, give a guarantee to the Powers that I will not annex a rood of the Sultan's territory, and that I will withdraw my fleet the moment I have compelled the Sultan to submit to the will of Europe.' Is it really to be seriously argued that the Powers would meet so reasonable a proposal with a declaration of war against England? The supposition is incredible and preposterous.

The next landmark in Lord Salisbury's record on the Eastern question is his action in 1877–78. The limits of space forbid my doing more than giving the salient points. In the early part of that historic controversy he indicated his scorn for the Russophobists by his 'large map' illustration; as he did a year ago, when there was a silly panic about Port Arthur, by declaring that there was room enough in Asia for both Russia and Britain. In the late spring of 1877 he carried to the Conference of Constantinople a paper of admirable instructions, signed by his chief, Lord Derby, but drawn up, I imagine, by himself. They covered the ground most satisfactorily, and were barbed with an ominous warning of coercion in case the Sultan rejected the reforms offered to him. But Lord Salisbury had scarcely left the shore of England when Lord Derby told the Turkish Ambassador that in no case would England join in a coercive policy, or give her sanction to its adoption by any other Power—stronger language than that used by Prince Lobanoff in August 1895, to which such portentous significance has been attributed. Musurus Pasha immediately telegraphed the important information to his Government, and received by return a telegraphic acknowledgment with the Grand Vizir's 'deep gratitude to Lord Derby,' and an assurance that 'the Sublime Porte reckons more than ever on the kind support of the Government of Her Britannic Majesty,' which thus offered 'a sure guarantee' of future help in time of need.

Thus it happened that when the Conference was opened Lord Salisbury found the efficient weapon with which his Government had armed him broken in his hand. But there was another weapon still left—the Russian army on the frontier, now alone 'the motive force of the Conference,' as Lord Salisbury called it in the

House of Lords after his return. But this weapon also was broken by two dexterous strokes. The Jingo Press of London, the *Pall Mall Gazette* in particular, laboured from day to day, with great skill, to assure the British public and the Sultan that the Russian army was in so disorganised and rotten a state that it could not fight Turkey. To this malign influence on Lord Salisbury's diplomacy he bears witness himself in the speech already referred to.

> To myself (he says) it appears that one of the causes which led the Turks to this unfortunate resolution [rejection of the proposals of the Powers] was the belief which was so sedulously fostered, I know not by whom but by irresponsible advisers, that the power of Russia was broken, that the armies of Russia were suffering from disease, that the mobilisation had failed, and that, consequently, the fear of war was over.

Undoubtedly there was an influential party then in England, as I shall show presently, which eagerly desired a war between Russia and Turkey, in the hope and belief that England might be pushed into it in alliance with the Sultan.

The other, and even more formidable, stroke which neutralised the diplomatic use of the Russian army as 'the motive force of the Conference,' was the speech in which Lord Beaconsfield threatened Russia with 'three campaigns' in the event of her making war on Turkey. This is not a matter of speculation or of inference. It is Lord Salisbury himself who complains, in a despatch to Lord Derby, 'that the Grand Vizir believed he could "count upon the assistance of Lord Derby and Lord Beaconsfield."' And the Grand Vizir himself (Midhat Pasha) declared afterwards, in an article in the *Nineteenth Century*, that the Sultan would never have rejected the proposals of the Powers or run the risk of a war with Russia if he had not counted confidently on the assistance of England. Still Lord Salisbury worked energetically with the Plenipotentiaries of Russia, who, after the Russian plan was rejected by England, retired behind Lord Salisbury and supported him loyally step by step, even to the 'irreducible minimum' to which he was reluctantly forced by instructions from home to pare down the excellent proposals which he had originally offered to the Conference. On one thing the Russian Plenipotentiaries and Lord Salisbury were thoroughly agreed—namely, that the Sultan would accept no proposals without coercion, as indeed he could not have done, since any scheme of reform that tends to put non-Musulmans on a footing of equality with Musulmans would be a violation of the theocratic laws of Islam, which no ruler can transgress without apostasy except under *force majeure*. Lord Salisbury's sagacity and knowledge told him that the key to the problem was an amicable understanding between Russia and England, and he directed his diplomacy to that end. But the pro-Turkish Press in London, with the *Pall Mall Gazette* at the head of it, started a campaign of slander against Lord Salisbury, and did its very best to belittle his authority abroad and his influence at home. The arrant nonsense that was distributed in London from day to day will now appear incredible, but was then largely believed. Lord Salisbury was the dupe of Ignatieff. His real object was union between the Churches of Russia and England, and he was sacrificing the honour and interests of his country to that dream. Lady Salisbury could not be seen in the same carriage with Madame Ignatieff, or shaking hands with the Russian Plenipotentiary, without the portentous fact being telegraphed to London as a proof of Lord Salisbury's folly or perfidy. This is the sort of stuff which the *Pall Mall Gazette* poured out almost daily in acid streams of vigorous English. It is comical reading now; but it had considerable effect at the time. Other papers followed the lead of the *Pall Mall*, and the campaign of depreciation and slander helped to undermine Lord Salisbury's position both at Constantinople and in London. For there were occult influences at work at the same time. It was no secret that Lord Salisbury's colleague at the Conference was more in sympathy with Midhat Pasha than with Lord Salisbury. And that fervid disciple of David Urquhart, who proved the sincerity of his convictions by the ruin of his fine estate in the Sultan's cause—poor Mr. Butler Johnston—was for months flitting about between the Sultan and the Porte, exhorting them to pay no heed to Lord Salisbury, since Lord Beaconsfield was heartily with them and would see them through their troubles.

Thus it was that Lord Salisbury's mission to Constantinople failed, and that Abdul Hamid, buoyed up by false hopes, was mad enough to engage in war with Russia. So sure was he of his ground that he thought he could afford to give vent to his spirit of vindictiveness by attempting to put an affront on Lord Salisbury. For when the latter called to take his leave of him, the Sultan pleaded a sudden attack of diplomatic toothache, and refused to see him. Mr. Frederick Greenwood has now raised a corner of the curtain which has hitherto veiled the intrigue that made Lord Salisbury's mission to Constantinople abortive. In a signed article in the *Pall Mall Gazette* of the 16th of last September, Mr. Greenwood makes the following statement:—

Disraeli's policy during the Russo-Turkish War was a policy of armed intervention. He would have fought the Russians in alliance with the Turks. If he could he would have raised Turkestan against the Russians at the same time for the relief of our Indian frontier: measures to that effect were considered, if not arranged. That was what he proposed to do and would have done but for the strong opposition of his colleagues in the Cabinet. His motive? . . . It is true that Disraeli was a Jew, was pleased with the grandiose, would no doubt have liked to link his name with a memorable Eastern enterprise, and was probably grateful to those Mahommedan Turks who were so good to his people. . . . Disraeli thought this policy good, because it bolstered up the British Empire, and did so not in keeping up Turkey, but in keeping Russia down.

I thought at the time of his journalistic campaign against Lord Salisbury that Mr. Greenwood had access to Cabinet secrets, and this article of his shows that I thought rightly. As he has not scrupled to divulge so much, it is better that the public should know a little more. Yes; a plan of campaign against Russia was really arranged after Lord Salisbury's mission to Constantinople. An attempt was to have been made to raise Turkestan against her in preparation for an invasion from India, and I believe that British troops were also to be landed at Trebizond and an attack made on Russia from that side also. That plan of campaign is in the Russian Foreign Office, for political secrets will out. Is it so very surprising that Russia should be exceedingly suspicious about the designs of England? As Mr. Greenwood's incomplete revelation is calculated seriously to prejudice Lord Salisbury's diplomacy at this critical moment, I will add that the man who took the lead against Lord Beaconsfield on that occasion, and defeated him in his own Cabinet, was Lord Salisbury. So at least Lord Carnarvon told me in the course of a quiet walk in the park of Longleat in the year 1878. I have not repeated it till now; but I think I am justified in revealing it under the circumstances. Is it possible to avoid the conclusion that Lord Salisbury's mission to Constantinople was never intended, by some one, to be a success, but merely to gain time for allied England and Turkey to get ready for Mr. Disraeli's 'three campaigns'? Of that policy itself it is really not necessary to speak at this time of day. I should imagine that Mr. Greenwood, that pathetic Abdiel of a lost cause, is now the only defender of it. He is still a believer in the possibility of 'keeping Russia down,' and emphasises his formula with Dantesque iteration. The possibility of keeping down a growing empire of 125,000,000 souls and boundless resources by an alliance with a moribund despotism of 17,000,000 Musulmans! A Mezentian alliance truly!

> Mortua quin etiam jungebat corpora vivis,
> Componens manibusque manus atque oribus ora,
> Tormenti genus! et sanie taboque fluentes
> Complexu in misero, longa sic morte necabat.*

I trust that I shall offend none of Lord Beaconsfield's admirers by humbly expressing my opinion that his policy on the Eastern question smacked more of the novelist than of the statesman. He tried to realise the dreams of 'Tancred.' And he succeeded, too, in part. That he imagined that he was serving the

* *Æneid*, viii. 485.

British Empire well at the same time I have no doubt. But suppose—for I have no knowledge on that subject—that Lord Salisbury could only defeat the Mezentian policy by a compromise which included the Cyprus Convention and the division of Bulgaria, then I think those transactions may wear a different aspect both for his countrymen and for Russia, so far as he is concerned.

I think I have said enough to show that Lord Salisbury, from his first speech on the Eastern question down to the Treaty of Berlin, has been an opponent of an alliance with Turkey, and a supporter of a friendly understanding with Russia. In my next article I think I can show that he has continued in that policy till now; and has exemplified it by a service which he has lately done to Russia even more signal than his defeat of Lord Beaconsfield's 'three campaigns.' It is a dramatic ending to a great political career if Mr. Gladstone's last appearance on a public platform has been in support of the Minister who, as a young nobleman, deserted Mr. Disraeli in order to support with his first speech on the Eastern question Mr. Gladstone's eloquent pleading for the liberation of Roumania from the curse of Turkish misrule.

CHAPTER VII.

LORD SALISBURY AND BISMARCK.

It really seems as if one required some sort of intellectual Röntgen tube to reach the intelligence of those nervous persons who in their unreasoning panic keep on declaring that separate action on the part of England would be to court a European war. Did Lord Salisbury court a European war when he took his own line on the Cretan question without the co-operation of the other Powers? Did Mr. Gladstone court a European war when he acted without the co-operation of the other Powers in 1880? On the contrary, separate action on the part of those statesmen averted the danger of European war, while it vindicated at the same time the honour of England. Lord Rosebery has lately upbraided Lord Salisbury for pursuing a policy which is 'neither spirited nor skilful.' Is it either spirited or skilful to tell the other Powers of Europe and the Sultan that under no imaginable circumstances will we separate from the Concert of Europe, even after Count Goluchowski has declared, as related in the Blue Book, that the policy of the Concert of Europe—at least as far as Austria can influence it—is to stand quietly by while the Sultan is proceeding to the 'extermination of the miserable Armenians'? How much wiser as well as more skilful is Mr. Gladstone's policy as expounded in his Liverpool speech :—

> While I admit that it is of the utmost importance that we should study every means of consulting the sentiments of other Powers, and of carrying them along with us, I do not believe that the way to carry them along with us is to show a servile determination under all circumstances, and whatever they may decide, to make their conscience the measure of our own.

A noble sentiment, cheered to the echo by Conservatives and Liberals alike. It now appears that the policy of showing the white feather is opposed to Lord Salisbury's not less than to Mr. Gladstone's, for the Liverpool resolution, drawn up in consultation with Lord Derby, 'assures Her Majesty's Ministers that they may rely on the cordial support of the citizens of Liverpool *in whatever steps* they may feel it necessary to take.'

Separate action may be of various kinds. It may consist in declining to be a party any longer to the fatuous policy of futile 'admonition' and 'representations,' which Lord Salisbury has himself denounced as worse than useless. It may consist in the cessation of diplomatic intercourse with a convicted assassin. It may consist in suggesting to the other Powers that England should act alone; and, if they menace her with armed opposition, to retire and throw on them, in the face of civilised mankind, the terrible responsibility of the consequences—a responsibility which they are by no means likely to accept. It is surely making too large a demand on our intelligence to ask us to believe that the adoption of any of these courses would be to court a European war. It would be, on the contrary, the best way to avoid it. The recent pacification of Crete is one instance of successful separate action on the part of Lord Salisbury, and some more will appear in the course of my narrative of Lord Salisbury's diplomatic management of the Eastern question.

Lord Beaconsfield seemed to think that the division of the Bulgaria created by the Treaty of San Stefano was the culmination of his triumph at Berlin. It is said that he ordered a special train to take him home on the morrow unless Russia yielded on that point. I doubt whether that policy ever commended itself to Lord Salisbury's mind. Why, then, did he sanction it? There are cases where a statesman must balance the claims of varying duties, and is obliged to choose the course which he considers, not the best abstractedly, but the one which, under the circumstances, he believes to be the least likely to do mischief. All statesmen, even the most powerful, must sometimes act on this principle of compromise. But let events speak for themselves.

In the year 1881 a deputation from the two severed divisions of Bulgaria made the round of the Courts of the six Powers, in the hope of persuading them to allow the reunion of the two provinces. A Liberal Government was then in office, and the deputation naturally came to London first. But Lord Granville, then Foreign Secretary, refused to see them. Greatly surprised and grieved, they called on me, for I was known to several of them before. I tried to make them understand how the very fact of Lord Granville being a member of Mr. Gladstone's Government made it all the more impossible for him, in his official position, to espouse their cause, or do anything that might expose him to the suspicion and imputation on the part of foreign Powers of intriguing to reopen the Eastern question. Both as a statesman out of office, and as one of the signatories of the Treaty of Berlin, Lord Salisbury could act with greater freedom. He received the Bulgarian deputation kindly, and, while refusing to encourage their hopes, advised them to be patient. Their mission, of course, was a failure at all the Courts, and they wrote to me in a mood of somewhat ominous despair. In my reply I said:—" There is nothing desperate in your case. Take a lesson from the union of the two Principalities of Roumania. Avoid giving any legitimate ground of complaint to the Porte or the Powers. Organise your finances. Get up a good army. Prove to Europe that you know how to govern yourselves; and then, one fine morning, unite yourselves without asking any one's leave, and you will find that, as in the case of Roumania, the same stupid dread of reopening the Eastern question, which will always prevent the Powers from combining to sanction your union, will equally prevent them from combining to undo your accomplished fact.' They took my advice. Years passed, and then one fine day Europe was astonished to find that divided Bulgaria had united itself in a quiet businesslike fashion, without tumult or bloodshed.

Lord Salisbury was at the time, as he is now, Prime Minister and Foreign Secretary. How did he act? He did not place his judgment and conscience at the feet of other Powers. He took no counsel of his fears, lest anybody should accuse him of courting a European war. Nor did he show any petty *amour propre* as to the undoing of what Lord Beaconsfield had ordered a special train to effect. He acted promptly and alone. He sanctioned the union of the two Bulgarias before any of the Powers had time to move, and thereby prevented, in all probability, a European war. Lord Rosebery would have consulted the European Concert before acting, beginning with the Sultan, and thereby done his best unwittingly to court a European war. Turkey had a treaty right to march troops into Bulgaria to undo the union, and would have had the support of Austria, Germany, and Servia in doing so. But Lord Salisbury's decision saved the situation. Even as it was, Austria egged Servia on to declare an unprovoked war against Bulgaria—Austria herself, as usual, lying low, in the hope of picking up some of the spoils won by others. But Austria underrated the strength and bravery of the Bulgarian army, and the military capacity of its gallant chief; and Servia got a sound beating for her pains, and was saved from disaster by the intervention of Austria. The Sultan was prevented from intervening by a warning from Lord Salisbury. So much for ' separate action ' !

All this is a matter of history. My next point is as yet, in its full details, one of the secrets of diplomacy. Lord Salisbury's warning to the Sultan in his Guildhall speech, and later at Brighton, has been characterised by some as a mere *brutum fulmen*. My belief is that Lord Salisbury meant business. It will be remembered that Mr. Goschen made a speech last March in which he said that England's ' splendid isolation ' was not compulsory, since she had refused invitations from some Powers to act with them on the Armenian question. What did Mr. Goschen mean ? I was on the Continent at the time, and was told on first-hand authority that Austria had proposed a demonstration of the fleets of the six Powers before Constantinople to bring the Sultan to reason on pain of deposition. Russia and France refused, doubtless suspecting some concealed design upon Constantinople. Austria and Germany then proposed that the other fleets should still carry out their programme; the fleets of England, Italy, and Austria passing the Dardanelles, while Germany lay in wait to join the three Powers in case Russia and France made any attempt to oppose them. Lord Salisbury, while ready to join in a naval demonstration by all the Powers, or by some of them with the acquiescence of the rest, refused to have anything to do with an enterprise which embraced the contingency of a combined attack on France and Russia.

Such is the story which I was told by one who was in a position to know, and there is nothing inherently improbable in it. The secular policy of Germany and Austria is to keep Russia away from Constantinople and the region of the Danube, and England has hitherto been good enough to play their game and fight their battle. The Franco-Russian alliance is a formidable fact for the two Northern Powers, and it would suit them well to get England and Italy to help them to seize Constantinople by a *coup de main*. The combination could have crushed the united fleets of France and Russia. England would

have been ensnared into the Triple Alliance, and
Germany and Austria would have been rid of
the nightmare of the Franco-Russian alliance.
Or, if it suited his game, the 'honest broker'
would have left his dupes in the lurch, and come
to terms with France and Russia. For Bismarck
is still the ruling spirit of the German Foreign
Office. It escaped notice at the time that the
German Emperor paid a flying visit to Friedrichsruh before sending the famous Kruger
telegram. Bismarck's method has always been
first to dupe and then to betray and crush his
victim. His nefarious acquisition of the Elbe
Duchies; his bamboozling of the Germanic
Confederation and absorption of the minor
States; his wars on Austria and France after
first lulling their suspicions with false promises
and hopes; his use of Russia to keep Austria in
check while he was crushing France, and then
his betrayal of her at the Congress of Berlin
by putting Austria in a position to dominate the
Balkan States and watch her opportunity to seize
Constantinople: these are examples of Prince
Bismarck's diplomacy. He is the greatest enemy
of England since the first Napoleon; and his
enmity springs from two causes. In 1870 Mr.
Gladstone refused to give implicit credence to
Prince Bismarck's story of the Bismarck-Benedetti draft treaty for the spoliation of Belgium,
and required both Prussia and France to sign a
treaty with England to respect Belgium on pain

of reckoning with England as an ally against the Power that invaded Belgium. In 1875 Lord Beaconsfield's Government joined that of Russia in preventing Bismarck and Moltke from an unprovoked war against France, whose rapid recovery from her great defeat surprised and alarmed them, and whom they wished this time, in Prince Bismarck's phrase, 'to bleed white.' 'I will not permit all the laws of the civilised world to be transgressed and Europe plunged into the horrors of war again,' said the Tsar to the French Ambassador at St. Petersburg.* 'The old Emperor,' said Lord Derby to the French Chargé d'Affaires in London, 'does not wish for another war, and was ignorant, as we have seen, of the plot going on around him. Prince Bismarck desires it, and is in a hurry to bring it on during the Emperor William's lifetime.'† It now appears that our Queen also intervened effectively by a letter to the German Emperor, for Prince Bismarck has lately published in his Hamburg organ his own insolent attack on Her Majesty and the Empress Frederick, in his reply to the Emperor's request for an explanation. Prince Bismarck seems to be a man who, spite of all his greatness, is unable to forgive a check or slight, and has vindictively pursued even the wretched printer

---

* See *Alexander II., sa Vie, son Œuvre*, p. 292.

† See M. Gavard's Notes in the *Correspondant* of November 25, 1894.

of a pamphlet unfavourable to the great statesman. He has never forgiven England for the checks of 1870 and 1875.

But there is a deeper reason for his hostility to Great Britain. His huge armaments are an intolerable burden to the Fatherland, and the conscription is driving crowds of able-bodied Germans every year into foreign lands. Germany therefore needs colonies rich and attractive enough to allure Germans, who would thus remain still available as soldiers. If Bismarck could only destroy the naval supremacy of England, he might oust her from South Africa and supplant her commercial marine primacy. He has accordingly devoted his ingenuity for the last quarter of a century to the task of provoking a war between England and Russia, or England and France—a war which would have the additional advantage of crippling for a time one of the Powers which he dreads. Hence the excitement of the Press of Germany and Austria just now, caused by the visit of the Tsar and Tsaritsa to Balmoral. Hence the *canards* about a Russian General inspecting the fortifications of the Dardanelles, and the Russian Dragoman secretly advising the Sultan to reject the proposals of the Powers. Austria and Germany are in mortal fright lest England and Russia should come to a friendly understanding, and their Press has begun again its congenial occupation of sowing distrust between them. But 'in vain is the net spread in the sight of any bird.' The people of this country have come to realise that the ownership of Constantinople is not a British interest, however much it may be an Austrian interest; and that, in any case, there is no difficulty which need keep England and Russia apart, or England and France either. A leading French paper the other day suggested that France might seek in Syria her compensation for the British occupation of Egypt. Why should she not? England is not likely to oppose her. In short, everything points to a new grouping of the Powers, based on a friendly understanding between England, Russia, France, and Italy.

CHAPTER VIII.

PRECEDENTS FOR SEPARATE ACTION.

I INSERT the following letter not only in fairness to Mr. Greenwood, but also in order to emphasise Lord Salisbury's service both to England and Russia on that occasion.

To the Editor of the 'DAILY CHRONICLE.'

SIR,—Canon MacColl, in an article printed in this morning's *Daily Chronicle*, says that I am 'still a believer in the possibility of keeping Russia down.' Since Canon MacColl must have read that article of mine from which he makes a meanly garbled extract (see the *Pall Mall Gazette* of September 16), I cannot imagine him unaware that this is not my case. The whole tenor and purpose of what I wrote, its intention and meaning in every line, is to the following effect:—Russia cannot be kept down; her ascendency over England and Europe—but particularly over England—is complete; and the last chance of keeping Russia out of the dictatorship which she now holds was lost when Disraeli's policy of 1877-78 was disallowed by his colleagues. Just where I say this Mr. MacColl's extract leaves off. Allow me to follow him with a few sentences from where he stops. 'Disraeli's anxiety was to prevent in 1878 what was fully accomplished in 1895, the absolute predominance of Russia in Europe and the East too.... His motive was the postponement to a far future of the dictatorship which England is now compelled to acknowledge. What is unintelligently called bolstering up the Turkish Empire was the seizing of an opportunity of rolling back the half-crippled Russian armies in ruin, breaking down the Russian prestige in Asia, and therewith destroying all idea of Russian ascendency for many a decade.' And then I say that 'no doubt Disraeli saw that this opportunity, if lost, would be the last,' and that it *was* the last. Europe must be turned topsy-turvy before another recurs.

So far, then, from believing it 'still possible to keep Russia down,' I complain that she has been allowed a position of absolute mastery which there is no present hope of shaking. What Canon MacColl dislikes, I fancy, is the further explanation that if Disraeli's policy had been permitted, and had been fairly successful, there would have been 'no Russian dictatorship in Turkey, and, at any rate for the present, no Russian mastery in Europe. To England would have been restored the most commanding voice at the Porte.' Nor can Mr. MacColl, in his heart, think that policy wrong which, had it been allowed, 'would have forestalled the Russian dictatorship under which the Armenians perish and the Sultan is shielded.' Or if he do think it wrong, how much the dictatorship must please him!

Trusting to your sense of fairness to print this answer to what you can see for yourself is an entirely unwarrantable misrepresentation, I am, your obedient servant,

FREDERICK GREENWOOD.

September 25.

I have too much respect not only for Mr. Greenwood's honesty and ability, but for the prudential rules of controversy, to lay myself wilfully open to the charge of 'entirely unwarrantable misrepresentation.' The truth is that I cut out as much of Mr. Greenwood's article as included even more than he has quoted in his letter to the *Daily Chronicle*. But finding that my article extended to such a length that I could find no room for my full quotation, I gave what I believed to be the gist of it, and gave also the reference to the number of the *Pall Mall Gazette* which contained the article, in order that the honesty of my quotation might be tested. I regarded Mr. Greenwood's opinion that the defeat of Mr. Disraeli's policy in 1877 had established for the future 'the absolute predominance of Russia in Europe and the East too' as a rhetorical exaggeration rather than the expression of his deliberate conviction. And I had more than surmise to guide me to that conclusion. For long after 1877—down to this very year, in fact—Mr. Greenwood has been urging this country to join the Triple Alliance, in order to prevent that predominance of Russia which he now tells us was irretrievably established by Lord Salisbury's defeat of Lord Beaconsfield's plot against Russia in 1877. I cannot see, then, that I have done him any injustice. As a matter of fact, Russia is not nearly as predominant in Europe now as she was from 1848 to the Crimean War.

But I must say a word on this scheme of 'seizing an opportunity of rolling back the half-crippled Russian armies in ruin, breaking down the Russian prestige in Asia, and therewith destroying all idea of Russian ascendency for many a decade.' England was to have achieved this easy triumph over a high-spirited nation of (at that time) 100,000,000 of human beings, and with no other ally than 'Abdul the Damned.' Napoleon tried that achievement with an army incomparably greater than any that England and Turkey could have put into the field, and failed disastrously. Has Mr. Greenwood forgotten that it took the combined military and naval forces of England, France, Sardinia, and Turkey more than two years to conquer Russia forty years ago, when Russia had scarcely any railways, and was otherwise less prepared for war than in 1877? Yet Russia is again, in his opinion, in a position of 'absolute predominance in Europe.' And while this deadly contest, of which Mr. Greenwood was so ardent an advocate, was going on, the 'honest broker' would be lying in ambush till Russia and England were exhausted, when he would step in to make terms with Russia at England's cost, and perhaps achieve his long-cherished purpose of reducing this country to the rank of a second-rate Power.

But what about the morality of the plot? Where would be England's *casus belli*? Russia made war on Turkey, with the approbation of Europe, for the liberation of millions of Christians suffering as the Armenians are suffering now, and she gave absolute guarantees of good faith which Lord Beaconsfield's Government accepted as satisfactory. Mr. Greenwood has now revealed the fact that in the midst of that most righteous war Lord Beaconsfield hatched a plot for 'rolling back the half-crippled Russian armies in ruin,' and riveting the yoke of Abdul Hamid on the necks of his half-delivered victims. Thus 'was lost,' according to Mr. Greenwood, an opportunity of giving England 'the most commanding voice at the Porte,' 'when Disraeli's policy of 1877-78 was disallowed by his colleagues.'

Mr. Greenwood thinks that he is honouring the memory of Lord Beaconsfield by thus exhibiting him in the character of a freebooter, smitten with 'midsummer madness,' instead of that of a civilised statesman ! If Lord Salisbury had done no other service to his country, he would deserve undying gratitude for having saved us from that deadly peril and everlasting infamy.

I will now proceed to show how complete a case Lord Salisbury could make for separate action if he thought it expedient to make such a proposal to the Powers. And let me say, in passing, that those show a singular kind of confidence in Lord Salisbury who tell him that they will support him as long as he acts with the other Powers, but no longer. We may assume that the resolution of the Liverpool meeting, which received the sanction of Lord Derby as well as Mr. Gladstone, is a fair reflex of Lord Salisbury's mind, and that resolution promised the Government 'cordial support' '*in whatever steps* they may feel it necessary to take' in discharging the nation's obligations. Lord Salisbury has thus a free hand from the country, and may exercise his own discretion undismayed by the timid counsels of the few who seem to think that the best way to strengthen his hands is to proclaim to the world that England can be frightened from her righteous purpose by the mere frown of some foreign Power. Nobody is urging Lord Salisbury to go to war. The country has declared that it trusts him to do the best that circumstances will admit of, and this not so much for the benefit of Lord Salisbury himself as for the purpose of showing foreign nations that this is no artificial agitation like those sometimes manufactured in Austria, Germany, and Turkey, but the spontaneous uprising of a free nation enjoying the advantage of a free Press.

And now let me indicate, out of the Blue Books of 1876-77, the case that England may make out for separate action if she thinks it right to propose it. In replying to Lord Derby's invitation to the Conference of Constantinople, Prince Gortchakoff, after expressing his general agreement with the bases of negotiations laid down, uttered the following warning against too formal a recognition of the independence of the Sultan, as likely to hamper negotiations :—

If the Great Powers wish to accomplish a real work, and not expose themselves to the periodical and aggravated return of this dangerous crisis, it is impossible that they should persevere in the system which permits the germs of it to exist and develop with the inflexible logic of facts. It is necessary to escape from this vicious circle, and to recognise that the independence and integrity of Turkey must be subordinated to the guarantees demanded by humanity, the sentiments of Christian Europe, and the general peace. The Porte has been the first to infringe the engagement which she contracted by the Treaty of Paris with regard to her Christian subjects. It is the right and duty of Europe to dictate to her the conditions on which alone it can on its part consent to the maintenance of the *status quo* created by that treaty ; and since the Porte is incapable of fulfilling them, it is the right and duty of Europe to substitute itself for her to the extent necessary to insure their execution. Russia can, less than any other Power, consent to renew the experiences of palliatives, of half-measures, of illusory programmes, which have led to the results which are under the eyes of all, and which react on her tranquillity and internal prosperity ; but if she is more directly and more sensibly interested in putting an end to it by real and adequately guaranteed improvements, she none the less considers this question one of general interest, calling for the concord of all the Powers with a view to its pacific solution. With reference to the personal views which she brings into the pursuit of this object, they are free from all exclusive *arrière-pensées* : the most positive assurances in this respect have many times been given by the Imperial Cabinet.*

What answer could· Russia and the other Powers make if Lord Salisbury were to present this admirable Russian despatch to them and advise them to act upon it now, *mutatis mutandis*? Or this, also from Prince Gortchakoff, on November 13, 1876 ?—

The Imperial Cabinet, finding itself in presence of a question where political interests should make way before the universal interests of humanity and European peace, has done its utmost to bring about an agreement among the Great Powers. For itself, it will neglect no effort in order that this agreement may bring about a practical and substantial result, and one which will

* *Turkey*, No. 1 (1877), p. 719.

satisfy the exigencies of public opinion and of general peace. But while diplomacy has been deliberating for a whole year with a view to reduce to practice the combined wishes of Europe, the Porte has had time to summon from the recesses of Asia and Africa the *ban* and *arrière-ban* of the disciplined forces of Islâmism, to arouse Musulman fanaticism, and to crush under the weight of its numbers the Christian populations who are struggling for their very existence. The perpetrators of the horrible massacres which have so shocked Europe remain unpunished, and at this very moment their example tends to propagate and perpetuate throughout the whole of the Ottoman Empire, and in full view of indignant Europe, similar acts of violence and barbarism. . . . His Imperial Majesty does not wish for war, and will do his utmost to avoid it; but he is determined not to halt before the principles which have been recognised by the whole of Europe as just, humane, and necessary, and which public opinion in Russia has taken up with the greatest energy, have been fully carried out and secured by efficient guarantees.

Could any one more accurately describe the present situation and the English position, even to the appeal to the public opinion behind him which the Autocrat of All the Russias was not ashamed to make? There is just one little difference — namely, that the crimes of the Sultan are now infinitely more heinous in character and in extent, as well as flaunted with greater insolence 'in full view of indignant Europe,' than they were in 1877.

On the 5th of the following December Prince Bismarck made a speech in the Reichstag.

After quoting this declaration of the Tsar, and denouncing the Bulgarian massacres as 'revolting to the conscience of the whole of Europe,' he said :—

Should the Conference not lead to any result, and should Russia determine to obtain by force of arms what she has failed to obtain by pacific means, we shall put no veto on her action, since the objects she pursues are also our own, and we have no reason to believe that she will pass the limits of those objects. No one shall succeed in disturbing our friendly relations with Russia, for the alliance of the three Emperors, formed some time ago, subsists to-day in its integrity.*

It was in face of that alliance that Lord Beaconsfield proposed, with Mr. Greenwood's energetic support, to make war on Russia in alliance with Abdul Hamid! The other Powers took the same view as Germany and Austria. The Foreign Minister of France, Duc Decazes, pledged France, in the event of Russia enforcing the will of Europe on the Sultan at the point of the sword, to a policy of 'absolute neutrality, guaranteed by the most absolute non-intervention.'†

Signor Depretis, Prime Minister of Italy, took occasion, in a speech to his constituents a short time before the Constantinople Conference, to reprobate 'an excessive prudence' which should sacrifice 'the grand principles of civilisation and humanity to the traditions of

---

* *Nouvelle Etude sur la Question d'Orient*, p. 22.
† *Turkey*, No. 25 (1877), p. 138.

diplomacy and the cold calculation of political interests.'

I do not believe that the nineteen years that have elapsed since then have destroyed the moral sense of Christian Europe. It is not dead, but sleepeth. Mr. Gladstone's noble speech will have done much to awake it; and if Lord Salisbury were to formulate England's case now on the basis of Russia's case (which received the sanction of Europe) in 1877, I believe that he would carry Europe with him. That would not mean war. There would have been no war in 1877 if the Sultan, as Lord Salisbury has told us, had not counted on the support of England. Let me then put an extreme case—though I believe, for my part, that Lord Salisbury will now be able, with a united nation at his back, to persuade the other Powers to adopt his policy of coercion. Let me suppose that he proposes to occupy some point of Turkish territory with the fleet till Turkey gives satisfaction to Europe, offering at the same time such guarantees of disinterestedness as Russia offered in 1877. That would not be war. It would be a pacific method, well known to diplomacy, of enforcing just claims, and often practised by all Governments. Surely no sensible man will say that the mere proposal of such a thing would provoke a European war. The supposition is preposterous, and those who hazard it on that ground are simply proposing to degrade Great Britain from her position as a great Power. The nation which has not the pluck to make so moderate a proposal to Europe has abdicated its position as a Power of the first class, and has gone out of its way to invite insult and aggression. The other Powers would be more likely to join England in such a pacific solution of the crisis that now threatens the very catastrophe which they fear—the downfall of the Turkish Empire —than in thwarting her proposal. My own belief is that, once Russia is convinced that England has now no plot against her, as in 1877, she will return to her old tradition of protecting the Christians of Turkey, and perhaps send troops into Armenia while the British Fleet co-operates wherever its action may be thought most effectual. The mere knowledge that such action was contemplated by Russia and England would bring the Sultan to his knees at once, as in 1880, and the question would be settled without bitterness or danger. It is the interest of every Power to settle it speedily, except Austria and possibly Germany. Austria has her eye on Macedonia, and it is not her interest to see any reforms introduced into Asiatic Turkey which would set a precedent for similar reforms in Macedonia. The late Lord Derby accused Austria to her face, as the Blue Books testify, of having got up and of keeping alive, for her own ends, the insurrection in Bosnia and the Herzegovina. So now her policy is to keep discontent and disaffection simmering in Macedonia, in the hope of some day getting the sanction of Europe to occupy Macedonia after the precedent of Bosnia. Germany, too, covets a good slice of Asiatic Turkey when the fruit is ripe for her plucking. She has once again declared that for her the Eastern question 'is not worth the bones of a Pomeranian grenadier.' I am sick of the Pomeranian grenadier and his bones. Nobody wants him, and I trust that his friends will now give him a decent burial and have done with him. But the plain truth is that Germany intends, with the aid of Austria and any other combination which she may succeed in forming, to play a leading part in the final solution of the Eastern question, and in a manner by no means to the advantage of France and Russia. All these considerations make for the peaceful settlement of the Armenian question through a friendly understanding between Russia, France, Italy, and Great Britain.

CHAPTER IX.

BRITAIN'S TRADITIONAL POLICY.

We have heard much of late about 'our traditional policy towards Turkey,' and about the Sultan of Turkey as 'our ancient ally.' Now the plain fact is that our traditional policy towards Turkey has branded that Government as a barbarous Power, beyond the pale of civilisation, and which, therefore, it was necessary to keep in decent order by the strong arm of coercion. Through the influence of Lord Palmerston this barbarous Power was admitted within the comity of European nations by the Treaty of Paris—'one of the greatest blunders, if not one of the greatest crimes, in history,' said Dr. Döllinger, a master of the subject, to me in the year 1877. But although Lord Palmerston unfortunately succeeded in persuading the Congress of Paris to admit an irretrievably barbarous Power into the political system of Europe, it was on condition that the Sultan should be put in leading-strings and obey the behests of the Christian Powers. In the House of Commons' debate on the Treaty of Paris in 1856 he went out of his way to explain that the maintenance of the Turkish Empire did not necessarily mean the maintenance of the Turkish race in that Empire. 'We did not engage,' he said, 'to maintain in the Turkish Empire this or that race—one dominant party or the other.' Lord Palmerston thought it impossible to get any fundamental change introduced into the administration of Turkey during the reign of Abdul Medjid, the Sultan of the Crimean War period; but he had great hopes of his successor, and wrote to the British Ambassador at the Porte urging some drastic reforms. He recommended the Sultan to put 'into execution the system of liberal toleration and progressive internal improvement established by his predecessor *on paper*... But the Sultan must begin by clearing out the harem, dismissing his architects and builders, and turning off his robber Ministers.'*

Such was the policy of Europe down to the Cretan Insurrection of 1866-67: diplomatic interference in the affairs of Turkey for the protection of the non-Musulman subjects of the Sultan, and, when diplomatic intervention failed, material coercion. It is the policy with which are associated the best traditions of British statesmanship, Liberal and Tory: Burke, the two Pitts, Fox, Lord Holland, Mackintosh, Canning, Peel, Lord Aberdeen, Lord Palmerston, Lord Russell, Mr. Gladstone, Lord Salisbury. A

* Ashley's *Life of Lord Palmerston*, ii. p. 213.

few typical examples will suffice. Lord Holland was as far removed as most men from a fanatical or intolerant temper, yet he did not hesitate to speak as follows :—

> The anti-social race which now enjoys the throne of the Constantines considers itself naturally at war with every nation with which it has not entered into a formal treaty of peace. Mr. Addison, who was not only a philosopher but one of the wisest and best men on the face of the earth, remarked upon the bad effect of the numerous journalists in this country, and went on to say that, though there was no absurdity to which people, by this itch for talking and writing politics, might not be brought, he did not believe it possible that there could be persons in England who could think that we were interested in the prosperity of the Ottoman Empire. . . . Almost every man who had held office and had authority stated that the opinion of Lord Chatham was that we should never have any kind of connection whatever with the Ottoman Porte, and that opinion was fortified during the Seven Years' War by a similar opinion of the King of Prussia. In 1772 our allies, the Russians, sent a great fleet into the Mediterranean for the purpose of overpowering the Turks. What was the policy of this country? To assist the Russian navy. That fleet was refitted in our harbours, and, with the munitions and implements which it received from us, burnt a Turkish town and fleet, and continued cruising in the Archipelago for no less than five or six years.

In the year 1791 there was a great debate in the House of Commons on a proposal by Pitt to join Turkey and Prussia in compelling Russia to restore to the Sultan some territory which she had extorted from him in the Crimea. Burke spoke against the proposal with his usual eloquence and force, and in a tone of pathetic solemnity characterised the proposal as 'the most extraordinary event that passed in that House since he had the honour to sit in it.' He 'could not account for' Mr. Pitt proposing anything so opposed to the traditions of British policy. An extract or two from the speech will show its drift :—

As in all probability this will be the last time I shall ever speak upon a political question in this House, I beg leave to intrude upon its patience a few minutes. It may arise from the prejudices of an old man that I cannot help feeling an alarm at any new principles of policy; but since I have sat in this House, I solemnly declare I have never heard anything so new as what I have heard advanced this evening. The confidence claimed by His Majesty's Ministers is new. The principle of alliance [with Turkey], and the doctrine drawn from thence, are entirely new. . . . I have never before heard it held forth that the Turkish Empire was ever considered as any part of the balance of power in Europe. They have nothing to do with European power. They consider themselves as wholly Asiatic. . . . They despise and contemn all Christian Princes as infidels, and only wish to subdue and exterminate them and their people. What have these worse than savages to do with the Powers of Europe but to spread war, destruction, and pestilence among them? The Ministers and the policy which shall give these people any weight in Europe will deserve all the bans and curses of posterity. All that is holy in religion, all that is moral and humane, demands an abhorrence of everything which tends to extend the power of that cruel and wasteful Empire. Any Christian Power is to be preferred to these destructive savages. . . . Russia is our natural ally, and the most useful ally we have in a commercial sense.

Fox took the same line in a powerful speech. The proposal to join the Turks and the Prussians in an attack on Russia he denounced as 'conduct so unreasonable, so unjust, so insolent as he had never before witnessed.'

It would be madness in us to show the most lively jealousy of the growing power of Russia in the Black Sea. But it might be said that if the Russians became masters of the Black Sea, they would soon appear in the Mediterranean. It was indifferent to him if they did, for then there would be three Powers in that sea, and as the two former were allies it was probable we might be assisted by the third [Russia].

Pitt carried his proposals in both Houses of Parliament; but the country declared so unequivocally against his pro-Turkish policy, that he dropped it incontinently, and henceforth was an advocate for a friendly understanding with Russia. One of the curious features of the debate in both Houses was the hearty denunciation of the conduct of Prussia, which, then as now, was apparently eager to sacrifice the freedom and happiness of the Christians of Turkey to her own sordid ends. 'The Prussians,' said Earl Fitzwilliam, 'were desirous to obtain possession of Moldavia [then in the possession of Russia] merely in order to give it up to the

Turks. But was it not better that it should remain in the hands of a Christian Sovereign than be subjected to the dominion of a Mohammedan Prince?'*

Sir James Mackintosh said in another debate :—

It was bare justice to Russia to say that her dealings with the Ottoman Power for the last seven years had been marked with as great forbearance as the conduct of Turkey had been distinguished by continued insolence and incorrigible contumacy. Facts proved that if Russia was to be blamed at all it was rather for the long patience she had exercised than for any premature interference. . . . The war against the Greeks was waged against defenceless women and children, with the superadded aggravation of the burning of villages, the rooting up of trees, the destruction not only of works of art but of the productions of Nature herself, as well as those of man.†

Sir Robert Peel, in a speech in the House of Commons on March 24, 1828, said :—

Previous to the signature of the Treaty (of July 6) an intimation was given to His Majesty's Government that it was the intention of Turkey to remove from the Morea the female part of the population and the children for the purpose of selling them in Egypt as slaves, &c. Distinct notification was given to Ibrahim Pasha that so violent an exercise of rights—if rights they could be called—that a proceeding so repugnant to the established usage of civilised nations never would be permitted by His Majesty, and that this country

---

* *Hansard*, vol. xxix. (1791), pp. 32–81.
† *Ibid.* Second Series, vol. i. pp. 400–1409.

would certainly resist any attempt to carry such an object into effect.

That was the manly and patriotic language of the Conservative party of that day, and indicates, as I believe, the spirit of the Conservative party of to-day. And Sir Robert Peel had the advantage of having a Liberal leader opposite him who supported him heartily, instead of beseeching him, for God's sake, to beware of courting a European war. The mere threat of Sir Robert Peel sufficed, for the Sultan knew he had to deal with a Government, backed by the nation, which had the will as well as the power to enforce its threat. Lord John Russell had two months previously (January 29) used the following language in the House of Commons :—

We believe the battle (Navarino) to have been a glorious victory and a necessary consequence of the Treaty of London, and, moreover, as honest a victory as had ever been gained from the beginning of the world. . . . Turkey was spoken of as an ancient ally. Now the fact was that there never had been any alliance between Turkey and this country prior to 1799, and it was not twenty years since Mr. Arbuthnot had been compelled to fly privately from Constantinople from his fear that his personal safety would be endangered by a violation of the ordinary rights of Ambassadors.

The alliance to which Lord John Russell referred was a very short-lived one, and there was no other till the Crimean War. 'The travelled Thane, Athenian Aberdeen,' was not a man to let either his tongue or pen run away with him; he was also one of the most experienced Foreign Secretaries that England has ever had, as well as one of the best. And it was on the eve of the Crimean War, and from the responsible position of Prime Minister of England, that he deliberately put on record the following opinion :—

Notwithstanding the favourable opinion entertained by many, it is difficult to believe in the improvement of the Turks. It is true that under the pressure of the moment benevolent decrees may be issued; but these, except under the eye of some foreign minister, are entirely neglected. Their whole system is radically vicious and inhuman. I do not refer to fables which may be invented at St. Petersburg or Vienna [in answer to Lord Palmerston], but to numerous despatches of Lord Stratford himself, and of our own Consuls, who describe a frightful picture of lawless oppression and cruelty. This is so true that if the war should continue, and the Turkish armies meet with disaster, we may expect to see the Christian populations of the empire rise against their oppressors; and in such a case it would scarcely be proposed to employ the force in the Levant to assist in compelling their return under a Mohammedan yoke.*

In a 'Memorandum on Greek Affairs sent to Lord Goderich' on December 6, 1827, Lord Palmerston said :—

It seems now to be perfectly certain that the Porte

* *Life of the Prince Consort*, vol. ii. p. 528.

is obstinately determined to refuse compliance with the demands of the Allies with respect to Greece; and unless therefore the Allies are prepared to abandon the objects for which they coalesced, and to expose themselves by so doing to the derision of the whole world, it becomes necessary for them to concert, in pursuance of the agreement they have entered into, such further measures as may be necessary for the accomplishment of the ends of the Treaty of London. Persuasion, reasoning, and threats having failed to sway the Porte, actual coercion must be resorted to.

Lord Palmerston had a nation at his back, as Lord Salisbury has now, and by presenting a determined front in tones which showed that he intended to have his way he got his way. Would he have succeeded if a chorus of puling voices had gone forth warning him that his language was likely to bring on a European war? It is not by waving the white flag in the sight of Europe that England has won her triumphs on the field of diplomacy or of battle. In the Hatt-i-Humaioun of 1856 the Sultan engaged to put his Christian subjects on a footing of perfect equality in all respects with his Musulman subjects. 'The Treaty of Paris,' said Lord Palmerston in the House of Commons' debate on the subject at the time, 'having recorded that that Firman has been issued by the Sultan, it is perfectly plain to my mind that it cannot be revoked. In fact, that it should be revoked is a thing which I hold to be as impossible, almost, morally speaking, as that the sun should go backwards.' Again :—

Hitherto the Sultan has been like a person with but one leg to stand on, and but one arm to defend himself; for one-half of his subjects have had no interest in maintaining his empire, and have been precluded from all participation in its defence. Now, however, if this Firman be but faithfully carried out, all the subjects of the Sultan will have equal rights, and will equally contribute to the defence of the empire.*

All the world knows that no Sultan from that day to this has taken a single step to fulfil the solemn promises made to Europe, and on which Lord Palmerston relied as on the stability of the laws of Nature. The lot of the Christian subjects of the Sultan has, in fact, become much worse. There was no need to 'revoke' the Hatt-i-Humaioun, for it never became a legally valid document. No political act of the Sultan has any validity for his Ministers or subjects till it has received the *Fetva* of the Sheikh-ul-Islâm, and the Sheikh-ul-Islâm will never give his sanction, without coercion, to any Firman of the Sultan which promises to put the non-Musulman subjects on a footing of equality with the Musulmans. For Turkey is a theocracy, and its politics are based on the unchangeable dogmas of a religious law which forbids absolutely and eternally (without coercion) the equality of the non-Musulman with the Musulman. Hatts and Firmans, therefore, are mere dust thrown in the eyes of Europe,

* *Hansard*, Third Series, vol. cxlii. pp. 125–126.

and are never meant to have any effect. It is their crass ignorance of this fact that has made the diplomacy of European statesmen such a ghastly failure in Turkey. Russian statesmen know the fact, and so does Lord Salisbury. Hence Prince Lobanoff's reference as 'unworkable' to the scheme of reforms which Lord Rosebery bequeathed to his successor, and hence Lord Salisbury's complaint that 'he found his hands tied' when he acceded to office. The Sultan will never accept without coercion any scheme of reform which has the smallest value; or if he does accept it he will never execute one particle of it without European control. And so it was that when Lord Palmerston found that the Sultan's promises were mere waste paper, he took advantage of the Syrian massacres to teach Turkey a lesson. He took 'separate action' very energetically, got France to join him, and sent a fleet to Syria, with Lord Dufferin as Special Commissioner, to punish the official organisers of the massacres, and to rescue the district of the Lebanon from the uncontrolled yoke of the Sultan. Russia, to her credit, volunteered to send a man-of-war to join the Anglo-French fleet as a visible token of sympathy.

I have now shown that the traditional policy of this country has been, not alliance with Turkey, but coercion of Turkey, sometimes in concert with the other Powers, or with some of them, and sometimes by separate action, coupled with an understanding with Russia as often as circumstances allowed it. That policy prevailed till 1867, when a contrary policy was for the first time adopted.*

* I have referred to Midhat Pasha's article in the *Nineteenth Century*, in which he says that Turkey would not have engaged in war with Russia if the Porte had not been encouraged to rely on British aid. To this must be added the message dictated by Server Pasha, Foreign Minister of Turkey, for publication in England when Turkey lay prostrate at the feet of her conqueror. Server Pasha declared that England was entirely responsible for the war, and Turkey would now become an ally of Russia. And one of the Turkish Envoys with him added: ' We were encouraged to go to war by England, and even to continue the war when our better judgment told us we had better make peace on any terms. We would have made peace before the fall of Plevna that would have satisfied Russia but for the counsels of the English Government. I do not refer to the official notes of Lord Derby. If we believed them we had nothing to hope from England; but it is not official notes diplomatists believe in most. It is " officious " notes. It is words whispered in the ear. It was the private conversations of Lord Beaconsfield with Musurus Pasha, of Mr. Layard with Server Pasha and with the Sultan, that led us on and deceived us. Server Pasha has documents which will prove beyond doubt all I say.'

Sir H. Layard and Lord Beaconsfield contradicted this at the time; but Server Pasha chose to resign rather than withdraw a word; and now Mr. F. Greenwood's revelations in the *Pall Mall Gazette* and the *Cornhill Magazine* prove that Server Pasha was strictly accurate.—See *Daily News* of Feb. 7, 1877, and Thompson's *Public Opinion and Lord Beaconsfield*, ii. p. 377.

CHAPTER X.

THE NEW POLICY AND ITS CAUSES.

I SAID in my last chapter that when Pitt found that not only the leading British statesmen of the day, but the entire British nation, condemned the anti-Russian attitude into which he had allowed himself to be momentarily betrayed under the influence of Prussia, 'he dropped it incontinently, and henceforth was an advocate of a friendly understanding with Russia.' As I have based my argument all through on authoritative proof, I had better fortify this statement also by unimpeachable evidence. In a subsequent debate in the House of Commons Mr. Pitt eulogised Alexander I. of Russia as 'the most magnanimous and powerful Prince' of his age, as shown by his sacrifices 'for the deliverance of Europe.' This eulogy was greeted by a solitary jeer from Mr. Tierney, upon whom Pitt immediately turned with the retort: 'Does it not promise the deliverance of Europe when we find the armies of our allies (the Russians) rapidly advancing in a career of victory, at once the most brilliant and auspicious that ever signalised the exertions of any combination?'*

This policy continued down to the Crimean War—a war into which England was cleverly manœuvred by three men—the Emperor of the French, who had a special reason of his own to break the power of Russia, as I shall explain in my next chapter; Lord Stratford de Redcliffe, who had a personal quarrel to avenge on the Emperor Nicholas; and Lord Palmerston, who appeared to have been mesmerised by the Emperor of the French. I have related elsewhere (and it is also alluded to in the Greville and Malmesbury Memoirs) a painful story told me in 1877 by the late Lord Bath, with permission to publish it; but it is worth repeating here. Lord Palmerston and the British Ambassador at the Porte succeeded, with the powerful aid of Louis Napoleon, in persuading the Cabinet of Lord Aberdeen to agree to the despatch of the French and English fleets to Constantinople, Turkey having before then declared war against Russia—a challenge which Russia, on the advice of France and England, did not take up actively, as negotiations for peace were still going on. It was at this critical stage that the three conspirators, eager for war, managed to manœuvre the allied fleets to Constantinople, in the hope of provoking Russia into some indiscretion which would give France and England a *casus*

* *Hansard*, vol. xxxiv. p. 1046.

belli against her, or (still better) which might provoke Nicholas at last to declare war against the two Powers. While the allied fleets, many of which were sailing vessels, were waiting at the Dardanelles for a favourable wind to take them up to Constantinople, Lord Bath arrived in his yacht. Admiral Dundas, in command of the two fleets, visited him, and begged him on his arrival at Constantinople to call on the Ambassador and tell him that the allied fleets were at the Dardanelles, and would arrive at Constantinople as soon as the wind permitted. 'On delivering my message,' said Lord Bath to me, ' Sir Stratford Canning (as he then was) jumped up, and, apparently oblivious of my presence, stalked up and down the room muttering aloud to himself : " Ah ! the fleets will soon be here. Once they are here there must be war. It cannot be avoided. I shall take care that it is not avoided. I vowed to have my revenge upon that man [Nicholas, who had refused to receive him as Ambassador at St. Petersburg], and now, by God, I've got it." ' Yes, indeed, he got it. Under his inspiration the Turks used all their ingenuity to provoke Russia to attack them. They employed their navy to carry Turkish Bashi-Bazouks to the coast of Circassia, from which they conducted a guerilla warfare against Russia, while the Turkish fleet manœuvred in bravado before Sebastopol. After one of these piratical expeditions and challenges the Russian fleet came out from Sebastopol to engage the Turkish fleet, which immediately took to flight. The Russian fleet pursued, and sank it in the harbour of Sinope—a legitimate and justifiable operation of war, if ever there was one. But it was immediately denounced by Sir Stratford Canning as 'the massacre of Sinope,' and the London Press took up the cry and hounded the Government on to war. Lord Aberdeen and most of his Cabinet tried to stem the tide, while the Emperor of the French and Palmerston did their uttermost to swell the cry for war. The former proposed that France and England should order the Russian navy not to issue from their ports on pain of being driven back by the fleets of France and England. Palmerston urged this policy on the Cabinet in vain, whereupon he resigned on the pretext of disagreement with his colleagues on a domestic question. There was a popular clamour for his return to the Cabinet, and Lord Aberdeen, yielding to the storm, took Palmerston back on his own terms—namely, the acceptance of the French Emperor's proposed insult to Russia. The insulting order was issued, and Nicholas, seeing that France and England were bent on war, refused to accept any more humiliations, and broke off diplomatic intercourse.

Russia knew that the French Emperor was determined on war, and gave up all hope of conciliating him. But up to this last fatal affront the Tsar still cherished the hope of avoiding war with England. In a Russian official 'Diplomatic Study on the Crimean War' (Vol. i. p. 337) I read as follows:—

M. Drouyn de l'Huys (French Foreign Minister) proposed to order the admirals (of France and England) to declare to the Russian naval authorities that the allied Governments were resolved to prevent a repetition of the affair of Sinope; that consequently any Russian vessel met with at sea would be invited to put back into Sebastopol, and that any act of aggression against the territory or flag of Turkey would be repelled by force.

Yet Turkey had declared war on Russia and committed sundry acts of aggression, including the seizure of a Russian town. 'The English Cabinet,' continues the 'Diplomatic Study,' hesitated to take so serious a step 'as that proposed by the French Government'; and believing that 'the English Ministers had not lost every sentiment of justice and honour,' the Russian Government made an appeal to them which is pathetic in its pleading. I continue the quotation:—

The Russian Government for its part declared to them that nothing could have been more ill-founded than the supposition that any offence had been intended to France or England. 'What had occurred,' said the Chancellor of the Empire to Sir Hamilton Seymour (British Ambassador), 'was an inevitable result of the position taken up by the two Powers, and of that which they had assigned to Russia. Turkey wages war on us: she begins a campaign before the period fixed by herself; she takes from us Fort St. Nicholas, which she still retains, and you reproach us for meeting hostility with hostility! Pray remember that we are at war with Turkey, and that no one has ever heard of a war in which such acts as those of which you complain do not occur. Moreover, our alleged *attack* was a *defensive* measure. It is notorious that the Turkish squadron was carrying ammunition and troops intended to help and arm the tribes which are waging war upon our frontiers.'

But the appeal was made in vain. The lie of 'the massacre of Sinope' inflamed the British public and frightened Lord Aberdeen to take Palmerston back into the Cabinet on his own condition, namely, that the Government should join the French Cabinet in flinging this affront into the face of the proud Nicholas.

I still quote from the Russian official account:—

Lord Aberdeen was completely overwhelmed by the public exasperation. This was so great that, at the opening of Parliament, Prince Albert, the Queen's husband, involved in the odium then attaching to the peace party, was the object of popular insult. Lord Aberdeen did not disguise from our Minister the state of affairs. 'I am accused,' he said, 'of cowardice, of betraying my country to Russia. I dare not show myself in the streets; I am done for.'

It would be improper to bring the name of the Queen into such a discussion as this gratuitously. But the Queen has herself let her subjects into her confidence, and revealed the part which herself and the Prince Consort took in this deplorable business. They were behind the scenes, and saw clearly the deadly peril of allowing the British fleet to join the French fleet in a hostile demonstration against Russia. The following extracts from the 'Life of the Prince Consort' show how much more prescient and wise than either the nation or the Cabinet were the Queen and the Prince Consort :—

It appears to the Queen that we have taken on ourselves, in conjunction with France, all the risks of a European war without having bound Turkey to any conditions with respect to provoking it. The 120 fanatical Turks constituting the Divan at Constantinople are left sole judges of the line of policy to be pursued, and made cognisant at the same time of the fact that England and France have bound themselves to defend the Turkish territory. This is entrusting them with a power which Parliament has been jealous of confiding even to the hands of the British Crown. It may be a question whether England ought to go to war for the defence of the so-called Turkish independence ; but there can be none that, if she does so, she ought to be the sole judge of what constitutes a breach of that independence.

The Prince Consort, writing to Baron Stockmar on November 27, 1853, says :—

The prospects of a peaceful settlement in the East do not improve. Lord Stratford fulfils his instructions to the letter, but he so contrives that we are constantly getting deeper into a war policy. Six weeks ago Lord Palmerston and Lord John carried a resolution [*i.e.* in the Cabinet] that we should give notice that an attack on the Turkish fleet by that of Russia would be met by the fleets of England and

France. Now the Turkish steamships are to cross over from the Asiatic coast to the Crimea, and to pass before Sebastopol! This can only be meant to insult the Russian fleet, and to entice it to come out, in order thereby to make it possible for Lord Stratford to bring our fleet into collision with that of Russia according to his former instructions, and so to make a European war certain. Of course this is merely surmise. Still there are under-currents without end. ... The consequence is a set of measures, which the late Lord Liverpool would have called 'neither here nor there.'

The biographer, Sir Theodore Martin, continues:—

On December 16 the political world was startled by the announcement that Lord Palmerston had resigned. On the 25th it learnt that his resignation had been withdrawn and that peace was once more restored in the Cabinet. It was at this time that the destruction of the Turkish fleet at Sinope by a squadron, which had run out from Sebastopol for the purpose, realised all that had been apprehended as likely to result from sending the combined fleet to the Bosphorus, where its presence was a defiance to Russia, but futile to prevent a serious disaster to Turkey.

On December 23 the Prince wrote to Baron Stockmar from Windsor:—

The defeat of the Turks at Sinope, upon our element—the sea—has made the people furious; it is ascribed to Aberdeen having been bought over by Russia, and Palmerston is the only English Minister! ... One almost fancies oneself in a lunatic asylum.

The Prince himself, as we have seen, did not

escape these dishonouring imputations. On December 27 he writes :—

> The defeat at Sinope has made the people quite furious. Treachery is the cry, and, guided by a friendly hand, the whole Press has for the last week made 'a dead set at the Prince' (as the English phrase goes). My unconstitutional position, correspondence with foreign Courts, dislike to Palmerston, relationship to the Orleans family, interference with the army, &c., are depicted as the causes of the decline of the State, the Constitution, and the Nation; and, indeed, the stupidest trash is babbled to the public— so stupid that (as they say in Coburg) you would not give it to the pigs to litter in.

The view which I have taken of the origin of the Crimean War ever since I studied its diplomatic history for myself is thus confirmed by the Queen and the Prince Consort. The Duke of Argyll and Mr. Gladstone are now the only survivors of the Aberdeen Cabinet, and they have both defended the Crimean War on the ground that it was waged in vindication of the public law of Europe against a violation of it by the Emperor Nicholas. This defence is justified by the facts as they were presented to these illustrious statesmen. If the true state of the case had been known to them, I am sure they would never have given their consent to a war which was hatched in the brain of the Emperor Napoleon for his own private ends, manipulated with consummate craft, in order to avenge a personal grudge, by the British Ambassador at

Constantinople, and forced on the British Cabinet by the dexterity of Lord Palmerston.

One more extract from the Prince Consort's writings must end this part of my subject. He sent to the Cabinet a singularly able and comprehensive Memorandum on the objects and aims of the Crimean War after it had, through the manœuvres which I have described, become inevitable. The drift of his policy may be gathered from the following passage:—

> The war ought to be carried on unshackled by obligations to the Porte, and will probably lead, in the peace which must be the object of that war, to the obtaining of arrangements more consonant with the well understood interests of Europe, of Christianity, liberty, and civilisation than the reimposition of the ignorant, barbarian, and despotic yoke of the Musulman on the most fertile and favoured portion of Europe.*

It thus appears that the original author of the 'bag and baggage' policy was the Prince Consort. Lord Aberdeen and his Cabinet were in favour of it, with the exception of Lord Palmerston, who denounced it as 'aiming at expelling from Europe the Sultan and his two millions of Musulman subjects'; as gross a misrepresentation as the criticism, twenty-three years afterwards, of Mr. Gladstone's policy. The Prince, like Mr. Gladstone, proposed to put an end to Turkish rule and administration in Europe. There was no question of expelling a single Musulman. Unfortunately, Lord

* 'Life of the Prince Consort,' ii. pp. 521-538.

Palmerston's opposition defeated the Prince's prescient and statesmanlike scheme. I am an admirer of constitutional government, but one must admit that it has its disadvantages and failures. It is impossible to read dispassionately the diplomatic history of the Crimean War without being forced to the conclusion that if the Queen and Prince Consort had been able to carry out their own policy unhampered by a Government, a Parliament, and an irresponsible Press, they would have settled the Eastern question on a durable basis without war.

I have now shown what the policy of England has always been, with the unfortunate exception of the Crimean War. That was, however, only a temporary interruption. The traditional policy of England down to the Cretan insurrection of 1867 was a friendly understanding with Russia, coupled with diplomatic intervention in the affairs of Turkey for the protection of the Christian population; and when diplomatic intervention failed, material coercion. In 1867 this policy was reversed, and a new policy laid down and acted on—namely, a policy of non-intervention in the affairs of Turkey, qualified by going to war against any Power which should attack her. The Porte must be left alone to deal with its subjects in any way it thought best for its own interests; or, if any advice at all was given, it must be only to the extent of urging the Turkish Government to suppress as promptly as possible every effort of the subject population towards freedom. I cannot for the moment lay my hand on any document in the Parliamentary papers of 1867 in which this policy is formally laid down. But it was laid down in several despatches by the Secretary for Foreign Affairs in 1876–77. The following is a specimen :—

> Her Majesty's Government have, since the outbreak in Bosnia and the Herzegovina, deprecated the diplomatic intervention of the other Powers in the affairs of the Ottoman Empire. Her Majesty's Government would not, however, assume the responsibility of advising the Porte, who must be guided by what they thought best, after due consideration, for the welfare of the Ottoman Empire. It was impossible to expect them (Her Majesty's Government) to do more than to state, if their opinion was asked, that they had better follow the policy which they thought most consistent with their own interests.

Even an intervention by Consuls

> was scarcely compatible with the independent authority of the Porte; it offered an inducement to insurrection as a means of appealing to foreign sympathy against Turkish rule, and it might not improbably open the way to further diplomatic interference in the internal affairs of the empire.

This policy is repeated and enforced in several of Lord Derby's despatches,* and in a speech to a deputation, headed by Mr. John Bright, on July 14, 1876. I quote from the report of the *Times* of the following day :—

> As regards intervention between Turkey and the

---

* See *Turkey*, No. 2 (1876), p. 96; No. 3, pp. 174, 188, 192, 236.

subjects of the Porte, or between Turkey and the semi-independent States which form part of the Turkish Empire, that is a question which has never been so much as entertained. We will endeavour to press that view on others, and I have every reason to hope that we shall succeed. . . . Now that, gentlemen, is in a few words our policy as regards this war now going on. We shall not intervene; we shall do our utmost, if necessary, to discourage others from intervening; but I do not believe that under the present circumstances it will be necessary.

'Our policy as regards this war now going on.' The 'war' was an uprising of a poorly-armed peasantry, driven to desperation by intolerable wrongs, against disciplined and well-armed troops, aided by what Lord Derby called 'armed bands of murderers and robbers.' And Lord Derby's policy was to form a ring round these unequally-matched combatants, neither intervening himself nor (to the best of his ability) letting others intervene. The Sultan had bound himself before the Areopagus of Europe, twenty years before, to place his Christian subjects on a footing of equality with the Musulmans; but he had flagitiously broken every item of his solemn engagement, and the oppression of the Christians had gone from bad to worse, and had at last become unbearable. They had therefore a clear right to rise in insurrection against a tyrannical and perjured Government; and the Powers had not only a right to intervene, they had a *casus belli* against the Sultan. Yet they contented themselves with pressing for moderate reforms, which the Sultan would undoubtedly have accepted if the Powers had been unanimous. But Lord Derby persistently opposed every suggestion pressed upon him by the other Powers with remarkable unanimity, yet shrank afterwards from the logical conclusion of his policy—a war against Russia—and called it 'the gunpowder and glory business.'

This was a new departure, a complete reversal of the traditional policy of England, and it dates, as I have said, from the Cretan insurrection of 1866-7, the year in which Lord Beaconsfield became Prime Minister. Austria then took the lead in urging the Powers to deal in a comprehensive spirit with the growing evils of the Turkish Empire. The Sultan had broken all his promises, 'and the Treaty of Paris had failed to provide sufficient guarantees for the better government of the Christians of Turkey.' Count Beust proposed accordingly, ' to put the populations of Turkey under the protectorate of the whole of Europe, by endowing them, under guarantees from all the Courts, with independent institutions in accordance with their various religions and races.'* All the other Powers agreed, but Lord Derby strenuously and successfully opposed every suggestion of intervention on behalf of the Christians of Turkey. The Government went even so far as to administer a severe

* See Émile de Girardin's 'La Honte de l'Europe,' p. 53.

reprimand to the gallant captain of a British man-of-war who, seeing a crowd of women and children running down to the shore with cries for help as they were being pursued by armed Turks, took them on board under protection of his guns. Thus a golden opportunity was thrown away for settling the Eastern question on somewhat of a permanent footing. Lord Salisbury was not a member of that Government.

I have quoted Lord Derby because it is his name as Foreign Secretary that occupies the chief place in this change of policy. And yet the policy could hardly have been Lord Derby's own. For in a speech at King's Lynn in 1864 he recommended a totally different policy, as the following extract will show :—

I believe the question of the breaking up of the Turkish Empire to be only a question of time, probably not a very long time. The Turks have played their part in history; they have had their day, and that day is over. I do not understand, except it be from the influence of diplomatic traditions, the determination of the elder statesmen to stand by the Turkish rule, whether right or wrong [this is not accurate]. I think we are making for ourselves enemies of races which will very soon become in Eastern Europe dominant races ; and I think we are keeping back countries by whose improvement we, as the great traders of the world, should be the greatest gainers ; and that we are doing this for no earthly advantage, either present or prospective.

The policy was of course Lord Beaconsfield's,

and Lord Derby was an apt pupil as long as the policy promised to keep things quiet all round and avert war. With all his ability and clearness of judgment within a limited range, Lord Derby lacked imagination and sentiment. Having surveyed the political situation in 1876, he came to the conclusion that war was impossible; France, Italy, Germany, England, did not want war; and as for Austria and Russia, her Slav soldiers would prevent the former from fighting Russia, while 'the condition of Russian finance' would restrain the latter. Lord Derby's unemotional and unimaginative nature made it impossible for him to realise either the unspeakable misery of the Christians of Turkey, or the wave of uncontrollable pity and indignation which roused the Russian people to such a pitch of enthusiasm that no Government could have held them back from going to the rescue of their kin in faith and race.

But what was Lord Beaconsfield's motive in reversing the traditional policy of England? I am anxious to say nothing which can vex any of his admirers. I, too, can admire his splendid pluck; his devotion to his race, regardless of self-interest; his indomitable perseverance in the face of what to most men might well seem insurmountable difficulties; his domestic virtues. But he had in abundance what Lord Derby lacked—a glowing Oriental imagination and lively emotions concealed under an impassive exterior. That he aimed at the glory of England I have no doubt. But he was with us rather than of us. It was in the East that his ideals lay and his strongest affections. He was a believer in the primacy of certain races; and probably thought that by 'rolling back Russia for many a decade,' as Mr. Greenwood says, he would give a new lease of life to Turkey, and bring the Arabs, whom he regarded as cousins, to the front.* He admired the English for their rough strength and courage, but despised them a little for their lack of ideality and pure blood, which placed them, as he expressed it, under the ban of 'that law of extermination which is fatal to curs.' He firmly believed in the resuscitation of the long-slumbering East; the idea pervades all his writings, and he probably imagined that he was himself predestined to set in motion the forces which would in course of time fulfil his dreams. For, with all his shrewdness and worldly wisdom, there was a strong vein of mysticism in Lord Beaconsfield's nature. It is thus that I interpret his reversal of

* 'For nearly five hundred years the true Oriental mind has been enthralled. Arabia alone has remained free and faithful to the divine tradition. From its bosom we shall go forth and sweep away the Tataric system; and thus, when the East has resumed its indigenous intelligence, when angels and prophets again mingle with humanity, the sacred quarter of the globe will recover its prominent and divine supremacy; it will act upon the modern empires, and the faint-hearted faith of Europe, which is but the shadow of a shade, will become as vigorous as befits men who are in sustained communication with the Creator.'—*Tancred*, page 428.

England's traditional policy on the Eastern question; and it is no small tribute to his genius that he succeeded, and that the present Oriental complication is so largely due to the reveries of an extraordinary and complex genius, whose cast of mind was more Oriental than English.

CHAPTER XI.

POLICY OF TSAR NICHOLAS.

'IT is really painful,' said Prince Gortchakoff in the midst of the crisis of 1877, 'to see two great States, which together might regulate European questions for their mutual advantage and the benefit of all, excite themselves and the world by an antagonism founded on prejudice or misunderstanding.'* In another despatch the same year he said—to Prince Bismarck's fierce indignation—that if only Great Britain and Russia would come to a friendly understanding, 'not a cannon could be fired in Europe without their consent.' It is England, not Russia, which has always put obstacles in the way of such understanding. A cordial understanding with this country on all questions, both in Europe and in Asia, was an article in the political creed of the Emperor Nicholas, which he held with almost the fervour of a religious dogma. He had witnessed the horrors of the Napoleonic wars, culminating, for him, in the patriotic immolation of Moscow, and he believed that the best security

* *Turkey*, No. 2 [1877], p. 736.

for peace lay in the union of the two Powers which then dominated between them both land and sea. For the purpose of threshing out all difficulties and differences between the two countries he came to London in the year 1844 on a visit to the Queen, and had frequent and friendly interviews with Sir Robert Peel and with his Secretary for Foreign Affairs, Lord Aberdeen. The result was a thorough understanding with the Conservative Government as regards India, Persia, Central Asia, and Turkey. On his return to Russia Nicholas instructed the Chancellor of the Empire, Count Nesselrode, to embody his understanding with the British Court and Cabinet in a Memorandum, which was sent to the Government of Sir Robert Peel. That most important State paper, I believe, has never been published by our Foreign Office; at all events, I have never been able to find any trace of it in the Blue-books. Lord Salisbury could do no better service to the cause of peace at this moment, if I may presume to say so, than by publishing the agreement arrived at between the two Governments in 1844, since it contains no infringement, as far as I can judge, of the rights of other Powers. I got a copy of the Memorandum twenty years ago from Baron Jomini—'the pen of the Foreign Office,' as he used to be called in St. Petersburg; and it throws such a flood of light on the traditional policy of Russia that the publication of so much of it as relates to Turkey may be useful at this moment. Here it is :—

Russia and England are mutually penetrated with the conviction that it is their common interest that the Ottoman Porte should maintain itself in the state of independence and of territorial possession now existing in that empire, this political combination being the one which best accords with the preservation of general peace.

Agreed as to this principle, Russia and England have an equal interest in uniting their efforts to strengthen the existence of the Ottoman Empire, and to avert all dangers by which its security may be threatened. With this object, the essential thing is to allow the Porte to live in peace, without agitating it by diplomatic worries, and without interfering in its internal affairs. To put this system in practice, two things must not be lost sight of. They are as follows :—In the first place, the Porte has a constant tendency towards freeing itself from the engagements imposed upon it by the treaties which it has concluded with the other Powers ; and it hopes to do this with impunity because it relies upon the mutual jealousies of the Cabinets. It believes that if it fails in its engagements towards one, the others will take up its quarrel, and will shield it against all responsibility.

It is essential not to confirm the Porte in this illusion. Each time that it fails in its obligations towards one of the Great Powers it is the interest of all the others to make it sensible of its fault, and to exhort it seriously to render justice to the Cabinet which seeks reparation. As soon as the Porte sees itself not maintained by the other Cabinets it will yield ; and the differences which may have arisen will disappear through the medium of conciliation, without any conflict taking place.

A second cause exists for the complications inherent in the situation of the Porte; the difficulty of bringing into accord the respect due to the sovereign authority of the Sultan founded on the Musulman law, and the concessions due to the interests of the Christian population of the empire.

This difficulty is not to be denied. In the actual condition of the European mind the Cabinets cannot with indifference see the Christian populations of Turkey subject to flagrant vexations and to religious intolerance. This truth must be impressed without cessation on the Ottoman Ministers, who must be persuaded that they can only count on the friendship and support of the Great Powers on condition of the Christian subjects of the Porte being treated with tolerance and mildness.

While they insist on this truth, the foreign representatives must, on the other side, use all their influence to maintain the Christian subjects of the Porte in submission towards the sovereign authority. Guided by these principles the foreign representatives must act between themselves in a perfect spirit of concord. If remonstrances are addressed to the Porte, they must bear a character of unanimity without any one Power putting itself forward exclusively.

Proceeding in this system with all calmness and moderation, the representatives of the Great Cabinets of Europe will have the best chance of succeeding without provoking such complications as might compromise the peace of the Ottoman Empire. If all the Great Powers adopt frankly this line of conduct they may hope with reason to preserve the existence of Turkey.

It is impossible, however, not to see what elements of dissolution are contained within this empire. Imperious circumstances may hasten its fall without its being possible for the united Cabinets to prevent such a result, inasmuch as it is not given to human foresight to trace beforehand a plan of action for such an unexpected case. It would be premature to take into consideration eventualities which may never be realised. In the uncertainty which weighs upon the future, one fundamental idea seems alone capable of practical application. It is this—that the danger which may result from a catastrophe in Turkey will be much diminished if, the case occurring, Russia and England understand one another as to the course to be pursued by both in common. This understanding will be all the more salutary, inasmuch as it will receive the complete assent of Austria. Between Austria and Russia a perfect conformity of principles as regards the affairs of Turkey already exists, the interests of both Powers being conservation and peace. To render the union more efficacious, the one thing to desire would be to see England associated with them in the same object. The reasons for aiming at the establishment of this accord are very simple. By land Russia exercises on Turkey a preponderating influence; on sea England occupies the same position. Isolated, the influence of these two Powers might do a good deal of harm; combined it may do much good. Hence the utility of a preliminary understanding before taking action.

This idea was adopted in principle during the stay of the Emperor at London. It has resulted in a conditional engagement to the effect that if anything unforeseen should occur in Turkey, Russia and England would concert together as to what course they should follow in common. The objects with which Russia and England would have to come to an understanding may be thus formulated:—

1. The maintenance of the Ottoman Empire in its present condition for so long a time as this political combination may be possible.

2. *If we see beforehand that it is breaking up, a preliminary understanding to be arrived at as to the establishment of a new order of things, destined to replace that which now exists*: and precautions to be taken in common, that no change occurring in the internal situation of that empire may threaten the security of our own States and the rights which the treaties guarantee to them respectively, or the maintenance of the European equilibrium.

With the objects thus formulated, the policy of Russia and that of Austria are closely bound together by the principle of complete solidarity. If England, as the principal maritime Power, acts in concert with them, there is reason to believe that France will find herself obliged to follow the course decided upon between St. Petersburg, London, and Vienna. All possibility of conflict between the Great Powers being thus averted, it may be hoped that the peace of Europe will be maintained even in the midst of such grave circumstances.

It is with the view of assuring this result to the interests of all that Russia and England should come to a preliminary understanding between themselves, as agreed upon by the Emperor with the Ministers of her Britannic Majesty during his stay in England.

Eight years later the Tsar came to the conclusion that the Turkish Empire could not be much longer upheld, and again he took Great Britain into his confidence as to the wisest course to pursue when the catastrophe came. With great frankness he unbosomed himself to Sir Hamilton Seymour, the British Ambassador at St. Petersburg, in a series of confidential conversations, which the British Government—I think unjustifiably—published at the beginning of the Crimean War in order to inflame public feeling, already too heated, against Russia. The Sick Man at Constantinople, said the Emperor, is on his death-bed. England and Russia are more concerned in the future of his empire than any other Powers. Let them come to an agreement as to what is best to be done when the collapse takes place. And he proceeded to sketch out a policy which most men who have studied the subject would now, I imagine, regard as sagacious and statesmanlike. France was to have her legitimate aspirations satisfied, and Austria also. As to England and Constantinople, the Emperor said :—

With regard to Constantinople, I am not under the same illusions as Catherine II. On the contrary, I regard the immense extent of Russia as her real danger. I should like to see Turkey strong enough to be able to make herself respected by the other Powers. But if she is doomed to perish, Russia and England should come to an agreement as to what should be put in her place. I propose to form the Danubian Principalities, with Servia and Bulgaria, into one independent State, placed under the protection of Russia; and I declare that Russia has no ambition to extend her sovereignty over the territories of Turkey. England might take Egypt and Crete; but I could not allow her to establish herself at Constantinople, and this I say frankly. On the other hand, I would undertake to promise, on my part, never to take Constantinople, if the arrangement which I propose should be concluded between Russia and England. If, indeed,

Turkey were to go suddenly to pieces before the conclusion of that Convention, I would not of course promise not to do so [*i.e.* temporarily].

On a subsequent occasion the Emperor said :—

I would not permit any Power so strong as England to occupy the Bosphorus, by which the Dnieper and the Don find their way into the Mediterranean. While the Black Sea is between the Don, the Dnieper, and the Bosphorus, the command of that strait would destroy the commerce of Russia and close to her fleet the road to the Mediterranean. If an Emperor of Russia should one day chance to conquer Constantinople, or should find himself forced to occupy it permanently, and fortify it with a view to making it impregnable, from that day would date the decline of Russia. If I did not transfer my residence to the Bosphorus, my son, or at least my grandson, would. The change would certainly be made sooner or later, for the Bosphorus is warmer, more agreeable, more beautiful than Petersburg or Moscow ; and if once the Tsar were to take up his abode at Constantinople, Russia would cease to be Russia. No Russian would like that. There is not a Russian who would not like to see a Christian crusade for the delivery of the Mosque of Saint Sophia ; I should like it as much as any one. But nobody would like to see the Kremlin transported to the Seven Towers.

That expresses the deliberate conviction and the deliberate policy of all far-sighted Russians, whatever sentiment as to the possession of Tsargrad may float here and there in the popular mind. Nicholas was right. From the possession of Constantinople would date the ruin of Russia, and every Russian Sovereign and statesman knows it. The true heart of Russia beats in Moscow and Petersburg. The removal of the seat of empire to Constantinople would de-Russianise the Empire of the Tsars as certainly as it de-Romanised the Empire of the Cæsars. Russia would become Byzantine, and any one who imagines that the Russian people would endure such degradation knows nothing of the passion of their patriotism. They would regard it much as a Briton would regard the realisation of Mr. Disraeli's dream—the transfer of our metropolis from London to Calcutta.

We may therefore dismiss from our minds all ideas about Russia hungering after Constantinople. What is true is that she would, as Nicholas said, 'spend her last rouble and her last soldier' in preventing any other Great Power from reigning on the Bosphorus. If, instead of allowing ourselves to be dragged into the Crimean War by Louis Napoleon, Sir Stratford Canning, and Lord Palmerston, we had come to terms with the Tsar in 1853, and joined him in creating a powerful Balkan State, perhaps in federation with an enlarged Greece, with Constantinople as a free city under the guarantee of Europe, there would have been an end of the Eastern question. How much bloodshed and treasure and misery would have been avoided if the British Government had agreed to settle the question once for all on such terms, instead of waging a wasteful war in the vain effort to bolster up a cruel, corrupt, and moribund despotism, which has been an unmitigated curse to mankind!

The brain which conceived the Crimean War was Napoleon's. No sooner had he been elected President of the Republic than he began to throw out ominous hints about undoing the Treaty of Vienna and rearranging the map of Europe. This was natural, for his ambition was to re-establish the Empire and found a dynasty, both of which were barred by the Treaty of Vienna, wherein the whole Bonaparte family was for ever proscribed from sovereign rank. Nicholas took alarm, for the Treaty of Vienna was to him a sacro-sanct document, on which reposed the peace of Europe. He opposed, therefore, the resurrection of the French Empire; but finding no support from any of the Powers, he agreed to recognise Napoleon as Emperor for life, but incapable of transmitting his title. Napoleon thus saw that there was no security for the throne which he was so anxious to establish unless he managed to break the power of Russia. And this feeling was intensified by the form in which Nicholas acknowledged his election to the Empire. For, while all the other Sovereigns saluted Napoleon as 'Monsieur mon frère,' Nicholas, true to his convictions, wrote 'Mon cher ami.' From that moment Napoleon determined to have his revenge and secure his dynasty. But there was no chance of this within the area covered by the Treaty of Vienna, for that might provoke a coalition against him.

He must find a field of battle elsewhere, and he found it in a series of aggressions on the rights of Russia in the Holy Places of Palestine; a stratagem which had the additional advantage of enlisting the sympathy of all Catholics in France and elsewhere. Fortunately for him, but very unfortunately for Great Britain, he found two accomplices of consummate ability to aid and abet him—the British Ambassador at Constantinople and the most popular member at that time of the British Cabinet. Such was the secret cause of the Crimean War. There was no telegraph in those days to Constantinople, and the Ambassador had a much freer hand than he would have now.

Has not the time arrived when Great Britain and Russia should draw a sponge over that business? And this country being, as I hold, in the wrong, ought to make the first move. Lord Salisbury is, as I have shown, in a very favourable position to make a new departure, or rather to revert to the traditional policy of both countries. Let him take it up at the point of Nesselrode's Memorandum and the Russian agreement with the Government of Sir Robert Peel. It is, moreover, Lord Salisbury's own policy, as I have shown, and he has given, as I have also shown, two signal proofs of goodwill to Russia. It was meet that France, which was the principal transgressor in the Crimean War, should be the first to make the *amende*. It now remains for England to do her part.

CHAPTER XII.

ISLÂM AS A RULING SYSTEM.

PEOPLE are coming round at last to the doctrine which I have been preaching by speech and writing for the last twenty years—namely, that any project of reform which has for its object the bestowal of any of the rights of citizenship on the non-Musulman subjects of the Porte can never receive the legal sanction of the Sultan without external coercion. The history of Turkey does not supply a single exception to that assertion. And the reason is that the Government of Turkey, like that of every Musulman State, is a strict theocracy. Its civil policy is based on religious dogmas which are unchangeable, and by which every orthodox Musulman is bound, from the Sultan downwards. Any proposal to put the Rayahs (*i.e.* non-Musulman subjects) on a footing of equality with the Musulmans is, in truth, a proposal to violate a fundamental article of the *religious creed* of Islâm, which no Sultan can do without apostasy, and consequently without the risk of a *Fetva* of deposition from the Sheikh-ul-Islâm, who is the guardian alike of law and religion in Turkey. Even well-educated persons in England, including leading statesmen and diplomatists, have such hazy notions on this subject that it may be useful to give a succinct summary of the facts.

In the belief of orthodox Musulmans the Koran differs from the Bible and all other religious books in one essential particular—namely, that it existed from all eternity in the Arab language on tablets in the highest heaven before the throne of the Most High. From those tablets it was copied by the Angel Gabriel in *suras* or chapters, and dictated to Mohammed in an audible voice, word for word as occasion required, in the course of twenty years. The revelation of the Pentateuch, on the other hand, was communicated to the mind, not the ear, of Moses through the medium of ideas which he was left free to deliver to men in any form or language which seemed to him good. Moreover, the Mosaic revelation did not profess to be final; on the contrary, it claimed to be preparatory and provisional, pointing explicitly to a greater prophet than Moses and to a future revelation in which the Mosaic dispensation should be developed and absorbed. That prophet was Mohammed, and that revelation the Koran, which is thus the last expression of the divine will to man, and therefore absolutely and eternally unchangeable. This doctrine is laid down in plain terms by Ibn-Khaldun,* the most

* Proleg. i. pp. 194-5.

learned and one of the most authoritative writers in the realm of Islâm. Himself an Arab, he held various offices under the Moorish domination in Spain; then travelled extensively in various Musulman countries in Asia and Africa, where he held converse with the most learned doctors of the law; became the prisoner and then the confidential adviser of Tamerlane; and settled down at last at Cairo, where he held office as Grand Mufti till his death some years afterwards. No higher authority on the doctrines and principles of Islâm exists in the Musulman world; indeed, it would be no exaggeration to say that there is none so high.

But it is not enough to consult the Koran alone for Islamic doctrine and law. You must take the Koran with the *Hadis* or body of Traditions of the sayings and doings of the Prophet, which are a supplement to the Koran and its infallible interpretation. These Traditions bear the same relation to the Koran which the infallible decrees of Councils bear to the Bible in Roman theology. You don't refute a believer in Papal Infallibility by quoting the Bible, for he believes in the Bible as interpreted by the Vatican decrees. Similarly, Moslem apologists in English newspapers take refuge in an irrelevant sophism when they challenge proof out of the Koran alone for any Islamic doctrine which they may find it inconvenient to acknowledge. For the Sacred Law of Islâm rests on the Koran *plus* the Traditions. Now among the irrevocable doctrines of the Sacred Law are the following :—If the Rayah refuse to become a Musulman he must choose between the cruel alternatives of death or tribute. If he become a Zimmi or Tributary it must be on certain painful and degrading conditions, of which the following will suffice as specimens :—He must pay a yearly capitation tax for the permission to live, and the form of receipt says that the tax is a ransom for the permission to *wear his head that year*; so that, if he is in arrear with his taxes, as the ruined Armenians are now, his life is forfeited. The Rayah's evidence cannot be received in a court of law against a Musulman. He is not allowed to bear or possess arms. He must provide three days' gratuitous hospitality for every Musulman official or traveller who asks for it. Travelling pashas and their retinue of rapacious servants, the ruffianly police, tax-gatherers, Bashi-Bazouks, dirty Dervishes, &c., are thus mercilessly quartered on the wretched Christians of Turkey, whose women (although this is not sanctioned by law) are at the mercy of these unwelcome guests. Should a Christian convert a Moslem to Christianity, both the Christian and the convert must suffer death. The Rayah must build no place of worship. If he obtain official sanction (which he never does without heavy bribes) he may repair or rebuild such places of worship as existed in the country when the Musulman conquerors took possession of it; but it must be on the same plan, sites, and dimensions as the old buildings.

It is sometimes said by persons who know nothing about the subject that the Musulmans of Turkey are more cruelly oppressed than the Christians. That is nonsense, for although Musulmans and Christians are all abominably oppressed under the horrible rule of the Sultan, there is this difference—that the Musulmans are oppressed contrary to law, and the Christians in obedience to the law. The former possess two remedies which are partially effective, and which are denied to the Christians: they possess arms, and can appeal to the law for protection. Moreover, the Christians, in addition to the disabilities which I have described, are subject to many taxes from which the Musulmans are free. I have mentioned the yearly capitation ransom tax. But they are liable to many other imposts which do not touch the Musulmans—for instance, forced labour *ad libitum* and a tax on every male Christian, from three months old to the day of his death, to provide a substitute in the army, from which the Christians are by law excluded. In brief, the Christians throughout Turkey are obliged—according to the unanimous testimony of British Consuls—to pay in legal taxation 67 per cent. of the produce of their soil and toil. There are, of course, innumerable extortions in addition. So that the wretched Christians could not manage to eke out even their miserable existence except by means of cheating and bribery. And then, forsooth, highly virtuous writers and speakers in England, who have never experienced any oppression or injustice, take up their song and parable against the servile and degraded character of the Christian subjects of the Porte! Who degraded them in so far as they are degraded? How many of their critics and slanderers would endure torture, dishonour, and barbarous death in defence of their faith, or of any doctrine, or principle, or cause whatsoever? Yet that is what the Christians of Turkey have done for centuries. There is a noble passage in his 'Memoirs of the Affairs of Europe,' by Lord Russell, which I quoted nearly twenty years ago, and which is worth quoting again:—

We are perpetually asked if the nations at present declaring their independence, or reforming their institutions, are fit to be free. It would be lamentable indeed if this plea were to be allowed to prevail in bar to the generous efforts of countries long oppressed by tyranny. It would indeed be a hopeless case for mankind if despotism were thus allowed to take advantage of its own wrong, and to bring the evidence of its crimes as the title-deeds of its right. It would be indeed a strange perversion of justice if absolute Governments might say, 'Look how ignorant, base, false, and cruel our people have become under our sway; therefore we have a right to retain them in eternal subjection and everlasting slavery.' But no! When I am asked if such or such a nation is fit to be free, I ask in return, Is any man fit to be a despot? The answer must be,

None whatever, neither Musulman nor Christian, neither in Greece nor in Columbia. It is the proved effect of despotism that wherever her horrid head appears, she creates the evils she affects to deplore. And although those who first shake off the chain may bear upon their frame the marks of the degrading links, yet these impressions will wear out, and, the first fury of the released captive once over, the vengeance of a slave will give way to the virtues of a freeman.

I have sometimes been called a fanatic on the subject of Islâm. I am no fanatic on that or on any other subject. I am an advocate of religious freedom in the widest sense consistent with the inalienable rights of mankind. My toleration ceases where the religious doctrines of one man invade the aboriginal rights of another, as they do, and have ever done, in every State, without exception, where Islâm has ruled supreme. The non-Musulman can never obtain the rights of citizenship, but is irrevocably doomed to a most cruel and degrading servitude, under Musulman rule. It is no answer to this to point to Christians and Jews occupying high posts under the Sultan, who is obliged to make use of them for lack of competent Musulmans, or because he finds it good policy to employ them. It sometimes happened under the serf system in Russia that a landlord educated one of his serfs and employed him to manage his property, or permitted him to strike out a career for himself. But that did not affect the condition of the serfs in general, or even of the emancipated serf, unless he was really manumitted. So in Turkey. The rare exceptions prove the rule as regards the mass; and even the privileges of the few can be withdrawn in a moment. They have no rights. The Sultan's present Ambassador in London, like his two predecessors, is a Christian; but he is not, and cannot be, a citizen of the Ottoman Empire, for the only gate to that citizenship is the profession of Islâm. The Turkish Ambassador, though a Greek Christian, is simply a Rayah advanced to high position by the arbitrary will of the Sultan, just as a slave on an American plantation might have been by his master, and his case proves absolutely nothing as to the legal *status* of the non-Musulman. Indeed, the position of the Rayah is worse than that of the slave on an American plantation or in the Roman Empire; for the American planter or the Roman slave-owner could have made, and sometimes did make, his slave a freeman. But even the Sultan cannot make a single Rayah in his dominions a freeman, since that is a privilege reserved to the Musulman alone. It is because our statesmen and ambassadors have been ignorant of this fundamental fact that their policy in Turkey, from Lord Stratford de Redcliffe downwards, has been such an abject and disastrous failure. I have been preaching this truth for years, and some among us are at last beginning to recognise it. It was refreshing to read in the *Morning Post*, of last September 17, a leading article which clearly grasped the situation, as the following extract will show :—

> Just as in the Christian West living things are divided into human beings and brute beasts, so where the Moslem is the master they are divided into believers and infidels, and the infidel human being is regarded as little better than the brute. And just as in a Christian country if the cattle become dangerous they would be slaughtered wholesale for the safety of the community, so in Turkey, whenever the Rayahs have been thought to be dangerous, a clearance of them has been made. It is impracticable in a Mohammedan country to appeal to a principle of humanity, for that would be to assert a brotherhood between man and man, which it is the essence of the Mohammedan religion to deny. In a Mohammedan State the Christian can have no part, for his recognition would imply the negation of Islâm. Accordingly, the most competent judges, Ranke, the historian of the modern changes in Turkey, and Moltke, the shrewd observer of the beginnings of the modern period, explained long ago that security for the Rayahs could never be had until they were placed under their own rulers and withdrawn from the authority of the Turks.

But we are sometimes told that we must be careful how we deal with the Sultan, who, as Khalif and Commander of the Faithful, is regarded with reverence and spiritual allegiance by the Musulmans of our Indian Empire. That is all a myth of very modern origin. Our Indian Musulmans are no more concerned with the Sultan of Turkey than they are with the Amir of Afghanistan or the Emperor of Morocco. For the Sultan is certainly not Khalif or Commander of the Faithful, nor has he ever been acknowledged as such in India or out of Turkey. Abdul Hamid has furtively and indirectly played at being Khalif; but to claim the title openly and formally would be heretical and illegal, and would certainly bring down upon him a Bull of excommunication and deposition, which would probably cost him his life. For his well-paid and pampered bodyguard would then desert him. The following are the legal titles of the Sultan, and it will be observed that Khalif is not one of them. He is, 'by the grace of the Almighty Creator, Lord of lords, Dominant Sovereign in Arabia, Persia, and Greece, Invincible and always Victorious, Emperor of Constantinople, Distributor of Crowns to the Great Princes of the Earth, Sovereign Master of the Two Seas and of all the Adjacent Countries, Lord of the Orient and the Occident, Protector of the Sacred and August Cities of Mecca and Medina, and of endless other Countries, Kingdoms, Empires, Isles, and Peoples.'

The two great divisions of the Mohammedan world are the Shiahs and Sunni, who regard each other as heretics. The former occupy Persia; there are some 5,000,000 of them in India, and some millions more are scattered over the rest of the Mohammedan world. To the Sunni division belong Turkey, Afghanistan, Morocco, Algeria and Tunis, the Soudan and most of Central Asia and Central Africa. By the Sacred Law of the

Shiahs the Khalif must be a lineal descendant of the Prophet. By the Sacred Law of the Sunni Musulmans the Khalif must belong to Mohammed's tribe, the Koreish. This is an irrevocable article of the faith of Islâm throughout the world. The great authorities in the Turkish Empire are the doctors of Mecca, with the Shereef (a descendant of the Prophet) at their head; and the doctors of the University of Cairo. The former represent the Arab feeling, which is one of veiled rebellion, often breaking out into open insurrection, against Ottoman rule. The latter is the most authoritative and influential seat of learning in the realm of Islâm. The principal text-book of Musulman theocratic law in the University of Cairo says :—

It is a condition that the Khalif be of the Koreish tribe. All admit this except the Khawárij (sect) and some of the Mutazilites. We all say with the Prophet: 'Let the Khalif be of the Koreish.' . . . It is therefore unquestionably established that the Khalif must be of the Koreish.

The Delhi text-book of Musulman Law, which expresses the belief of the Musulmans of India, says :—

It is a necessary condition that the Khalif be of the Koreish tribe.

I have already referred to Ibn (*see* p. 139) Khaldun as, on the whole, the most learned Mohammedan extant authority on the law and religion of Islâm. He has a dissertation on the qualifications of the Khalifat, and goes at length into the necessity of the Khalif belonging to the tribe of Mohammed. Quoting the answer of Abu Bakr, when he was saluted as 'the lieutenant of God'—'I am not the lieutenant of God, but the lieutenant of the Prophet of God'—Ibn Khaldun says that the Khalif 'has taken the place of the inspired legislator (Mohammed), being charged with the maintenance of religion, and by that means with the government of the world.' 'The office is called indifferently by the words Khalifat or Imamat. The Khalif is called Imam because, as the whole congregation imitates the movements of the Imam, who conducts the public prayers, so the whole world of Islâm imitates the movements of the Khalif, who is therefore called also *the Grand Imam*.' The whole Musulman world is thus religiously bound to obey the orders and follow the example of the Khalif. So that if, for example, he gives the signal for the massacre of Christians anywhere, he is to be obeyed without demur, not merely in the territory which owns his authority, but everywhere. For one of the essential attributes of the Khalif is to claim, as Ibn Khaldun says, 'to govern the world.' He claims, in fact, a universal papacy, in a more rigorous and unqualified sense than was ever dreamt of by the most arrogant of the Popes. It follows that if the Khalif were to call upon the Musulman subjects of the Queen to rise in rebellion, they would be bound to obey him. It is an *imperium in imperio* which makes the Khalif supreme in every State where there are Musulmans enough to obey his will with a fair prospect of success. It would therefore be a very serious matter for Great Britain to acknowledge the Sultan as Khalif and Commander of the Faithful, for it would mean the acknowledgment of him as supreme ruler of India. But we need not disturb ourselves, for the Musulman world has been without a Khalif for nearly four hundred years; and the Sultan of Turkey is absolutely disqualified by race for the office. 'The great majority of the doctors,' says Ibn Khaldun, 'persist in regarding the condition of being a Koreishite so essential a qualification that they insist upon it even in the case of a Khalif otherwise unfit to direct the affairs of the Musulman people'—*i.e.* supposing all the Koreishites had become effete and incapable of ruling. Ibn Khaldun himself does not go so far as that; but adds that, while there are Koreishites fit to rule, 'it is the unanimous opinion of the ancient doctors' that the Khalif must be of the Koreish tribe. He gives the following account of the origin of this essential qualification :—

The condition of being a descendant of the Koreish was adopted, in the journey of *Skifa*, by the Companions of the Prophet. That day the Ansars [the people of Medina] wished to elect Saad Ibn Abada as Khalif. ' Let there be an emir chosen by us,' they said, ' and another by the Koreish tribe.' To this the Koreishites opposed the saying of the Prophet: 'Let the Imams be taken from the Koreish tribe.' To which they added: 'Our holy Prophet recommended us to do good to those who do good to us, and to pardon the offences which we have received from you. Now, if you were strong enough to rule the other tribes, the Prophet would not have made that recommendation.' The Ansars were convinced, and renounced the project of raising Saad to the Imamat. There is also found in the *Sahih* the following saying of the Prophet: 'Let not the authority depart out of the Koreish tribe.' I could cite any number of texts to the same effect.*

The truth is, the illiterate camel-driver of Mecca knew very little about the world outside of Arabia, and in his ignorance he imagined that the Arabs, if welded together into one nation, might supplant the Christian empire by a Mohammedan empire, and eventually rule the world through the Arab race in general and its noblest and bravest tribe—his own—in particular. He went a long way towards the fulfilment of his dream; but his prevision did not embrace the rise of other races who, subduing the warriors of Arabia, should then embrace their religion and found kingdoms and dynasties in utter disregard of the conditions which he had laid down as to the qualifications of the Khalifat. The Musulman sovereigns of Hindustan, Persia, Central Asia, even of Andalusia and Sicily, paid no heed to those qualifications. So that even before the Khalifat became extinct in fact it had

* *Prolegomena*, pp. 387-397.

virtually ceased to be a living power. In any case the Ottoman Sultans are certainly excluded from the Khalifat, for they are not Arabs at all, still less of the Koreish tribe.

Moreover, the Khalifat is elective, not hereditary—another insuperable barrier to any claim on the part of the Sultan. It may suit the self-importance of some Indian Musulmans in this country to pose as champions of Islâm; but they are either grossly ignorant of the doctrines and history of Islâm, or are members of rationalistic sects, like Mr. Justice Ameer Ali, who is a Mutazilite. In no sense can they be regarded as representing the beliefs and feelings of the Musulmans of India, whose loyalty depends on our just treatment of them, and not on our conduct towards the Sultan of Turkey, in whom they are no more interested than in any other Musulman ruler. Was the loyalty of her Musulman subjects in any degree shaken by Russia's crushing war against Turkey in 1877? On the contrary, she did not hesitate to employ Musulman troops under Musulman officers against the Sultan. Was the loyalty of our Indian Musulmans stimulated by our defence of the Sultan against Russia in the Crimean War? On the contrary, it begot the Mutiny. The ringleaders of the Mutiny underrated our power when they saw that it took us two years, in union with France, Sardinia, and Turkey, to beat Russia, and they thought their chance had come for driving us out of India and recovering the domination of Islâm. The stability of our rule in India rests on the recognition of its justice and strength; and that recognition would be accentuated by our compelling the Sultan to fulfil his engagements, and not by weakly condoning his offences out of deference to the feelings of our Indian Musulmans. The mass of them care nothing about the Sultan; but the emissaries of sedition, whom this Sultan has been employing for years to sow the seeds of another mutiny, will be encouraged by any sign of fear in our press or among our public men. Mr. Forster made an admirable reply to this Indian Musulmans argument in 1876, from which I am tempted to quote :—

There is another danger than this which is held before us, and we are reminded not merely of our Indian Empire and the necessity of keeping up our intercourse with India; but we are told: 'You have thirty or forty millions of Musulman population in India; what will they think unless you support the leader of their faith?' Well, I doubt their having those feelings. I believe that fear to be immensely exaggerated. But true or false, founded or unfounded, I maintain that it is a danger which we cannot afford to take into account. There is no man who more feels than I do the duty of maintaining that great empire. . . . But I will never consent to hold that power upon the condition that England's verdict upon right or wrong should depend, not upon the consciences of its own people or upon the actual right or wrong of the matter, but upon the opinion and action of our fellow-countrymen in India. One hears that argument sometimes made use of by those who talk of a spirited foreign policy, and who are advocating our Imperial rule. There would be an end of our Imperial rule if we consented to such humiliation as that. It is one of those dangers which no country could afford to take into account; it is a fear which we must not regard. We cannot consent to govern India upon the ground that our policy is to be dictated, not by the justice of the matter, but by the prejudices or fears of any of our Indian subjects. And do you imagine for one moment that such policy would be successful? What would become of our *prestige* if it were discovered that we thus were guided in our actions? The shrewd and skilful Oriental would quickly find out the reason of our action, and would exaggerate our fears and talk of English *prestige*. English *prestige*, indeed, would be gone in India; and, after all, it is not the Musulman only we have to deal with. An enormous majority are Hindus, and what would they think of that country which governed its relations to Christian Europe upon a regard to Musulman prejudices?

These menaces and fears about the Musulmans of India are as dishonouring to them as they are discreditable to the few Englishmen who help to propagate them.

The Turkish government is thus seen to be *sui generis*, a heteroclite monster among the various species of despotism. In the Mohammedan system of policy we may trace three eras. The first was a pure theocracy, lasting through the lifetime of Mohammed who, like Moses and Joshua, appeared in the double character of military chief and inspired legislator. The second was the government of the Khalifs. They, too, bore the double sceptre of temporal and spiritual power, but pretended to no personal communication with the Almighty; the religious character of their acts and decrees reposed on the Koran and Traditions, of which they were themselves *ex officio* expounders and interpreters. The temporal power of the Khalifs was destroyed by Houlakon Khan, son of Genghis Khan, in A.D. 1258. But the spiritual attributes of the office survived nominally till A.D. 1516, in the descendants of the Fatimite Khalifs resident in Egypt. The Khalifat was then abolished by the Ottoman conqueror of Egypt, Selim I., and has been in abeyance ever since. This is the third era of the theocratic government of Islâm. Since then the temporal and spiritual powers have been separate and distinct in every Musulman State, the reigning Sovereign exercising the temporal power, and the Ulema, represented by the Grand Mufti or Sheikh-ul-Islâm, representing the spiritual power.

In order to insure the prompt obedience of their subjects, the Khalifs were accustomed to give to the principal acts of their Government the sanction of religion by affixing to their decrees and legislative acts the sacred seal which assured to the True Believers acting under it the glory of supporting their faith if triumphant, or the crown of martyrdom in case of death. In order to compass the same end, the Ottoman

Sultans were obliged to solicit the aid of the Ulema—*i.e.* the sacred hierarchy, who are at once the guardians and interpreters of law and religion throughout the Musulman world. They exercise their functions under every Musulman ruler through the Grand Mufti, or Sheikh-ul-Islâm. The Ulema thus represent the theocratic character of the Government of Turkey, and their *Fetva*—equivalent in effect to a Papal Bull —is given by the Sheikh-ul-Islâm, and has become a fundamental law of the empire; for without it no political act of the Sultan possesses the smallest validity. So indispensable is the Sheikh-ul-Islâm's *Fetva* that the Sultan who should dare to put any Hatt, Firman, or Iradé of his in motion without it would be treated as an infidel, and hurled from his throne by a *Fetva* of deposition.

The importance of this will be seen at once when I add that all the treaty engagements of different Sultans from the Crimean War till now are sheer waste paper in the eyes of every orthodox Musulman, for not one of them has been sanctioned by a *Fetva*. They are, therefore, legally as dead as a Bill passed through the House of Commons, but thrown out by the Lords or vetoed by the Sovereign. Hence the utter futility and folly of relying on any promise or engagement of the Sultan without European control to secure its execution. The Sultan cannot keep his engagements, if he would, without external coercion. But the same sacred law, which forbids him to yield without coercion on pain of apostasy, commands him to yield without a blow when confronted by superior force, 'lest damage should ensue to Islâm.' Coercion is therefore the only effective policy, and the kindest. When exercised by superior power it invariably secures submission without firing a shot. It is pitiable to read the despatches even of so strong a man as Lord Stratford de Redcliffe from his ignorance of this elementary fact in the government of Turkey. He goes groping about in the dark, extorting promises from the Sultan, and then complaining of breaches of faith; not knowing that the Sultan could not have fulfilled his promises till he was menaced by *force majeure*. Let me give an example. Several Muslim converts to Christianity were put to death in different parts of Turkey while Lord Stratford de Redcliffe was Ambassador at Constantinople, even during and after the Crimean War. The Ambassador received peremptory instructions from his Government to demand the abolition of the law which doomed to death the convert from Christianity and his converter. Lord Stratford de Redcliffe's despatches show that he had not even a glimmer of the facts which lay at the root of the question, namely, that the law, of which he demanded the repeal, was an immutable dogma of religious faith. And so he went on blundering as follows :—

> The Turkish Government know well, as I have often told them, that the regeneration of this empire is, humanly speaking, impossible while the principles and forms of legislation applied to administrative and judicial matters are invested with the inflexibility of divine truths. It has been found necessary to ascribe a suspending or dispensing power to the head of the State, and in the exercise of that prerogative lies a principle of vitality capable of imparting fresh vigour, under new forms, to the most decayed institutions. Soliman the Magnificent departed as much from the established maxims of the Koran, when he made his first durable treaty with France, as Abdul Medjid would do in setting his seal on the perpetual abolition of penal enactments against apostasy. That great and glorious monarch perceived the necessities of his empire in their very germ, and with the foresight of genius laid the first stone of that broad causeway over which the Western nations were in due season to advance to the successor of his descendants, not only with the pomp and powers of war, but yet more effectually with the arts of peace and the miracles of science.*

This is a specimen of the magniloquent nonsense (written in 1855, while the Crimean War was going on) with which Lord Stratford de Redcliffe was accustomed to deceive himself and his employers. The Ambassador was entirely in error in supposing that the Sultan possessed ' a suspending or dispensing power' as regards any article of the Sacred Law. Nor was Soliman's treaty with France a proof of it. That

* *Eastern Papers*, pt. xvii. pp. 26-28. *Cf.* Lord Aberdeen's despatches to Sir Stratford Canning in 1843 and 1844.

treaty, like the treaties of Paris and Berlin, doubtless violated the law of the Koran on paper; but all such treaties, as I have already explained, not having received the *Fetva* of the Sheikh-ul-Islâm, were mere waste paper, having no validity whatever in law for any Musulman. The controversy ended, as it had ended eleven years previously, in the Sultan promising the British Ambassador, that although the law sanctioning persecution of Christians and death of apostates was irrepealable, yet it would be allowed to become obsolete. As a matter of fact, it went on unimpeded, although the executions took place privately. But in the year 1880 a case was brought to light by accident. An enlightened member of the Ulema, Ahmed Tewfik Effendi by name, a professor in a college at Constantinople, was suddenly flung into a dungeon and condemned to death by the Sheikh-ul-Islâm for revising, in a purely literary sense, some pages of a Turkish translation of the English Book of Common Prayer; and it required the intervention of the Great Powers and three months' diplomatic pressure to get the punishment of death commuted to banishment to Chios, where the man would have been put quietly to death if he had not been able to escape to England by the aid of some Greek fisherman. In this case also the Sultan admitted to Sir Henry Layard, after repeated lies, that the law could not be abolished, and that he had no power to interfere

with it. And Sir Henry Layard, who knew
Turkey well in other respects, was quite surprised.
He admits, however, that there has been no
change from Sir Stratford Canning's day to his
own, and devotes a long despatch to the task
of proving and illustrating his assertion. The
despatch opens thus :—

> In looking back to the despatches addressed by
> Lord Stratford de Redcliffe (then Sir Stratford Canning)
> to Lord Aberdeen relating to the execution of an
> Armenian youth, who was beheaded in 1843 as an
> apostate from Islamism, I have been very much struck
> by the remarkable resemblance that the circumstances
> of that case bear to those of the affair of Ahmed
> Tewfik Effendi. By substituting for the names of the
> principal actors in that tragedy those of present Turkish
> statesmen, I might almost have used the very words of
> Lord Stratford's despatches in addressing your lordship
> [Lord Salisbury] with respect to the present instance
> of Turkish fanaticism.

How is it that so practical a people as the
English appoint men to the posts of Secretaries
for Foreign Affairs and Ambassadors to Turkey
who do not know the rudiments of the Constitution
of the Ottoman Empire? To send an Ambassador
to Paris without knowing a word of French
would be nothing to the absurdity of our dealing
with Turkey. The true parallel to it would be
the appointment to a Regius Professorship of
Greek of a man who did not know the Greek
alphabet. Russia acts very differently, and till
we imitate her common sense we shall go blun-

dering on, extorting promises from Sultan after Sultan, and then wondering that nothing comes of it. 'An Amurath an Amurath succeeds'; but what avails it while the system remains? It is the Ulema who hold the key of the position, for it is in them that all sacerdotal, judicial, and legislative functions are centred. And they are a very powerful corporation too. More than three-fourths of the soil of Turkey belong to them. Their property, moreover, is exempt from taxation, and they are the only class whose property is hereditary in the family. Lord Salisbury is the only Foreign Secretary for fifty years who understands the theocratic system of Turkey, and that is one reason why I cannot believe that he will go on indefinitely relying on a policy of barren promises on the one hand and futile admonitions on the other.

And now let me conclude this part of my subject with one caution. Neither here nor anywhere else have I ever written or spoken a word which, taken with its context, can furnish the slightest excuse for the accusation sometimes recklessly made against me, namely, that I advocate a crusade against Islâm as a religion. The Musulmans of India enjoy perfect religious liberty, including polygamy; and I am glad of it, much as I dislike polygamy as degrading to woman and injurious to man. But the Musulmans of India are not allowed to practise slavery, though it is sanctioned by their religion; nor are

Musulman judges allowed to reject Christian evidence against Musulmans, though that also is sanctioned by their religion. I draw the line where the British Government has drawn it in India; liberty for the Musulman to practise his religion without let or hindrance up to the point where his religion invades the sacred sphere of natural justice, as it does in Turkey. I should object to Christianity on the same ground with just as much emphasis. Moreover, the government of Turkey is, as I have shown, an ecclesiastical government, which I consider the worst possible form of government in the civil sphere, even when it is Christian ecclesiasticism; much more when it is an ecclesiastical government which professes to be theocratic. For then it follows that the regulations which fix the *status* of the Christians are not simply civil ordinances which admit of amendment, but dogmas of religions which are absolutely immutable so long as the Musulman Power rules supreme. I object to a system of that sort, not because it is Musulman, but because it is inhuman.

CHAPTER XIII.

MR. GLADSTONE'S LIVERPOOL SPEECH.

I MUST now deal with the change which has been made in the situation by Lord Rosebery's speech in Edinburgh. On my return to England in the end of August from a yachting cruise, during which I saw the newspapers very irregularly, the first piece of news that met my eyes was the horrible massacres in the streets and environs of Constantinople, of which the entire responsibility has been charged upon the Sultan by the unanimous declaration of the foreign Ambassadors accredited to his Court. I merely passed through London on my way to fulfil an engagement in Ireland; and during my ten days' residence in that country I was agreeably surprised to find the whole Irish nation, without distinction of creed or party, aflame by this sanguinary defiance of the Powers of Europe by the craven puppet who occupies his throne by their sufferance. Whig and Tory, Roman Catholic and Orangeman, Parnellite and anti-Parnellite, were united for once in demanding the punishment of the criminal and the rescue of the ancient people whom, like Haman in his plot against the Jews, Abdul Hamid has doomed to extermination. From England and Scotland, too, could be heard the premonitory symptoms of a storm of indignation which might, as I believed, be guided, but could not be repressed. I was myself inundated with letters from all parts of the country, appealing to me, in my capacity of Honorary Secretary of the Grosvenor House Committee, to organise an agitation which had now become inevitable. I had hitherto done my best to preach patience, and I assured my correspondents that I believed Lord Salisbury was doing his best to move the other Powers to some effective action for putting an end to the hideous orgies of the Sultan. One gentleman, a Conservative in politics, suggested that if the Great Powers of Europe, with their mighty hosts, had not the courage to put this criminal lunatic under restraint, diplomacy should, in this country at least, be superseded by voluntary efforts, as in the Greek war of independence; and he offered, for his own part, 5,000*l.* towards the purchase of arms to be distributed among the helpless Christians in parts of Turkey accessible by sea; to be followed perhaps by bands of volunteers. I give this as one out of many proofs of the white heat which the public indignation had reached.

Seeing that an agitation was now inevitable, and that it might do mischief if left to run its course without any guidance, I returned to London by way of Hawarden in order to confer with Mr. Gladstone, who, having retired from public life, might be able to speak with greater freedom. He thought that the agitation, judiciously controlled, might help to convince foreign nations that this country was moved solely by a disinterested desire to put an end to the horrors which had been going on for two years in the Asiatic provinces of Turkey, and might thus strengthen the hands of the Government in their endeavour to move the Concert of Europe to some efficacious action.

It was in the hope of contributing to this result that Mr. Gladstone, after much hesitation, allowed himself to be persuaded to address a meeting at Liverpool, convened by the Mayor, Lord Derby, on a requisition signed by men of all parties in politics and religion. The resolution which Mr. Gladstone was asked to move was as follows:—

That this meeting trusts that her Majesty's Ministers, realising to the fullest extent the terrible condition in which their fellow-Christians are placed, will do everything possible to obtain for them full security and protection; and this meeting assures her Majesty's Ministers that they may rely on the cordial support of the citizens of Liverpool in whatever steps they may feel it necessary to take for that purpose.

That resolution is on the lines of the advice which Mr. Gladstone gave to me for the guidance of meetings in general—namely, to avoid everything that might seem to dictate a policy to the

Government, and be content with offering them the cordial support of the country in any effective steps which they might take for protecting the Armenians. Mr. Gladstone followed in his own speech at Liverpool the advice which he gave to me. The most microscopic ingenuity cannot point out a sentence in that speech which dictates any specific course of action to her Majesty's Government. He said indeed—what is merely a political truism, on which Lord Salisbury has repeatedly insisted—that in dealing with the Sultan the only effective policy is coercion; but he was careful to abstain from urging any particular kind of coercion. As his speech has been so persistently misrepresented, it is necessary to make some quotations from it. After reading the resolution which Lord Derby had put into his hand, Mr. Gladstone proceeded:—

> It appears to me, my Lord Mayor, that resolution has great merits. It is firm, and at the same time it is cautious, and it does not take into our hands that which does not belong to us. It expresses our confidence that her Majesty's Ministers will do everything that is possible for the purpose of attaining a great end. It shows very well that we have not the information or the other advantages necessary for pointing out those means in detail, but it assures the Government that every measure which it may adopt for the advancement of that great end will have our warm, ungrudging, unhesitating support. Ladies and gentlemen, it is upon the ground of that resolution that I invite you to place yourselves, and I think you will allow me to say, in the first place, the terms of the

resolution are of course to be interpreted in accordance with the rules of common sense, and when we say we hope her Majesty's Government will adopt every possible measure, we mean every measure which is possible consistently with reason. I therefore think that although the resolution does not say so, yet it is not the intention of this meeting to express a desire that everything that in the nature of things is abstractedly possible should be done. The rules of prudence must be observed, and the rules of prudence, I think, as has often been said in the course of this discussion, neither require nor permit—nor does duty, in my opinion, either require or permit—that we, for the sake even of the great object we have in view, should place ourselves in a condition of war with united Europe, or should take measures which would plunge Europe generally into a state of war. With that proposition I cordially agree; but when I speak of a state of war in that sense I mean a real state of war, and I don't mean those phantasms of European war which every one—not so much in this country as in other countries—who wishes to stop beneficial measures on behalf of Armenia conjures up before our eyes in saying that any country that takes into its own hands, exercises its own judgment, and makes itself in the last resort the judge of its own duty—that every such country must reckon upon plunging Europe into war. I do not say that. I say everything that is reasonable—everything that is possible. I say that it would not be reasonable to do that which would imply war with Europe or plunge Europe into war; but I completely deny that it means that England is, under all circumstances, to abandon and forego her own right of ultimate judgment upon her duties and her powers, and to be dragged at the chariot-wheels of the other Powers of Europe, or of some of them, who have possibly other points of view, and who may not take at present entirely the same view with ourselves. As to this idea of war—the idea that the threat of war in insignificant newspapers and by random gossiping about from one place to another, even if among the places be included the doorways of some public departments—to suppose that that implies that all independent action on the part of this great country is to be made chargeable for producing war in Europe is, in my opinion, a mistake—almost more deplorable perhaps than any of those mistakes that have ever before been committed in the history of diplomacy. Therefore, my Lord Mayor, while I fully admit and recognise that the possible measures—all measures that are possible—do not include a policy which gives just cause of complaint to the Powers of Europe, because I grant that if they had just cause of complaint, of course they would have a title to object to our action and to enforce their action by the use of all their military means—I will not admit that we are on that account to forego our own convictions and our own duties, or to take our own measure of those duties from that which may be said and felt abroad. We have an independent part to play. We have often undertaken to play that part on behalf of our own interests. Let us see now what are the obligations incumbent upon us; because, while I admit that it is of the utmost importance that we should study every means of consulting the sentiments of other Powers and of carrying them along with us, I do not believe that the way to carry them along with us is to show a servile determination under all circumstances, and whatever they may decide, to make their conscience the measure of our own. The first question is: Have we the title and would it be politic—should it be found impossible to obtain the assent of the other Powers—have we a title, a just title, according to the law of nations, to threaten Turkey with coercion? Coercion, ladies and gentlemen, does not of itself mean war. Coercion justly and judiciously employed has often been the means of averting war.

Mr. Gladstone, of course, admitted that coercion might conceivably lead to war; but he believed the contingency so remote as hardly to merit serious discussion. The Concert of Europe he regarded as 'a powerful and an august instrument for good.' But suppose the Concert of Europe was to go on doing nothing beyond sending impotent remonstrances to the Sultan after each fresh horror—even after the object-lesson which he offered them by the massacre of thousands of Christians before their eyes in the streets of Constantinople—was Great Britain to remain indefinitely an accomplice in that policy? Rather than that—*everything else having failed*—he suggested the withdrawal of our Ambassador from Constantinople and the dismissal of the Turkish Ambassador from the Court of St. James's. But this suggestion he was careful to preface as follows :—

Now, I earnestly hope, and more than hope, and I have every trust, that England will not be called upon to act alone in this matter; but the right to act alone I, for one, will never be a party to renounce. It is a case where the cause of complaint is not sufficient only, but fearful in its amount, intense in its character, and where we confine ourselves strictly to the measures that such cause of complaint may entail. Now in the natural course of things I am not going to advise her Majesty's Government. It would be going entirely out of my line of duty, and inviting you, I think, to go beyond the purpose of this meeting; but there are certain measures that when a determined intention is entertained one must suppose hypothetically to come in the natural course of events. I will first of all suppose then that every effort to obtain direct and active co-operation from any Power of Europe has failed. That is a large supposition—but supposing that—because I am going to suppose everything against my own arguments in order that you may be enabled to measure the worst of what could possibly happen. Well, of course, the first thing would be to require Turkey to fulfil her obligations, and to require that by what may be called a peremptory demand, and not by one of those demands that are first of all delayed for a certain time in deference to the Porte, and then delayed in deference to a Commission, and then, pending the report of the Commission, delayed until the report of the Commission begins to be considered. The proceeding that I hope will be adopted, and I feel sure should be adopted, is the method of what is termed peremptory demand, which is taken, and can properly be made, when the title is unquestionable and the necessity urgent. Well, then, upon the failure to comply with that demand, I apprehend the first step to be taken must be the recall of our Ambassador from Constantinople, and the corresponding dismissal of the Turkish Ambassador from London. I apprehend that that is not creating a European war.

The suspension of diplomatic relations 'would,' in the first place, 'be a withdrawal of countenance and an escape from responsibility as far as it goes.' Should further action be deemed necessary, Mr. Gladstone suggested the proposal by

England of a self-denying ordinance on the part of the Powers, as in the case of the Crimean War, and he might have added in England's proposal in 1880 to seize Smyrna till the Sultan fulfilled his engagement under the Treaty of Berlin. Would the Powers, or any of them, have any just ground of complaint, still more any *casus belli* against England thus far ?

Well, ladies and gentlemen, according to some anonymous articles in the newspapers, and according to reports destitute of all authority, and due probably to the imagination or to selfish aim in some other quarter, or to pure error of judgment, we are told that such a proceeding as I have sketched is to create a united war with Europe against us. Gentlemen, I again say that in my opinion such a proposition is more or less to say that which is cruelly unjust to all the Powers of Europe—is saying little short of, even if it does not approach the limits of, absolute absurdity; because it would be a declaration, and a declaration supported by measures of violence, to the effect that there was no power on the part of a State which had obtained concessions by treaty to exact the observance of those concessions. I therefore don't believe, and don't entertain for a moment, this phantasm which is raised to alarm us if our nerves happen to be in a peculiar state of weakness—this phantasm of European war against measures unselfish, just, and directed to the stoppage of brutal and horrible massacres on an unexampled scale. I do not believe that Europe, or any part of Europe, will make war to insure the continuance of these massacres; but if they are not to continue, and if security is given against them, that is all we want. But that security must be effective ; it must be real ; it must not be visionary ; it must not be limited to the exaction of promises upon paper, with which we have too often and too long been contented.

But assuming what Mr. Gladstone regarded as a violent absurdity and a moral impossibility, what then?

Now, supposing however, my Lord Mayor, that this monstrous supposition were to come about, and that where we had in a binding form limited our own proceedings to the suppression of mischief in its aggravated form, then the suggestion is that a threat of war by the European Powers is to be at once thrown in our face. This supposition I am considering. Ladies and gentlemen, I am going to make a frank confession. If the people of England find themselves confronted by a distinct announcement of such a war in order to secure the maintenance of the present state of things in Turkey, they would have to consider their position. Supposing they came to the conclusion, because this is the most unfavourable supposition, that it was their duty to desist from all effort of procuring effectual change in Turkey—suppose they frankly owned that they were not prepared to incur the responsibility of plunging Europe into war—supposing they said, ' We cast upon you who are willing to undertake it the responsibility of giving countenance to those detestable and horrible proceedings, we wash our hands of them, we will have nothing more to do with them, we will never give countenance, we will never give neutrality, we will not acknowledge as a sovereign within the family of nations the ruler who is himself the responsible agent of these monstrous acts—but we are not prepared to urge Europe on to war, and we will do what was done by France in 1840, without loss of honour, retaining our own judgment and retaining our own right of enforcing that judgment when we see our way to do it—but we will not plunge Europe into war, and we will leave to those who bring about this state of things the responsibility which belongs to them,' would not that be better than the indefinite continuance of the present situation?'

Mr. Gladstone carried the whole meeting with him without distinction of party and without a dissentient voice. And Sir A. B. Forwood, a strong Tory, who had been doubtful as to the prudence of asking Mr. Gladstone to speak, was so convinced of the soundness and moderation of his speech that, in seconding the resolution, he said :—

The question was what step England was to take in dealing with those dreadful excesses in Turkey. He agreed with Mr. Gladstone that this country had the right to threaten coercion in the event of the Sultan not taking steps to stop the massacres.

The result, then, of Mr. Gladstone's reluctant intervention—an intervention urged upon him by the citizens of his native town, irrespective of political differences, and headed by the Lord Mayor, a distinguished Conservative statesman—was to lift the question out of the murky atmosphere of party, and to unite all creeds and parties in a national demonstration against the horrors in Turkey and in support of the Government 'in whatever steps they may think it necessary to take' to discharge the duty and vindicate the honour of the country. It would hardly have been possible to speak at length on such a subject without throwing out some suggestions, and Mr. Gladstone made some suggestions. But to make a suggestion is one thing; to urge a particular course of action on the Government is quite another; and Mr. Gladstone carefully avoided the latter. Like the resolution which he moved, he left the Government a free hand to choose out of a variety of alternatives the course which seemed to them best. And in order to leave no loophole for hypercritics to say that he was recommending a policy which would lead to a European war, he assumed for argument sake what he regarded as the impossible contingency of a European combination against England to prevent her vindication of her treaty rights. In that case this country could with dignity follow the example of France in 1840, and—throwing on the other Powers the responsibility of whatever might happen—decline to act any longer with them in a policy which he believed to be bad and mischievous, as Lord Salisbury did in the case of Crete. 'I declare, in my judgment, it would be far better even to run the risk, which I believe to be no risk at all, of recession than to continue the present state of things, in which we become ministers and coöperators with the Sultan by insuring his immunity and encouraging him to continue his monstrous acts.' But the decision, either way, must rest with the Government. It was for the people of Liverpool to assure the Government 'that we at least will not shrink from giving support to the most energetic conduct of the

Government within no bounds except those prescribed by reason.' Is it possible to imagine, under the circumstances, a speech more moderate, more prudent, more patriotic, and less provocative of a European war? Its moderation was acknowledged on all hands, and the Liberal press especially was enthusiastic in unstinted praise of it.

CHAPTER XIV.

LORD ROSEBERY'S EDINBURGH SPEECH.

A FEW days afterwards Lord Rosebery startled the world by announcing his resignation of the Liberal leadership. The principal reason which he gave was Mr. Gladstone's speech, and the evident agreement of the party with Mr. Gladstone rather than with himself. The reason was as surprising as the resignation. For Mr. Gladstone's views on the Turkish question in general and the Armenian massacres in particular had been public property for months and even years. The public therefore awaited with eager curiosity the speech in which Lord Rosebery promised to make a clean breast of it; and when the speech came it proved the greatest surprise of all. It deserves, from an oratorical point of view, all the praise which has been bestowed upon it. It is, in my humble judgment, far superior to any previous oratorical effort of Lord Rosebery; and that is no light praise. It would be difficult to give it higher praise than to say that it confused the issues in the minds of many, and 'made the worse appear the better reason, to perplex and dash maturest counsels.' I believe it hardly influenced the lower *strata* of society at all, except antagonistically—an opinion for which I have already given some reasons. Lord Rosebery also succeeded in propagating an entirely erroneous representation of Mr. Gladstone's speech, but a representation which of course he believed to be the true one. It is a striking instance of supplanting the natural and grammatical meaning of language by unintentionally reading into it one's own preconceived notions.

The reader, then, being now in possession of the arguments of Mr. Gladstone's speech, I will proceed to examine Lord Rosebery's in the light of reason, of facts, and of his own previous policy. I shall endeavour to do so with the same courtesy which he exhibited in attacking Mr. Gladstone's speech, and with the same frankness. But I must begin by expressing my sincere regret in finding myself in antagonism to Lord Rosebery on any subject. It has been my lot to fall, like many others, under the spell of his attractive personality. I have received many kindnesses from him, and never an unkindness. I believed that he had a great future before him, and I hailed his advent to the Premiership as a man not only of ideas, but of ideals also, and lofty moral convictions. I have talked and corresponded with him on the question of Armenia, and I believed, and believe still, in the genuine sincerity of his indignation at the wrongs of the Armenians, and of his desire to redress their wrongs. It is not his motives which I question, or his humanity, or his patriotism, but his policy and political prescience. I believe that his speech has done a most serious, perhaps a fatal, injury to the cause of the Armenians, and has already sent numbers of them to torture and death. Mr. Gladstone's great speech, the unanimity of the meeting to which it was addressed, the meetings that followed, and Lord Hugh Cecil's excellent letter, touched the consciences of the people of Europe, roused their Governments from their criminal apathy, and made the Sultan pause in his career of massacre. Lord Rosebery's speech, together with the applause with which it was greeted by the entire Ministerial press and by some leading organs of the Opposition, went far to neutralise the effect of the Liverpool demonstration, and to give foreign Governments and the Sultan the impression that the agitation against the Armenian horrors was not, after all, a spontaneous outburst of national indignation and sorrow, but merely the fleeting exhibition of an artificial excitement organised in the interest of the Government. Truly a good way of strengthening Lord Salisbury's hands!

And now let us consider the salient points of Lord Rosebery's criticism of Mr. Gladstone's speech. The fallacy which underlies and vitiates his whole criticism is contained in the following passage of his Edinburgh speech:—

Against the possibility of solitary intervention in

the affairs of the East I am prepared—the party who support the interests of peace must also be vigilant, and must also be prepared—to fight tooth and nail if they do not wish that policy to be carried out. Mr. Gladstone speaks—urging, as I think, indirectly, some idea of this kind—he speaks of the phantasm of a European war being excited by no such thing. I believe it is no phantasm at all: I am convinced, as far as my information and my knowledge goes—and up to recently I think that knowledge and information were sound, although the situation may have changed for the better—I do believe that there was a fixed and resolute agreement on the part of the Great Powers of Europe—of all of them or nearly all of them—to resist by force any single-handed intervention by England in the affairs of the East.

This is an expansion of a sentence in Lord Rosebery's speech at the Eighty Club on the 3rd of last March:—

On August 13, he [Lord Salisbury] had had a telegram from St. Petersburg saying that under no circumstances would Russia allow or countenance any vigorous action on this question of Armenia.

I shall consider Lord Rosebery's interpretation of this telegram presently. But I wish first to get to the bottom of his passionate denunciation of 'solitary intervention,' or 'separate action,' as he variously calls it. When did Lord Rosebery conceive this horror of separate action on the Eastern question? Dates are important. There are indications in Lord Rosebery's speech at the Eighty Club, eight months ago, that he was himself then in favour of solitary action. He twitted Lord Salisbury for his strong language about the Sultan, and ' the great and mysterious activity of the ship Dryad ; and when we had been buoyed up by the activity of this vessel, and by the speeches of Lord Salisbury, and by the assurances of the European Concert, and by the declarations of the Ministerial press, that all was well because of these declarations, when Parliament is about to assemble the whole collapses like a house of cards.' Again :—

I say that, in the first place, they used language deliberately which could only be justified by the gravest results. I say, in the second place, that no results followed that language, except possibly an aggravation and an increase of massacre and misgovernment in that country. And, in the third place, I charge them with an entire want of resources in dealing with this question—with an entire poverty of methods in dealing with it. For, after all, diplomatic pressure is not limited to war, or bombardment, or blockade. I am not going to enlarge on these three points ; for the first and second are self-evident, and the other I cannot discuss. But no one can read the recent correspondence without seeing that as regards all idea of putting pressure on the Sultan, *there has been an absolute destitution of any idea except getting other Powers to join with us in putting pressure upon him, and when that failed there has been an absolute negation of any action at all.*

Surely the plain meaning of that is, that when diplomatic pressure on the Sultan failed by means of the European Concert, the British

Government ought to have acted independently, and there is a hint that the separate action should take the form of blockading some Turkish port. But if I am right in my interpretation of the Eighty Club speech, how are we to reconcile it with Lord Rosebery's letter of the 26th of last September, in which he says: 'I trust to diplomatic action, strenuous, self-denying, and supported by an unanimous nation, to bring the Powers, or some of them, into line. If that fails, nothing will succeed'? Here surely we have that 'absolute destitution of any idea except getting other Powers to join us in putting pressure upon the Sultan, and when that failed there has been an absolute negation of any action at all,' which Lord Rosebery censured in his Eighty Club speech.

Now when Lord Rosebery wrote his recent letters and made his Edinburgh speech recommending the methods of diplomacy alone, and protesting vehemently against separate action, he knew that diplomacy by means of the Concert of Europe had 'failed,' that its resources had been exhausted in vain. Here is his own indictment against the Concert of Europe:—

What is the result? The Porte has triumphed all along the line. That is a grave and terrible result. The last state of the Armenians is far worse than the first. And as a result of the complete Concert of Europe, of which we have been so often assured, and which, it was boasted in the speech at the Guildhall, was under the leadership of Great Britain, we come to the final summing up. I know no summing up more terrible in the whole of diplomatic history. It occurs in a despatch from Sir Edmund Monson, in Vienna, after a conversation with the Austrian Minister of Foreign Affairs, Count Goluchowski. Sir Edmund Monson writes, under date of January 14 this year: 'No one can more clearly than himself' (that is, Count Goluchowski) 'perceive the horrors of the situation, nor feel more acutely the bitterness of the incapacity of Europe to ameliorate it.'

Count Goluchowski's language is, in fact, considerably stronger than the extract quoted by Lord Rosebery. I have quoted it at length in a previous chapter, and need only requote two sentences here:—

In presence of this heartrending prospect it is intelligible that numbers of humane people are revolted at the idea that Europe is powerless, and, regardless of consequences, would wish that action should be taken by some or even one of the Powers to put a stop to the extermination of the miserable Armenians. But practical statesmen are bound to consider the situation from another standpoint.

In other words and plainer language, Austria, which together with Germany has hitherto dominated the European Concert, is prepared to stand calmly by, and, if she can, force the Concert of Europe to stand calmly by, while the Sultan proceeds to 'the extermination of the miserable Armenians,' whom the Sultan himself reckoned to amount in August 1893 to 1,000,000, and whom M. Hanotaux, in his recent speech, estimated at 3,000,000. But let me proceed with Lord Rosebery's comments on Count Goluchowski's conversation with the British Ambassador :—

That is a pregnant, a terrible sentence. It is the declared abdication of Europe in the affairs of the Ottoman Empire. This is what we have come to after nearly nineteen centuries of Christianity, with a Europe which counts her armies on a footing of war not by thousands, nor by hundreds of thousands, but by millions and by millions, in face of a population not reckoned at above twenty-eight millions.* So that in all probability it is not too much to say that Europe, every part of which worships the same Christ, and believes in the doctrines of the same New Testament, through one way or another, is prepared, on the verge of the twentieth century, to relinquish its suffering fellow-Christians to the cruel mercies of barbarous Kurds, directed or connived at by a still more barbarous Government. That is the result—a grave and terrible result. I do not apportion any blame; I do not ask this Club, as a party Club, to utter any verdict. I do ask them, however, to consider this question; not to let it pass in silence, as some of us naturally do, as one of the gravest and most shameful in the history of civilisation; but at any rate to remember that, if they wish to appeal to the people of Great Britain, I believe there is no question which appeals to the hearts and the minds and the consciences of this country as this question of Armenia.

A fine and an impressive passage, which warmed my heart when I read it. But the orator who thus reproached the Concert of

* Excluding Egypt, the Musulman subjects of the Sultan, who are alone available for Lord Rosebery's argument, do not much exceed sixteen millions.

Europe for its cruel callousness himself now tells us that we must by all means act with the Concert. Count Goluchowski, voicing the Concert of Europe, has told the world, in the despatch which both Lord Rosebery and I have quoted, that the horrors which have taken place in Armenia and Anatolia are 'appalling,' and that he expected greater horrors yet to come, till they culminated in 'the extermination of the miserable Armenians.' He was very sorry for the Armenians; 'but practical statesmen are bound to consider the situation from another standpoint.' Which means that Austria had other interests, which she considered too important for her to run the smallest risk in stretching out a hand to save perhaps millions of human beings from ruthless extermination under every circumstance that could add horror and bitterness to death. Lord Rosebery has now apparently become a convert to the Austrian statesman's political doctrine. What other interpretation am I to put on the following passage in the Edinburgh speech?—

. The policy of this country consists, if you like it, of a thousand portions or a thousand interests, and we cannot allow nine hundred and ninety-nine of these portions to be sacrificed to the remaining one, however important.

And Lord Rosebery gave emphasis to this declaration by adding:—

I do not say that I am unwilling to draw the sword

in a great and necessary cause. I have myself, while a Minister, incurred the risk of war. I do not believe that any British Minister, with reference to the vast interests consigned to his charge, can avoid the risk of war. But I say that any British Minister who engages in a European war except under the pressure of the direst necessity, except under circumstances directly and distinctively British, is a criminal to his country and his position.

The Paris papers of the following day informed us that Lord Rosebery ran this grave risk for the sake of a strip of territory in Siam which I believe Lord Salisbury has conceded to France. Now imagine for a moment what that risk was: a war with France, who had Russia at her back, with Germany lying in ambush, to spring perchance from her lair when our troops and fleets were engaged elsewhere, in order to occupy the Transvaal as a *point d'appui* for establishing her domination in South Africa. I shall endeavour to show presently that there might be separate action of an efficient kind in Turkey that would involve no appreciable risk of war. But the risk which Lord Rosebery says he was willing to run menaced the integrity of the British Empire. And all for a strip of debatable land which it would take an expert to point out upon the map, and which France now possesses without any damage to British honour or interest!

Most of us still remember the indignation caused in England by a despatch from the British

Ambassador at Constantinople in 1877, in which he said :—

> We may and must feel indignant at the needless and monstrous severity with which the Bulgarian insurrection was put down; but the necessity which exists for England to prevent changes from occurring here, which would be most detrimental to ourselves, is not affected by the question whether it was 10,000 or 20,000 persons who perished in the suppression. We have been upholding what we knew to be a semi-civilised nation, liable under certain circumstances to be carried into fearful excesses; but the fact of this having just now been strikingly brought home to us all cannot be a sufficient reason for abandoning a policy which is the only one that can be followed with a due regard to our own interests.*

Lord Rosebery goes far beyond this. He accepts—with grief and horror, but as a political necessity—the extermination of all the myriads of Armenians under Turkish rule rather than run the smallest risk of injuring British interests. I do not forget that Lord Rosebery has assured us that he trusts to ' diplomatic action, strenuous, self-denying.' But while diplomatic action has been ' strenuous ' for two years in firing paper pellets at Abdul Hamid, he has been even more ' strenuous ' in massacring the Armenians. Lord Rosebery might just as well trust to diplomatic action stopping the ravages of a man-eating tiger. And Count Goluchowski said as much in the despatch which made such a profound im-

* *Turkey*, No. 1 (1877), p. 197.

pression on Lord Rosebery. 'Every kind of admonition,' said the Austrian Minister, 'had been given to the Sultan, and his Excellency did not see what more could be said to him than has already been repeatedly urged.' But Austrian interests might perchance suffer, and therefore, rather than that, perish the Armenians!

But are material interests—are pounds, shillings, and pence, and extension of territory and trade—the only British interests? Are not moral obligations an interest? Are not duty and honour interests? But Lord Rosebery denies that we are bound by any obligation of duty or honour to succour the perishing Armenians. This is what he said in the Edinburgh speech:—

Now Mr. Gladstone holds that we are bound in honour by the Cyprus Convention to intervene, and that if having—I think I state the arguments fairly—and that if having taken certain responsibilities upon ourselves we do not discharge those responsibilities because other Powers prevent us, then that the word 'honour' should be erased from our dictionary. Well, I confess that I do not hold that we are bound in honour to the Cyprus Convention. I have always felt, and I have always acted when at the Foreign Office on this presumption, that the Sultan, not having fulfilled or tried to fulfil any one of his pledges to that Convention, we have equally been released from ours.

But what about the Armenians? 'These sheep—what have they done?' Have we no obligations of duty or honour towards them? In the Treaty of San Stefano, Russia compelled the

Sultan to grant satisfactory reforms to the Armenians. But Russia knew the worth of Turkish promises; therefore she stipulated that Russian troops should occupy Armenia till the promised reforms were carried out. On the initiative of England the Congress of Berlin substituted, with the reluctant assent of Russia, the bare promise of the Sultan for the specific engagement of the Treaty of San Stefano. But Prince Gortchakoff pleaded earnestly for permission for the Russian troops to remain till at least the Sultan had made a fair beginning of carrying out his promises. Again England took the lead in assuring the Russian Chancellor that the Concert of Europe would see that the Armenians received no damage from the withdrawal of the Russian troops. And Russia acquiesced. Yet Lord Rosebery assures us 'that the Sultan not having fulfilled, or tried to fulfil, any one of his pledges to that Convention, we have equally been released from ours!' I am astonished. Armenian delegates were permitted to present their nation's case to the Congress of Berlin, and the Congress promised to protect them. Have the Armenians discharged us of our obligations under both Treaty and Convention?

But was Lord Rosebery always of opinion that the Anglo-Turkish Convention was 'a dead letter,' that it fell 'still-born' from its authors' hands? The following quotation from his Eighty Club speech last March supplies the answer:—

If our means are so inadequate, why did you make the Convention to protect these frontiers? Why did you take the separate and solemn responsibility of the Cyprus Convention for the condition of the suffering Christians of the East? We are now to understand that our means are not equal to it; or that our means in 1878 were greater than they are now. You know that they are twice as great. If there was no promise and guarantee, it is enough to make some of us open our eyes.

Nor is the Anglo-Turkish Convention the only subject in this connection on which Lord Rosebery has turned his back upon himself. I have shown conclusively that down to the eve of Mr. Gladstone's speech at Liverpool Lord Rosebery was himself a convinced advocate of separate action in case the Concert of Europe failed to stop the bloody work of Abdul Hamid. That seems to me a necessary inference from the evidence which I have produced. But we are not left to inference alone. On the 15th of August, 1895, Lord Rosebery delivered a speech on the Address in the House of Lords, from which I quote as follows:—

Then we come to the other subject with which the late Government had much to do—the subject of Armenia. That is raised outside the domain of party politics. I do not for a moment doubt that the noble Marquis feels as strongly as we do the necessity of obtaining from the Government of the Sultan adequate and permanent guarantees that there shall be no possible recurrence of the atrocities which have horrified the conscience of Europe. I believe action in that sense is as vitally necessary both for the interest of the Government of the Sultan itself as for the protection of the unhappy Christians of Asia Minor; for one thing at least is certain, that the recurrence of these outrages tends to shorten the life of the Sultan's Government in the midst of the civilised communities in which it is placed. . . I am well aware that it is not an easy matter to preserve a European concert. It is possible, as we have seen rumoured in the papers, that the Governments of France and Russia may not unreasonably be afraid to waken that uneasy phantom of the Eastern question by any vigorous measures in support of the policy of the British Government. But I believe and I hope that such is not the case; if it were, unfortunately, to be true, I am at any rate convinced of this—that the noble Marquis, *in proceeding even alone to deal with this question vigorously and efficiently*, will find that he has behind him, not a party, however overwhelming, but the entire nation at his back.

This goes considerably beyond anything that Mr. Gladstone said in his Liverpool speech. The solitary action which Lord Rosebery here recommends from his responsible place as leader of the Opposition and ex-Prime Minister and Foreign Secretary, is devoid of any of the qualifications and safeguards with which Mr. Gladstone surrounded his suggestion. Moreover, Mr. Gladstone did not believe in any risk of war from the policy which he favoured as a *dernier ressort*. Lord Rosebery does believe in not merely the risk, but the certainty, of a great European war from the solitary action which he nevertheless recommended in the autumn of last year and in the spring of this. Yet he now tells us that 'any British Minister who engages' in such a war 'is a criminal to his country and his position.'

I am perplexed and bewildered. And my bewilderment is increased on learning that Lord Rosebery resigned the leadership of the Liberal party because Mr. Gladstone made a speech at Liverpool in which he gave a general support to Lord Rosebery's own policy on the Armenian question, though in more guarded and reserved language than Lord Rosebery considered it necessary to use in the House of Lords.

CHAPTER XV.

POLICY OF SEPARATE ACTION CONSIDERED.

But now let us for a moment consider on its merits the policy of 'separate' or 'solitary' action. The phrase is Lord Rosebery's. I do not think that Mr. Gladstone has used it; nor have I done so myself, except in criticism of Lord Rosebery's speech and letters. It is a phrase which is susceptible of various meanings, and it is a pity that Lord Rosebery did not define his meaning. His idea of 'separate action'—and it is the idea with which he has managed to inoculate a large section of the public mind—is the forcible passage of the Dardanelles by the British fleet, and seizure, perhaps bombardment, of Constantinople. I am not aware that any responsible person has made any such proposal. Certainly Mr. Gladstone has not. Now it may be taken as an axiom, for reasons given in this volume, that the Sultan will never ameliorate the lot of his Christian subjects except under the stimulus of external coercion. But coercion need never pass the border of menace if prosecuted in the form of an ultimatum to be answered by the

Sultan within a fixed date, provided the ultimatum is issued conjointly by all the Powers, or even by one of them, with the acquiescence of the rest, or of a majority of them. The power of declaring war, or even accepting a declaration of war, does not rest with the Sultan, but with the Sheikh-ul-Islâm—one among other decisive proofs that the Sultan is not Khalif. The prerogative of peace and war belonged of right and fact to the office of the Khalif as Commander of the Faithful. But when the Khalifat was abolished this right was transferred to the Ulema, who are now the custodians of law and religion in every Musulman State, exercising in each State their power through the Grand Mufti or Sheikh-ul-Islâm. It is laid down in the *Multeka*—which is to the Turk what the decrees of the Vatican are to the Roman Catholic, a religious law without appeal—that the Sultan cannot make war even in self-defence without a *Fetvâ* (which has the force of a Papal Bull) from the Sheikh-ul-Islâm. And the Sheikh-ul-Islâm does not grant his *Fetvâ* till he is assured that the resources of the Sultan are such as to afford a reasonable prospect of success. 'The *Fetvâ* is now so indispensable a preliminary to any political act that the Sultan who should dare to omit it would be declared an infidel by a *Fetvâ* issued by the Mufti himself; and such a proceeding would be sufficient to excite against him both the populace and the soldiery, and to precipitate him at once from his throne.'* In the war of 1877 the Sultan was obliged to ask leave of the Sheikh-ul-Islâm before he could accept the Tsar's declaration of war, and the permission was given on condition that the Sultan 'is assured that his State possesses the force necessary to resist the enemy, and that the war may possibly have a result favourable for his country.'†

In dealing with the Sultan, therefore, the European Powers make the fundamental and fatal mistake of treating him as a free man. He is not a free man. There is a power behind the throne whose behests he must obey on peril of excommunication and deposition. The Ulema's *Fetvâ* would instantly absolve all his subjects from their allegiance to him, and not a soldier in his army, not even in his well-paid and pampered bodyguard, would dare fire a shot in his defence. I insist on this crucial fact because it is the key which fits all the wards of every form of coercion. The Sultan cannot resist an ultimatum from any Power that has a force superior to his own. But any naval Power, even Denmark or Greece, is superior to the Sultan at sea, and could paralyse his empire, for he has not a single man-of-war fit

---

* Eton's *Survey of the Turkish Empire*, edition of 1809, p. 22. One of the very best books ever written on Turkey. The author spent more than twenty years in official positions in different parts of Turkey and Russia, and made a thorough study of the Eastern question in all its bearings.

† *Turkey*, No. 26 (1877), p. 7.

for battle. I saw all his navy four years ago rotting in the Golden Horn, without crews or equipment. There was not a single ship in the fleet fit to go to sea to carry the Sultan's Firman to the new Khedive, and the Sultan was consequently obliged to send his private yacht. The explanation is that the navy took a prominent part in deposing the present Sultan's uncle, and Abdul Hamid has consequently left his fleet, practically dismantled, in confinement in the Golden Horn. He is therefore completely at the mercy of the smallest naval Power in Europe.

Now let me venture to suggest several kinds of separate action on the part of England which could not possibly involve the smallest risk of war. And let me begin with the precedent of 1880—the proposal to seize some Turkish port with the British fleet till the Sultan yielded to the will of Europe, accompanying the proposal with an engagement on the part of England to retire when the Sultan yielded, and in any case not to profit by the manœuvre. I should be surprised to learn that the other Powers opposed so moderate a proposal, and one certain to bring the Sultan to reason without firing a shot, and thus serve the policy even of selfish Austria by prolonging the territorial *status quo*. In any case none of the Powers could take umbrage, still less make so considerate a project a *casus belli*.

But suppose the Powers, from motives of

jealousy, rejected the British proposal. It would then be open to Lord Salisbury to propose that some other member of the Concert should take the proposed action. I cannot believe that the Powers would be so foolish as to veto separate action on the part of all the members of the Concert, subject to the conditions which I have named. But let us face even that possibility. Lord Salisbury might then propose that, as some of the Powers at the Conference of Constantinople in 1877 proposed that Swiss troops should be invited to occupy Bulgaria till the scheme of the Conference was put into working order, so now Denmark or Greece should be asked to occupy some portion of Turkish territory till the Sultan accepted whatever scheme the Powers agreed upon for the protection of the Sultan's Christian subjects.

These are all examples of separate initiative on the part of the British Government, proving to demonstration its pacific and disinterested intentions. If (which I do not believe) they all failed to win the approval of the Powers, it would then be open to the Government to fall back upon its inherent right to take a material guarantee, under whatever fair safeguards the Powers might suggest, to compel the Sultan to fulfil his treaty obligations. Can any one believe that the Powers would combine to oppose this by force of arms? Is it conceivable that they would set so dangerous a precedent in international law as to declare that no Power has a right, without leave of the rest, to vindicate its own treaty rights by force of arms if necessary, giving the others Powers guarantees, such as Russia gave England in 1877, to respect their interests? It is incredible. Still more incredible is it that the Triplice and Duplice, to quote the Continental phraseology, should make common cause against England for enforcing what they all profess to desire, and without any *arrière-pensée* on the part of this country. The most conspicuous feature in the relations of the Continental Powers with each other at present is their mutual suspicions. Bismarck's revealed treachery towards his colleagues in the Triple Alliance has sown a rank crop of mutual suspicions among all the Powers, which makes it morally impossible that they should combine against England once they were satisfied, as they could be without difficulty, that she had no sinister designs. Despite the inspired press of Vienna and Berlin, my belief is that at this moment Britain is the least suspected Government among the Great Powers. The Triplice and Duplice are pretty evenly matched, and the sword of Great Britain thrown into either scale would make the other kick the beam. And we are to suppose that either side would give the other such an overwhelming advantage by proposing a combined war against the Power which has this trump card to play! I find it difficult, to imagine the state of mind which can give a moment's credence to so wild an improbability. Three of the Great Powers objected to England's separate action with regard to seizing Smyrna in 1880, yet none of them opposed her; and the knowledge of England's intention sufficed, as such knowledge always will suffice, to compel the Sultan's submission.

Another example of separate action is Lord Salisbury's refusal to join the Powers in blockading Crete, which, so far from provoking war, prevented it. It is not to the Concert of Europe, as both Sir Michael-Hicks Beach and Mr. George Curzon have asserted, that we owe the pacification of Crete, but to Lord Salisbury's separate action. We all desire to act by means of the Concert of Europe; but separate action on the part of one of the Powers may be the means now, as it has been in the past, to set the Concert in motion. It will be time enough to talk of the peril of war when the Triple and Dual Alliance unite in warning us of it. 'When the sky falls we shall catch larks,' and when this threat of war, for so inadequate a reason, comes from mutually antagonistic Powers, I shall believe it, but not before. The Bluebooks, as I shall show presently, do not reveal a hint of such a thing. I have a prejudice in favour of patriotism, and it does not seem to me patriotic to proclaim to all the world that we are afraid to vindicate our treaty rights lest there should be a combination of foreign Powers to forbid us. That surely is the best way to invite the combination. An Evangelical precept bids us turn to him who smites us on the one cheek 'the other also.' But I know no precept in Christian ethics which bids us offer the cheek before any one has threatened to strike us. Yet is not this precisely what the panic-mongers have been doing? I can imagine no policy better calculated to weaken our influence in the councils of Europe. At the worst—if I must seriously discuss a chimera — there would be no shame or dishonour in declining to fight single-handed against Europe in defence of the Armenians; but there would be infinite shame and indelible dishonour in remaining in a Concert which should sanction Count Goluchowski's ignoble and wicked policy of watching with folded arms, albeit with sorrow, while the Sultan goes merrily forward with his resolution to exterminate the Armenians. Would Lord Rosebery have this country remain a member of the European Concert on Austria's condition, namely, to do absolutely nothing but send the Sultan diplomatic 'admonitions,' which the Austrian Minister himself declares to be perfectly useless? I infer from Lord Rosebery's Edinburgh and Colchester speeches that he would. He even objects to our removing the British Ambassador from Constantinople, and supports his objection with the following reasons :—

I must say that I do not agree with the proposal to withdraw our Ambassador from Constantinople. In the first place, it withdraws our presence from the European Concert. It necessitates our handing over our interests to the Ambassador of some friendly State; but friendly as that State may be, I should prefer those interests remaining in the hands of our own Ambassador, more especially when I observe the tone of the European Press. In the next place, we lose the only remaining method by which we can influence the policy of the Sultan. You may say it is a feeble and ineffectual method, but it is, after all, the only method, and in the present shocking state of affairs in the East I should think long and carefully before I could cut myself free from the matter. In the next place, if you withdraw your Embassy it will have an even more regrettable effect: it would deprive your Consuls in Asia Minor—throughout the Turkish Empire indeed—of almost all their use and employment. They would be reduced to commercial functions, they would be thwarted and harassed at every turn by the Turkish authorities, while at present they do in some respects act as an assistance and a guide to those suffering Armenians who still look to England for help, and are at any rate, and have been in the past, the only channels, I think, through which trustworthy information as to their condition has reached the outer world. I say, then, I am unwilling by the withdrawal of the Ambassador to cut myself off from those inevitable incidents. But I will go a step further in deprecating this policy. It is one of the ways by which, without meaning it, you may drift into war. The withdrawal of an Ambassador and the dismissal of the corresponding Ambassador is, after all, in its essence a great affront offered by one empire to another.

Let us glance at these reasons. 'In the first

place, it withdraws our presence from the European Concert.' But if Austria is still to dominate, as she has hitherto dominated, the European Concert, our presence there will serve no other end than that of giving a tacit sanction to the extermination of the Armenians. No one has recommended the withdrawal of our Ambassador except as a *dernier ressort* following on the proved failure of diplomatic efforts. Those efforts have been going on for several years, accompanied by a steady *crescendo* of the Sultan's iniquities. Continued impunity, tacitly sanctioned by the presence of the Ambassadors, has emboldened him, like a tiger which has tasted human blood, to go on by leaps and bounds in his career of crime. Is there no indignity—to use no harsher word—to the majesty of this great realm, and to the humane and pure Sovereign who wields the sceptre of that majesty, in going on recognising as an equal and a brother the greatest criminal of the nineteenth century, a wretch compared to whom Jack the Ripper might almost be regarded as a respectable person? A year ago the Ambassadors at Constantinople unanimously accused him to his face of having sanctioned, where he did not actually order, the massacres that had taken place up to that date. Knowing that their accusation would end in mere words, he enjoyed his triumph over Christendom and gave orders for more massacres, indulging his thirst for blood nearer and near

Europe in a spirit of bravado, till at last he made the streets of his capital, under the eyes of the Ambassadors, crimson with the blood of innocent men, women, and tender babes. Eight months ago Lord Rosebery declared that the Sultan had 'triumphed all along the line.' The line has been terribly enlarged since then, and the Sultan's triumph has proceeded *pari passu* with his unpunished crimes. Is this to be allowed to go on till the last Armenian has been butchered and the butcher has begun to sharpen his weapons for the rest of his Christian subjects? And is England to go on sitting supinely in a Concert which permits it? I understand Lord Rosebery to say Yes. He is an admirer of Cromwell. Does he think that Cromwell would have continued to accredit indefinitely an Ambassador to such an inhuman monster? What saddens and amazes one is the insensibility of civilised Europe to the unspeakable shame of holding intercourse with a man whom the Ambassadors of the Great Powers have twice publicly branded—a year ago and again after the recent massacres in Constantinople—with the responsibility of crimes the most frightful in character and extent that have stained the annals of the nineteenth century. How trivial are the reasons which Lord Rosebery urges in favour of holding diplomatic intercourse with Abdul Hamid compared with the burning shame of it! But let us consider the rest of them.

The withdrawal of the British Ambassador would reduce our Consuls in Asia Minor 'to commercial functions.' What other purpose have they served during this reign of terror? Have they prevented a single massacre? Not one, zealous and brave as they have shown themselves. The Consular delegates with the infamous Turkish Commission did infinite harm, and no good whatever. Lord Rosebery's argument betrays, for a man of his intelligence, a singular lack of appreciation of the Oriental character, and of the Sultan's character in particular. He is a man whose cowardice is equal to his cruelty; and suspiciousness, which is innate in the Oriental character, is aggravated in Abdul Hamid by his abject fears. The unknown is full of vague terror for him. Like a beast of prey, he would suspect a trap in so strange an experience as a breach of diplomatic intercourse, and would fear a blow in some unexpected quarter. Every movement of the British fleet would make him tremble. While England remains in the European Concert he feels safe. He regards her as a wild elephant surrounded and kept in order by five tame ones. And unparalleled success has inspired him with such confidence in his own cunning that, while he has a British Ambassador at Constantinople and a Turkish Ambassador in London, he believes he can go on befooling John Bull *ad libitum*. Leave him severely alone, and the probability is that his uncertainty as to what

England may do, coupled with the impossibility of getting any information, would influence him more than all the 'strenuous' diplomatic pressure, multiplied tenfold, to which alone Lord Rosebery trusts.

But our Consuls, adds Lord Rosebery, are 'the only channels through which trustworthy information as to the condition of the Armenians has reached the outer world.' That is an unlucky argument for Lord Rosebery to use, for he took care while in office, first as Foreign Secretary, and then as Prime Minister, that not a ray of information should reach the outer world from the reports of our Consuls in Asia Minor. Appeals, urgent and repeated, were made in the Press and in the House of Commons for the publication of the Consular reports; but every appeal was met either with silence or with a curt and peremptory refusal. That argument may therefore, I think, be dismissed.

Lord Rosebery's last objection to the withdrawal of our Ambassador from the Porte is that it would be 'a great affront offered by one empire to another.' An affront offered by Great Britain to Abdul Hamid! Are the susceptibilities of that personage to be the measure of our duties? Or is Lord Rosebery afraid that Abdul Hamid would declare war upon us?

I think I have now shown that neither Mr. Gladstone nor any other responsible person among sympathisers with the Armenians has proposed or suggested any kind of action that could by remote possibility provoke a European war; while, on the other hand, Lord Rosebery himself has been till now an advocate of solitary action on the part of England of a more unqualified and unguarded sort than any policy that can be inferred from Mr. Gladstone's speech. Surely the least that Mr. Gladstone had a right under the circumstances to expect from his successor and erstwhile intimate friend was that he should have conferred with him before accusing him of recommending a policy which might lead a Minister into conduct 'criminal to his country and his trust.' And was it fair, without a word of inquiry, to make Mr. Gladstone responsible for Lord Rosebery's resignation of the Liberal leadership? Where was Mr. Gladstone's offence? In speaking at all? Lord Rosebery can hardly have meant to suggest that in retiring from political life Mr. Gladstone became bound to remain for ever silent on all questions of public interest. Did Mr. Gladstone attack Lord Rosebery's policy? On the contrary, he abstained from any criticism whatever upon it, and the policy which he shadowed in outline is far less obnoxious to the reproach of separate action than that which Lord Rosebery himself suggested to the Government a year ago from his responsible place of leader of the Opposition. Besides, as leader of the Opposition, Lord Rosebery was not responsible for Mr. Gladstone's speech. If anyone had a right to complain of Mr. Gladstone's intervention, it was Lord Salisbury.

But Lord Salisbury has made no complaint; nor is there any reason to suppose that he has regarded Mr. Gladstone's speech this year at Liverpool, or last year at Chester, as injurious to his diplomacy. He knows at least that both were intended to have a contrary effect. Or is Lord Rosebery's grievance to be found in the fact that Mr. Gladstone has rallied the Liberal party behind Lord Salisbury, and thus given him a position of political strength such as few Prime Ministers have enjoyed in this country? Under Mr. Gladstone's inspiration the nation has given Lord Salisbury the powers of a dictator in this question—powers so great that he could shed off colleague after colleague who should venture to oppose him, and be all the stronger for the riddance. It is a unique position, and involves a unique responsibility. Yet it ought not to be a grievance to Lord Rosebery, since he declared at Colchester that his policy was Lord Salisbury's policy. In short, after looking at the question all round, I fail to find in Mr. Gladstone's speech any justification for Lord Rosebery's resignation and subsequent onslaught on Mr. Gladstone's intervention. That he found the leadership of his party intolerable to him on other grounds he took no pains to conceal; and to my humble thinking his position would now be infinitely stronger if he had placed his resignation on its true cause, instead of making Mr. Gladstone the scapegoat of other offenders.

CHAPTER XVI.

ALLEGED COMBINATION AGAINST ENGLAND.

LET us now examine the grounds of the alleged combination against England. Lord Rosebery said at Edinburgh that 'there was a fixed and resolute agreement on the part of the Great Powers of Europe—of all, or nearly all of them—to resist by force any single-handed intervention by England in the affairs of the East.' Again, 'There is no doubt a certain concord that reigns over the aspect of Europe at this moment. But that concord is chiefly directed, not in your favour, but against you.' At the Eighty Club, on the 3rd of last March, Lord Rosebery said: 'On August 13 Lord Salisbury had a telegram from St. Petersburg, saying that under no circumstances would Russia allow or countenance any vigorous action on this question of Armenia.' In a letter dated September 17, Lord Rosebery speaks of 'the declaration of Russia in August 1895, that she would oppose separate action on the part of any Powers'; which he explains in a letter of September 26 to mean 'the declaration of Prince Lobanoff, recorded in the despatch of

August 9'—a declaration which is, in Lord Rosebery's opinion, 'perfectly clear to anyone conversant with diplomatic language.' This is all the information on which Lord Rosebery professed to rely down to his Colchester speech three weeks later. In that speech he said that *he knew* there was this alarming combination against England to resist by force any separate action which she might propose. Had he received any fresh information which carried his knowledge beyond the Blue-books? I have good authority for stating that the only fresh information which he possessed—since it was the only fresh information in existence—is the fact that at their recent interview in Vienna, Prince Lobanoff and Count Goluchowski agreed that it was possible to maintain the territorial *status quo* in Turkey for some years to come, and that they mutually pledged their respective Governments to use their best endeavours to maintain it. This pledge would oblige the two Powers to resist any separate action aimed at the destruction of the territorial *status quo*. It pledged them to oppose no other kind of separate action. I called public attention to this all-important distinction in the end of September, and a few days afterwards (Sept. 29) the *Times's* Vienna correspondent confirmed my information on official authority. The Austrian Government declared categorically that the only agreement arrived at between Russia and Austria was to 'maintain the *status quo* in Turkey,' and added, that if the British fleet were to pass the Dardanelles without any designs against the *status quo*, the Northern Powers would not oppose it.

We are thus driven back on Prince Lobanoff's declarations on August 9 and 13, 1895, as the sole source of Lord Rosebery's sensational assertion that any kind of separate action on the part of England would be resisted by force of arms by 'all, or nearly all,' the Great Powers of Europe. Let us look at those declarations.

On reporting a conversation with Prince Lobanoff on August 9, 1895, the British Ambassador at St. Petersburg writes:—

On my asking Prince Lobanoff how far the Russian Government would be prepared to go in putting pressure on the Sultan in the event of his Majesty refusing to take any steps at all, his Excellency replied that he authorised me to state to your lordship that the idea of the employment of force was personally repugnant to the Emperor ; and, in answer to my further inquiries, his Excellency said that the employment of force by any one of the three Powers would be equally distasteful to the Russian Government.

Four days later (August 13) the Ambassador reports:—

Prince Lobanoff informed me, in reply to my question how far the Imperial Government were prepared to go in pressing these reforms upon the Sultan, that both the Emperor and himself were strongly against force being used by any or all of the Powers.

P

Here, then, we have Lord Rosebery's entire evidence for his opinion that there is a combination 'of all, or nearly all,' the Great Powers to attack us in case of separate action on our part. But the evidence to which he appeals indicates neither suggestion nor hint of any such combination. On the contrary, there is no special reference to England at all. The Russian Government objected, fourteen months ago, to the employment of force by any or all of the Powers against the Sultan *to enforce an unworkable scheme of reforms.* It is plain from the Bluebooks that by the employment of force Prince Lobanoff meant the invasion of the Sultan's dominion by an army, or the occupation of Constantinople by a naval force. Russia was suspicious, and had good reason to be suspicious, of the intentions of the Triple Alliance and of England, and she therefore objected to any action which might have the effect of upsetting the Turkish Empire, or which might possibly end in the seizure of Constantinople by a *coup de main.* It is probable that Russia had wind of the plot (described in a previous chapter) which Austria and Germany were then hatching against her—the plot of inveigling England in a naval combination with the Triple Alliance, which had for its ultimate object the crushing of the Russian and French fleets, and the consequent delivery of Austria and Germany from the incubus of the Dual Alliance; England having been meanwhile entrapped as a partner into the Triple Alliance, which would then be secure against any adverse combination. But there is nothing in either of Prince Lobanoff's declarations to suggest that he would oppose such separate action as Russia herself sanctioned in 1880, namely, the seizure of a material guarantee by one of the Powers, which need not be England, and might be Russia herself.

I pointed out at the time that Lord Rosebery had read into Prince Gortchakoff's language a sense which that language did not bear, and was referred in reply to some esoteric meaning in 'the language of diplomacy,' which had eluded my understanding. I venture to plead humbly in self-defence that I have not studied the history of the Eastern question for twenty years in the diplomatic documents of Great Britain, France, Russia, Italy, and Germany and Austria occasionally, without having acquired some knowledge of diplomatic language; and my experience is that the language of diplomacy is merely the language of grammar and common sense, varying in perspicacity or obscurity according to the literary skill of the diplomatist, and not by reason of any linguistic freemasonry. However, let us test the matter.

In 1876-7 the question of coercion agitated, as it does now, the Chancelleries of Europe. Lord Derby, then Minister for Foreign Affairs, was asked repeatedly, as Prince Lobanoff was asked last year, whether England would support a policy of coercion to force the Sultan to grant reforms in Bulgaria. I will give his answer on three separate occasions. He said to an English deputation:—

We shall not intervene; we shall do our utmost, if necessary, to discourage others from intervening.

In a despatch to the British Ambassador at St. Petersburg he said:—

The Russian Ambassador called to-day and asked me whether, in the event of war breaking out between Turkey and Servia, her Majesty's Government intended, as he had been led to believe, to adhere to a policy of strict and absolute non-intervention. I said that such was undoubtedly the case; but that it must be clearly understood that her Majesty's Government entered into no engagement to continue to abstain from intervention in the event (which, however, I could not assume as probable) of a different course being pursued by other Powers.*

On the day before the Conference of Constantinople opened Lord Derby wrote to tell Lord Salisbury 'that her Majesty's Government had decided that England will not assent to or assist in coercive measures, military or naval, against the Porte.' †

All these declarations of Lord Derby are very much stronger and more peremptory than the very mild language of Prince Lobanoff, on which Lord Rosebery has fixed such portentous significance.

* *Turkey*, No. 3 (1876), p. 351.
† *Ibid.*, No. 2 (1877), p. 56.

Did Lord Derby then mean that he would oppose by force any separate action on the part of Russia? Let Lord Derby answer for himself. Reporting an interview with the Turkish Ambassador, Lord Derby says:—

I had informed him that, although her Majesty's Government did not themselves meditate or threaten the employment of active measures of coercion in the event of the proposals of the Conference being refused by the Porte, yet that Turkey must not look to England for assistance or protection if that refusal resulted in a war with other countries.

Perhaps we shall find that Prince Lobanoff also has supplied us with a clue to the right understanding of the language on which Lord Rosebery has rested his case. Such a clue I find in a despatch from Sir Philip Currie, dated August 29, 1895, and in a despatch from the British Ambassador at St. Petersburg, dated August 28, 1895. Lord Salisbury saw at once that the scheme of reforms which he inherited from his predecessor was not only useless, standing alone, but mischievous in addition. He proposed, therefore, that instead of an international Commission sitting at Constantinople, a Commission of Surveillance should be sent to Armenia, composed in the manner described in Sir Philip Currie's despatch:—

The Sublime Porte have received a telegram from their Ambassador at St. Petersburg stating that Prince Lobanoff informed him on the 27th inst. that Russia accepted England's proposal to appoint a Commission of Surveillance, consisting of three Europeans [representing Russia, France, and England] and four Turks, under the Treaty of Berlin. Prince Lobanoff had said this was the smallest concession which he should make to your lordship's demands, *and that unless he did so England and Turkey would be left alone face to face.*

On the previous day the British Ambassador at St. Petersburg sent a despatch in which he reports a conversation from Prince Lobanoff, from which I make the following quotation. On hearing of Russia's acceptance of Lord Salisbury's proposal, the Turkish Ambassador hastened to ask if it was true.

Husny Pasha had become much perturbed on hearing that this was the case, and had expressed his surprise and regret that the Russian Government had adopted such a course. Prince Lobanoff had replied that there was nothing surprising in the matter, as the action now taken was entirely justified by the Treaty of Berlin, and the Turkish Government had only themselves to blame for not having introduced reforms earlier. They had, he believed, been led to hope that the recent change of Government in England might have brought about a modification of the views of Her Majesty's Government, and that your lordship would be less inclined to press the demands of the Ambassadors on the Porte. In this, however, the Turkish Government had been mistaken, and in his Excellency's opinion the demands which had been put forward were the minimum which your lordship, in view of the state of public opinion in England, could accept. Prince Lobanoff said that it was rather hard that Husny Pasha should reproach him after the line he had taken in attempting to moderate the action of Her Majesty's Government, who at one time seemed on the point of taking isolated action in the matter, which he feared might have led to great complications and, indeed, have reopened the whole Eastern question.

Here, then, we have it on Prince Lobanoff's own authority that the alternative of his accepting the minimum of Lord Salisbury's demands was 'isolated action' on the part of England in which 'England and Turkey would be left alone face to face.' * This was a fortnight after the mild remarks of Prince Lobanoff out of which Lord Rosebery has conjured up a vision of war, ruin, and massacre that ' would transcend twenty Floddens, and that angel of death who appeared, or was said to appear, in Edinburgh before Flodden, would appear in every hamlet, every village, every town in the United Kingdom to summon your sons or brothers, the flower of your youth and manhood, to lose their lives in this European conflagration.' This is telling rhetoric, addressed by an ex-Prime Minister and Foreign Secretary to an audience entirely ignorant of the facts; but it is unsubstantial as 'the gossamers that idle in the wanton summer air' when confronted with the evidence out of which the rhetoric is spun.

So much, then, for the appeal to Prince Lobanoff. The dead Chancellor has interpreted his own language, and his interpretation is precisely the reverse of Lord Rosebery's. The truth is that Prince Lobanoff's attitude on the

* *Turkey*, No. 1 (1896), pp. 135–137.

Armenian question was determined by the management of that question by Lord Rosebery's Government. In order to understand the Prince's point of view, and do justice to it, we ought to have a clear idea of the negotiations which preceded the fall of the Rosebery Cabinet. This I shall now endeavour to offer to the reader with as much conciseness as may be consistent with an accurate presentation of the facts.

CHAPTER XVII.

A BAD BEGINNING.

JUST before Lord Salisbury went out of office in 1892 he published a Blue-book on Armenia which proved beyond all doubt that the Sultan had been then for more than a year carefully organising a massacre of the Armenians. After encouraging the Kurds and Musulmans in general to harass the Christians in their property, their lives, their religion, and their honour, apparently for the purpose of goading them into some indiscretion which would give him an excuse before Europe for raising the cry of sedition and 'diminishing the population'—to quote the Turkish euphemism for massacre—he formed the Kurds into a cavalry force of 30,000, gave them his own name, the 'Hamidiè,' and set over them as officers the greatest ruffians to be found in Asia Minor. A certain Hussein Agha had been for some time Mudir of Patnoss in Armenia. The crimes of this man were notorious both for their number and for their brutality. A dry catalogue of them fills more than a folio page of a Blue-book, and in sending the black list to Lord Salisbury the British Ambassador described

Hussein as 'a monster.' Let me give a few specimens of his misdeeds as reported by the British Consul at Erzeroum in 1891 :—

Fifteen days ago, Hussein Agha, with his nephew, entered by night the house of an Armenian named Caspar, in Patnoss, with the intention of carrying off Caspar's daughter-in-law, a very beautiful young woman. The inhabitants of the house cried out for help, on which Hussein drew his revolver and fired, killing the woman on the spot.

Here you have an illustration of the ordinary lives of the Christians under Turkish rule. The Governor of a large district takes a fancy to the beautiful young wife of a Christian, goes with his nephew to carry her off to his harem, and because her husband and relatives cry out for help, punishes what he considers the insolence of the 'Christian dogs' by shooting the young woman dead on the spot. That happened, remember, not in a season of disturbance or excitement, but as an ordinary incident in the lives of the Christians. They are daily exposed to these outrages. Every village, almost every house, has its tale of similar tragedies. And the criminal was an official of rank, the Governor of a district. Here are a few more examples of Hussein's method of administering the district of Patnoss :—

About four or five years ago [this was written in January 1891] Hussein was robbing and plundering. He set fire to nine villages, killed ten men, and cut off the right hands, noses, and ears of eleven more, some of whom could, if necessary, be produced as witnesses. He carried off 2,600 sheep, nine horses, many cattle, and property of all sorts. From the house of Avani's brother (who was present while the tale was told) he took £500 worth of property, and blinded his mother with a gun. . . . A year ago Hussein carried off and ravished five Christian girls from Patnoss. On his return from Van he continued in his old courses, and during the months of September and October forcibly collected £300 in the district of Patnoss.*

When Lord Salisbury received the despatch containing the record of this man's crimes he read it to the Queen, and instructed the Ambassador to demand the criminal's punishment. What was the Sultan's answer to this righteous demand? The same answer which he made when Lord Derby demanded in 1876, in the name of the Queen, the punishment of Chefket Pasha, the hero of the massacre of Batak. He immediately decorated Chefket and promoted him to a place of honour in the palace. So now he took no notice of Lord Salisbury's denunciation of Hussein; but when the equipment of his newly-formed Kurdish cavalry was complete he invited a representative deputation of them to Yildiz Kiosk, where he fêted them for a week, and then sent them back to their homes with orders to 'harry the Armenians.' Hussein was among the honoured guests. The Sultan raised him to the rank of pasha, and gave him a high command in the Kurdish cavalry; and he has

* *Turkey*, No. 1 (1892), pp. 6-25.

been one of the worst scourges of the Armenians ever since. Am I not right in thinking that if an insult like this were offered to the Queen by any European Sovereign the immediate result would be the recall of our Ambassador at that Sovereign's Court? Why is this savage barbarian to be treated with a forbearance which would not be accorded to any European Sovereign?

Such was the state of things which Lord Rosebery found when he became Foreign Secretary in 1892. The Sultan was doing his utmost to provoke the Armenians into some show of resistance which would give him a plausible excuse for the massacres which he had been for some time organising. In addition to letting loose the Kurds upon them, he sent agents to preach sedition and tempt some of the tortured Armenians into some kind of rising. All this is in the Blue-books. Yet our Government took no precautions.

Then came the Bitlis massacres in the early autumn of 1894. Two months later rumours of it began to filter to the outer world through the cordon of troops with which the Sultan surrounded the district. Now, how did the Government deal with this massacre? They had early information of it through their own Consuls; but not a ray of information did they suffer to reach the public. Parliament and the public ought, in my humble judgment, to demand from whomsoever it may concern some justification for the wholesale suppression of the Consular reports from Armenia all through the lifetime of the late Government. It is to Lord Salisbury that we are indebted for our knowledge of the transactions of that period. I must pass over them lightly, merely indicating the finger-posts which point the way.

It may be laid down as an axiom in dealing with the Turkish Government, that you should never recede from any demand which you may think it right to make. You should act like the Sibyl when she offered her books at a fixed price to Tarquin. Raise your terms with each refusal, and you will soon find that there will be no more refusals. Lord Rosebery's Government unfortunately acted on the opposite rule of always yielding when the Sultan objected. The Sultan personally accused a British Vice-Consul in Armenia of inciting the Armenians to rebellion. Sir Philip Currie replied with spirit that he would at once send Colonel Chermside, military attaché at the Embassy, to investigate the charge. If true, it would involve the immediate dismissal of the Vice-Consul. If false, the charge must be withdrawn with an apology. The Sultan immediately withdrew the charge, and then the Government weakly yielded to the Sultan's 'fixed resolve not to allow the departure of Colonel Chermside' into Armenia. 'Fixed resolve,' indeed, 'not to allow' an official of the

British Embassy to investigate a dishonouring charge made against a British Vice-Consul! The Sultan knew that Colonel Chermside's mission would confirm the reports of the massacres, and the British Government weakly played into his hands. The more he objected, the more ought they to have insisted on Colonel Chermside's mission.

But the suppression of the Consular Reports did not avail. Private enterprise supplied in part the information which the Government refused. The revelations made by the special correspondents of some of our leading journals so oused public opinion that the Government feic hey must do something. And what did they do? They sanctioned a purely Turkish Commission, appointed by the Sultan, to inquire into the truth of reports sent to them by their own Consuls. On November 26, 1894, Sir P. Currie wrote to Lord Kimberley:—

> Mr. Hallward reports in detail the same horrors as those described in the *Times* of November 17. Mr. Graves, in his covering despatch, confirms the truth of the facts given by Mr. Hallward.*

Did the Government think that a Commission appointed by the Sultan was more trustworthy than her Majesty's Consul at Erzeroum and Vice-Consul at Van? Nor did the evidence of the British Consuls stand alone. The British

---

* *Turkey*, No. 1 (1895), p. 29.

Ambassador at Vienna wrote to Lord Kimberley on December 12, 1894 :—

The reports received by your lordship are entirely confirmed by the news received from the Austrian Consul at Trebizond, who fears evidence will not be given against the offending parties owing to the existing reign of terror.*

On December 18, 1894, the British Ambassador at St. Petersburg wrote to Lord Kimberley :—

On the receipt of your lordship's telegram of the 6th inst. I did not fail to communicate the substance to Count Kapnist, who said that the Russian Ambassador at Constantinople had telegraphed the reports of the horrible massacres in the vilayet of Bitlis, and the unsatisfactory manner in which the Porte had announced the appointment of a Commission to inquire into them.†

Yet, in face of this cumulative evidence that 'horrible massacres' had taken place, the British Government clung to the Sultan's Commission of Inquiry. And they urged the other Powers to join in it. Austria and Germany declined on the ground that they had no Consuls in Armenia. Russia and France agreed out of friendship for England, but with a timely warning that no good could come of a purely Turkish Commission. Did Lord Rosebery's Government really imagine that a Commission nominated by the Sultan and consisting of creatures of his own would make an honest inquiry? If, indeed, their

* *Turkey* No. 1 (1895), p. 48.   † *Ibid.*, p. 58.

credulity reached so sublime a height, the Sultan took care to undeceive them speedily. On November 23, 1894, Sir Philip Currie wired as follows to Lord Kimberley :—

The Ottoman Government have published decrees conferring decorations on the Mufti of Mush, who is said to have incited the troops against the Christians, and on Zeki Pasha, the Commandant of the 4th Army Corps. The Mutessarif of Mush, who protested against the massacres, has been dismissed. The appointment of the Commission has been officially notified in the press. The notice states that the Commission is sent to inquire into the criminal conduct of Armenian brigands, and denies absolutely the truth of massacres.

Here is in substance the official notification referred to in Sir Philip Currie's telegram. It is in the form of a circular addressed by the Sultan's Foreign Minister to the Turkish Ambassadors at Foreign Courts :—

My preceding communications have informed you that, in consequence of the criminal acts committed by a body of Armenian insurgents in the districts of Sassun and Talori, regular troops were sent to the spot to punish the guilty, and order and tranquillity have been restored. But unfortunately certain organs of the European press, allowing themselves to be misled by unfriendly inspirations, are publishing intelligence which is imaginary and opposed to the truth. In view of this inconceivable attitude, the Imperial Government has decided to send to the spot a Commission of Inquiry, composed of their Excellencies the General of Division, Abdullah Pasha, Aide-de-camp to his Imperial Majesty the Sultan, our August Sovereign; the

Director of the Savings Bank, Enmer Bey; the First Secretary of the Correspondence Bureau of the Ministry of the Interior, Medjid Effendi; and Hafviz Tewfik Pasha, General of Brigade of the Headquarters Staff attached to his Majesty.

This was a direct and most insolent challenge to Europe in general, and to England in particular. How was the challenge met? Immediately on receipt of Sir Philip Currie's telegram Lord Kimberley replied as follows:—

The announcement with respect to the Bitlis Commission, reported in your telegram of to-day, is so grave in its nature that Her Majesty's Government must give it their serious consideration without any delay. I must, however, at once express my surprise and pain at hearing that the inquiry is represented as one into the criminal conduct of Armenian brigands, and not into the truth of the reported massacre of Armenians; that even before the inquiry has been made the report laid before the Sultan and the Turkish Government by your Excellency has been declared publicly to be false; that decorations have been given to two Turkish officers concerned in the recent events; and that the Mutessarif who protested against the massacre has been deprived of his appointment. Your Excellency shall receive instructions after I have consulted my colleagues, as the matter cannot possibly be left in this position.

No fault can be found with this language. It is worthy of an English gentleman, and Lord Kimberley repeated it three days later to the Turkish Ambassador in London, with the addition of the following menace:—

I said I could not impress upon him too earnestly

the gravity and extent of the consequences to which this entire nullification of the promised investigation might give rise. It was even possible that it might develop into an European question.

Let the reader consider the gravity of the facts with which we are now dealing. Her Majesty's Government instructed their Ambassador at the Porte to lay before the Sultan the report—sent by a British Consul, and confirmed by Austrian, Russian, and Italian authorities—of atrocious massacres committed by order or connivance of the Sultan's officers, and demand an impartial inquiry. As if, forsooth, the inquiry of their own Consul, confirmed by other Consuls, had not been impartial! The Sultan dexterously avails himself of the doubt thus thrown by implication on the impartiality of the Consul by his own Government; denounces the report as 'imaginary and opposed to the truth'; and announces the appointment of a Commission of Palace parasites to inquire into 'the criminal conduct of Armenian brigands.' Sir Philip Currie protested to the Grand Vizir

that if steps were not taken to satisfy Her Majesty's Government that the Sultan's promise would be fulfilled they might find it necessary to claim a right under the LXIst Article of the Treaty of Berlin to send Colonel Chermside to inquire into the treatment of the Armenians, and that they might also be forced to publish the Consular Reports from the Asiatic provinces, which had been so long withheld.

But the Grand Vizir 'held out no expectation of the announcement being made here in a different form.'

Here, then, we have the Sultan giving the lie direct to the British Ambassador, and consequently to the Government and Sovereign whom he represented. Before the days of invertebrate diplomacy such an insult to the majesty of Great Britain would have been met by an instant demand for retractation and apology, or for the Ambassador's passport, accompanied by the dismissal of the Sultan's Ambassador from the Court which his master had so wantonly insulted. And Lord Kimberley's language, which I have quoted, leads one to think that he had something of the kind in contemplation. But he 'consulted with his colleagues' in Cabinet Council, and as a result of that consultation sent what is euphemistically called ' a protest,' which mildly expresses the 'great regret and surprise' of her Majesty's Government at the affront which the Sultan had offered them by the official announcement of the Commission.

Such an announcement, which is wholly at variance with the Sultan's assurances, renders it impossible for her Majesty's Government to accept the Commission as being of a nature to secure an impartial and satisfactory investigation of the facts of the case.

This, together with the threat—never fulfilled—of publishing the Consular Reports, ' which had been so long withheld,' was all that the Government could screw up their courage to. And they still urged the Sultan to proceed with a Commission which they had themselves condemned as an infamous imposture in the words which I have just quoted. It is amazing. Italy, which had reluctantly accepted England's invitation to sanction the Sultan's Commission, withdrew at once as soon as the Sultan published the character and intention of the Commission, and appointed Signor Monaco as Consul-General, with instructions to make an independent inquiry of his own. The Sultan tried to stop that inquiry by alternate cajolery and bullying, as in the proposed inquiry by Colonel Chermside. But the Italian Government, unlike the British, went its own way, regardless of the Sultan, and Signor Monaco made a thorough investigation, extending over the whole area of the massacres, instead of being limited to the narrow district prescribed by the Sultan's Commission. He made an exhaustive report, and estimated the number of victims at that date at 50,000, instead of Mr. Shipley's ridiculous estimate of 900. That estimate, as I have said, was limited to a small part of the area of the massacres. And even as regards that small district, Mr. Shipley himself admits that 'the inquiry, particularly as regards the events in the Talori region proper, was carried out by the Turkish Commissioners in a wholly inadequate manner,' so that 'it was impossible to fix even approximately the number of victims. If this was the case as regards districts which, in company with the Commission, we visited in person, the above observation will of course be much more applicable to the Talori region, which we had no opportunity of visiting, and from which only four witnesses independently of the ten prisoners were examined before the Commission.' The pity is that Mr. Shipley, having no data to guide him except the suborned evidence produced by the Turkish Commissioners, should have hazarded a guess and presented it in an official report. One remark will show the fallacy of his rule-of-thumb method of inquiry. He arrives, without trustworthy evidence, at the number of houses in villages which were entirely destroyed. Then he reckons the average number of inmates in a house at ten, subtracts the number of survivors, and so gets his result. But ten is a ridiculously low figure for the inmates of an Armenian house. Twenty to thirty would be nearer the mark. Several families often live under one roof: grandparents, children, and grandchildren.

But I am not concerned at present with Mr. Shipley's honest, but entirely untrustworthy, report. What I am dealing with is the management of the question by Lord Rosebery's Government. Italy, as we have seen, declined to have anything to do with such a Commission as the Sultan had appointed. Her Majesty's Government denounced it as an imposture, but still relied upon it. The Russian and French

Governments had no faith in it from the beginning; but after the official notification of its object they declined to send delegates of Consular rank to watch its proceedings. The British Government followed suit, and the Commission was thus accompanied by Russian and French dragomans and by a young English Vice-Consul, who was a stranger to the country and could not speak the language.

The Commission proved such a cruel farce that the Russian, British, and French delegates sent the following identic telegram to their Embassies :—

As Murad's examination is concluded and the Commission of Inquiry refuses definitely to summon the witnesses last suggested by us, we have closed the inquiry, in accordance with your Excellency's orders.

Nevertheless the British Government took the lead in getting the delegates to continue dancing attendance on the Turkish Commission, thus giving indirectly their official countenance to its iniquitous proceedings.*

Nine precious months were thus worse than gratuitously wasted; and the outcome of it all was a scheme of reform which Prince Lobanoff, with his thorough knowledge of Turkey, pronounced to be 'unworkable.' The British Ambassador at St. Petersburg reports (August 9, 1895) :—

Prince Lobanoff reminded me that he had never

* *Turkey*, No. 1 (1895), pp. 27, 29, 32, 33, 39, 40-43, 110, 117, 118, 121-3, 203-4.

concealed from me his opinion of the scheme of reforms drawn up by the Ambassadors at Constantinople, which he considered unworkable.*

Unworkable it certainly was, as I proved in detail in some criticism on it in the *Times* as soon as it was published. But it was not merely unworkable, it was mischievous in addition. The reforms were based on the numerical proportion of Christians and Musulmans in the area embraced by them.

This was a provision charged with deadly peril to the Christians unless the Powers took immediate steps to stay the hand of the assassin. But they did nothing, and the order went forth from Yildiz Kiosk to massacre the Armenians—within the area of the reforms, to begin with. The result is given in the following telegram from the British Ambassador at Constantinople to Lord Salisbury on December 13, 1895 :—

It may be roughly estimated that the recent disturbances have devastated, as far as the Armenians are concerned, *the whole of the provinces to which the scheme of reforms was intended to apply*; that over an extent of territory considerably larger than Great Britain, all the large towns, with the exception of Van, Samsun, and Mush [exceptions no longer], have been the scenes of massacres of the Armenian population, while the Armenian villages have been almost entirely destroyed. A moderate estimate puts the loss of life at 30,000. The survivors are in a state of absolute destitution, and in many places they are forced to become Musulman. The charge against the Armenians of having been the

* *Turkey*, No. 1 (1896), p. 121.

first to offer provocation cannot be sustained. Non-Armenian Christians were spared, and the few Turks who fell were killed in self-defence. The participation of the soldiers in the massacres is in many places established beyond a doubt.*

Mark the words which I have put in italics. The Foreign Minister of Italy told me in Rome last February that he had just received a despatch from the Italian Ambassador at Constantinople informing him that the Grand Vizir had presented a report to the Sultan on the state of Armenia, in which the Sultan was assured that he need not trouble himself about the scheme of reforms, 'since the Musulman element was now in a majority everywhere.' The Sultan, as I have proved from the Bluebooks in my pamphlet on 'England's Responsibility towards Armenia,' had begun in 1891 to prepare for one of those massacres of Christians which are periodical in Turkey. He made a start in the Sassun district; and but for the scheme of reforms that massacre might have satisfied his lust for blood for a season. But the reforms being based on the numerical proportions of the two creeds, he determined to defeat it by reversing the proportions; and he has done it very effectually not only in Armenia, but throughout most of Anatolia. This ought to have been foreseen by the authors of the scheme, and their first care—knowing the kind

* *Turkey*, No. 2 (1896), p. 210.

of man they had to deal with—should have been to provide against it. From the very first Russia frankly expressed her opinion that nothing would come of either the Turkish Commission or the subsequent scheme of reforms. But the British Government, for some inscrutable reason which I cannot fathom, clung to the Commission and the reforms, as if they believed them to be an infallible panacea for the wrongs of Armenia. Thus Lord Rosebery says, in his Eighty Club speech last March :—

> We had obtained with some difficulty from the Sultan a Commission of Inquiry into the massacres that occurred, on which Europe was intending to form an authoritative opinion as to whether they had occurred or had not occurred, as the Porte alleged, as the act of the Ottoman Kurds, or on the provocation of the Armenians themselves, as the Porte also alleged. Until we obtained that information we were not in a position to take action, and I say, then, that our connection with the whole of that investigation ended when we were still in process of negotiation. We had already obtained the concurrence of France and Russia in our policy; we had already obtained the concurrence of France and Russia in our scheme of reforms; and I may add that it was not till two months after we left office that Russia made this solemn declaration to which I have already adverted [against coercive measures].

My entire belief in Lord Rosebery's sincerity makes this passage very hard reading for me. It is—like his interpretation of Mr. Gladstone's Liverpool speech—an example of his faculty of reading into acts and words, not what they really contain, but his own preconceived notions on the subject.

After being himself an ardent advocate of separate action, it suddenly occurred to Lord Rosebery that separate action would lead to 'a great European war'; and so, without pausing to consider whether there might not be various kinds of separate action which could not possibly lead to a European war, he fell upon Mr. Gladstone's exceedingly moderate and well-guarded speech as if it were a challenge to mortal combat flung in the face of united Europe. So here he reads into the Turkish Commission and the scheme of reforms, not what was in them, but what he wished to see in them. 'We had obtained with some difficulty from the Sultan a Commission of Inquiry into the massacres that had occurred.' In matter of fact, they had obtained nothing of the kind. What they succeeded in obtaining was a 'Commission to inquire into the criminal conduct of Armenian brigands,' coupled with an 'absolute denial of the truth of massacres.' A Cabinet Council was called to repel that slap in the face from the Sultan, and the repulsion took the form of a mild expression of 'surprise and regret.' And when the Sultan peremptorily refused to alter the purpose and scope of the Commission, the British Government accredited a special delegate to accompany the Commission, and prevailed on France and Russia to follow its example. Italy refused to do so, as inconsistent with its self-respect. Was not the Sultan justified, after that experience, in believing that the British Government would, for the sake of what it believed to be British interests, meekly stand any amount of kicking?

Yet Lord Rosebery sincerely believes that a Commission, sent by the Sultan for the publicly avowed purpose of absolutely disproving the reports of massacres and finding the Armenians guilty, would enable Europe 'to form an authoritative opinion as to whether' there had been any massacres at all! And all this time the Government had their own Consular reports, confirmed by Russia, Italy, and Austria, that there was no doubt at all about the massacres. Nor is it quite accurate to say that the Government 'obtained the concurrence of France and Russia in their scheme of reforms.' France followed Russia as a matter of course, and Russia declared the Commission useless, and the scheme of reforms 'unworkable' and 'objectionable,' though she gave a qualified assent to both, to oblige the British Government.

The initial mistake—vitiating all that followed—was not to have started by coming to an understanding with Russia, which would then, I believe, have been quite easy. The Turkish Commission and scheme of reforms were not practical politics: they were the veriest trifling with a great question which needed very different treatment, as Prince Lobanoff, indeed, insinuated with the courtesy of a trained diplomatist. In truth, it is officially admitted in the Blue-books that the Commission and scheme of reforms were, in the first place, intended as expedients to meet the demands of public opinion in England. What was it that Russia objected to? Prince Lobanoff made it perfectly plain. In a despatch from the British Ambassador at St. Petersburg to Lord Kimberley, dated June 14, 1895, I read :—

> Prince Lobanoff then repeated to me at some length the language which he held to me on the 4th inst., and which I had the honour to report in my despatch of that day's date. He said that Russia would only be too happy to see an improvement of the Turkish Administration, and greater security for the lives and property of the Christian subjects of the Sultan, but she would object to the creation in Asia of a territory where the Armenians should enjoy exceptional privileges. According to the scheme of the Ambassadors, this territory would be of very large extent, embracing nearly the half of Asia Minor. . . . He could understand that Her Majesty's Government, on account of the distance between England, or indeed any English possessions, and the territory in question, should view the matter with some indifference; but Russia could not consent to the formation of a new Bulgaria on her frontier.

What Lord Rosebery means by saying, in face of this, and more that follows : 'We had already obtained the concurrence of France and Russia in our scheme of reforms'—I cannot understand. But let us look at the telegraphic despatch of June 4, to which the Ambassador refers :—

> In conversation with me this afternoon Prince Lobanoff, speaking very openly about Armenia, said he had never looked upon the presentation of the scheme of reforms as an ultimatum to the Sultan, or considered that, in the event of the Sultan declining to accept it or making counter-proposals, the Ambassadors would be justified in using threatening language. Russia would certainly not join in any coercive measures. . . . His Excellency expresses the hope that your lordship will consult him with regard to any measures that may become necessary after consideration of the reply of the Sultan; in no circumstances, however, will the Russian Government adopt coercive measures or consent to the creation in Asia Minor of a district in which the Armenians should have exceptional privileges, and which would constitute the nucleus of an independent kingdom of Armenia, such being evidently the object the Armenian Committees have in view.

On the same day the British Ambassador explained more fully in a written despatch to Lord Kimberley his conversation with Prince Lobanoff. The following extract will give the gist of the conversation :—

> Prince Lobanoff said that he would speak to me frankly on the subject. He said that although the three Ambassadors at Constantinople had elaborated and presented to the Sultan a scheme of reforms for Armenia, this by no means gave them the right of resorting to coercive measures, or indeed to threatening language, if the Sultan declined to accept it, or put forward counter-proposals. He had never concealed from me his opinion that the proposed scheme was open to objection, and he certainly never considered it in the

light of an ultimatum to the Sultan, which was to be followed by coercive measures if his Majesty refused to accept it. . . . His Excellency hoped that a full consideration of the Sultan's reply might enable the three Governments, who were in a better position than the Ambassadors at Constantinople, to consider the question calmly, and come to an understanding on the subject, and he trusted that your lordship would consult him as to the course which should be pursued ; but he feared that her Majesty's Government, urged on by public opinion, or rather the so-called public opinion which he believed had been the work of the Armenian Committees, would be inclined to adopt a course with which Russia could not associate herself. The fact was that the Armenian Committees in London and elsewhere aimed at the creation in Asia Minor of a district in which the Armenians should enjoy exceptional privileges, and which would form the nucleus ('noyau') of a future independent Armenian kingdom ; and to this Russia would not and could not agree.

The origin and cause of these conversations with Prince Lobanoff are explained by Lord Kimberley in the following despatch to the British Ambassador at St. Petersburg :—

The Russian Ambassador called here to-day, and informed me that he had received instructions from Prince Lobanoff to make the following communication to me :—

'Her Majesty's Ambassador at Constantinople had announced to his Russian colleague that in the event of delay in the answer of the Porte to the project of reforms for the Armenian provinces of Asiatic Turkey, which had been submitted to the Sultan by the three Powers, the British Government, having regard to the excited state of feeling in this country on the subject of the Armenians, would be compelled to have recourse to measures of constraint.'

Prince Lobanoff had in consequence telegraphed to M. de Nelidoff that in no case would the Russian Government associate itself with such measures.

I said that Sir Philip Currie had sounded his colleagues as to the steps which could be taken to put pressure upon the Porte, but her Majesty's Government had not come to any decision as to the course which they should pursue if their demands were not complied with.

On June 19 Lord Kimberley telegraphed to the British Ambassador at St. Petersburg proposing 'to demand an explicit reply from the Porte within forty-eight hours on the project of Armenian reforms.' The reply was 'that the Emperor was unable to agree to this proposal, as His Majesty did not think there was sufficient ground for making a communication of such gravity, especially in view of the consequences which might result if the reply of the Turkish Government should prove unfavourable.' On the following day Her Majesty's Government resigned, and the negotiations passed into Lord Salisbury's hands.*

Such, then, was the state of affairs when Lord Rosebery's Government went out of office. The British Government had proposed a Turkish Commission to verify the reports of its own Consuls, and accredited a British delegate after the Sultan had officially announced that the

* See *Turkey*, No. 1 (1896), pp. 71, 73, 81, 87.

Commission was to be sent 'to inquire into the criminal conduct of Armenian brigands.' Russia, while thinking the Commission certainly useless, and probably mischievous, agreed to send a delegate to accompany the British and French delegates; but asked the British Government to explain its intentions after the sham Commission had finished its farcical investigation. But the British Government apparently had no plan; at all events, Russia's question remained unanswered. Russia made another attempt later. Alarmed by the collapse of China and the victorious campaign of Japan, Russia solicited the coöperation of England alone in settling the affairs of the Far East. The British Government refused, and a report immediately appeared in the papers that the British squadron in the China seas was to be strengthened. Russia evidently became suspicious of England's intentions, and invited France and Russia to the partnership which she had in vain offered to us exclusively. The reticence of the British Government as to its intentions regarding Armenia alarmed Prince Lobanoff, and the scheme of reforms confirmed his fears. He pronounced it, quite truly, 'unworkable,' and he jumped to the conclusion—which he frankly avowed—that the real aim of Lord Rosebery's Government was to create 'a new Bulgaria' on the Russian frontier, to grow eventually into 'an independent kingdom of Armenia,' including Russian Armenia. It was in fact, in his opinion, a crafty development of the anti-Russian policy of the Treaty of Berlin and the Anglo-Turkish Convention. Hence his opposition to any coercion of the Sultan into acceptance of a scheme of reforms which he honestly, though erroneously, regarded as a sort of Trojan horse charged with mischief to his country. And the point at which the late Government left the negotiations to their successors was an endeavour, in spite of Russia's protest, to coerce the Sultan—apparently single-handed—to accept a scheme of reforms to which Russia was bitterly opposed, and which, without European control, was absolutely impotent for good, but, as the event has proved, pregnant with tragical ills to the Armenians. If our Government had begun by inviting Russia to suggest a plan for pacifying Armenia in cöoperation with England, and had accepted Russia's invitation to join her in arranging matters between China and Japan, there is hardly room for doubt that the Armenian question would have been settled eighteen months ago, and the subsequent horrors would have been prevented.

Prince Lobanoff readily accepted Lord Salisbury's subsequent suggestion of a fundamental and beneficial change in the scheme of his predecessor, instead of a cumbersome mixed Commission sitting at Constantinople to watch the execution of reforms by Turkish officials in Armenia. Here is Lord Salisbury's proposed substitute :—

No genuine surveillance could be exercised by an authority seated at Constantinople; it must be some authority locally resident at Van, Bitlis, or Erzeroum, or at some other suitable spot in the disturbed country. If a Commission of four Turkish members and three Commissioners nominated by the three Powers [Russia, France, and England] were appointed to reside in the Armenian provinces, with full authority to investigate and report, some security would be obtained for the adoption of reforms, and a means of remedy provided, should misgovernment again prevail.

That one suggestion is worth more than a score of such schemes of reforms as that for which the late Government was apparently ready to risk a quarrel with Russia. But the suggestion came too late. After accepting it, it was pointed out to Prince Lobanoff by the Russian Ambassador at Constantinople 'that a claim to be represented on the Committee [of Surveillance] might be put in by the other Powers who signed the Treaty of Berlin.' Prince Lobanoff objected to a Committee on which the Triple Alliance was to be represented.* This is another proof of the initial error of not having made a friendly understanding with Russia the first step in the negotiations. That secured, the rest would have been easy. But there seems to have been no idea of any definite policy at all. What is needed in Turkey is not a long and complex project of

* *Turkey*, No. 1 (1896), p. 135.

reforms on paper, but European officials empowered to enforce the execution of reforms already repeatedly granted in words by the Porte. Let the Hatt-i-Gulhané, or the Hatt-i-Humaioun be carried out, and there is no need for more. Each of those solemn engagements by past Sultans put the Christians of Turkey, on paper, on a footing of equality with the Musulmans, including the right to bear arms and enter the army. But they have both been in every particular dead letters—the one for nearly sixty, the other for forty years. Let me give one example. In the Iradé which the Sultan published lately to enforce on the Musulmans a capitation tax for arming the Musulman population—the Christians being invited to contribute voluntarily (we know what a despot's invitation means) towards the purchase of weapons for their own destruction—it was said that the Musulmans would doubtless contribute cheerfully 'in virtue of the special position which they held, as being alone privileged to serve in the army.' Yet in the Hatt-i-Humaioun the Sultan solemnly promised to admit the Christians into the army. How did he keep his promise? By doubling the tax which the Christians had previously to pay to provide substitutes, and enforcing that tax on all males from three months old till death, instead of from adolescence as before. Christians are thus still excluded from the army, and forbidden to bear arms, and they are heavily fined in addition to the end of time for having been the innocent cause of the Sultan perjuring himself! * How is it that the Great Powers go on from year to year and from generation to generation enduring these insults from a barbarous and decrepit Power which continues to live by their sufferance? And how can they expect the Sultan to give heed to their admonitions when they have in practice made him and his predecessors the chartered liars of European diplomacy? They would not endure from one another half the insults that they quietly pocket from the craven criminal of Yildiz Kiosk. Let them only insist on the Christians being allowed to enjoy their treaty right to bear arms, and they may postpone other reforms for the present. It is the helplessness of the Christians that tempts their oppressors to massacre them. Let them be armed, and the Sultan will think twice before he orders another massacre. But the Armenians, with arms in their hands, would rise up in rebellion? On the contrary, the unanimous testimony of our Consuls for years past is that the Armenians, under anything like tolerable government, would be among the most loyal of the Sultan's subjects. Possessed of the means of self-defence, they would settle down quietly— I will not say as contented citizens, for as

---

* See *Eastern Papers* (1856), pt. xviii. p. 46; and *Reports received from Her Majesty's Ambassadors and Consuls on the Condition of Christians in Turkey* (1867), p. 26.

Christians they cannot be citizens of the Ottoman Empire, but—as contented subjects. At all events, it would be much better for the Christians of Turkey if the Great Powers of Christendom were to wash their hands of the whole business and leave them alone than engage in these most humiliating interventions, which have always the same issue: a crop of fresh promises on the part of the Sultan, which remain absolutely unfulfilled till the next massacre, when the comedy is again solemnly repeated.

Why will not the statesmen of Europe take the trouble to understand that the Sultan *cannot* give the elementary rights of civilised existence to his non-Musulman subjects unless he is coerced? When hard pressed he will make any number of promises; but he cannot, even if he would, fulfil any of them.

'Turkey never changes,' as Prince Lobanoff said last year, until the Sultan is forced to change. But the exhibition of superior force, with the determination to use it, will always suffice. The Sultan is then obliged to yield in virtue of the same law which forbids him to yield without compulsion. It is one of the simplest of all political questions, if statesmen and diplomatists would only emancipate themselves from misleading traditions and look at plain facts without official spectacles. It was only the other day that the Chancellor of the Exchequer flung a gibe at the clergy for their interference in this question. The clergy were all very well in matters of religion, he thought; but on political questions they were the worst advisers in the world. He forgot that the Eastern question rests on a very different foundation from a Chancellor of the Exchequer's Budget. Its basis is mainly moral. It goes to the roots not only of Christian duty, but of the moral law on which human society rests. And it is just because statesmen and diplomatists have persistently forgotten that rudimentary fact that they have made such an egregious mess of the Eastern question. If the clergy, even the most ignorant of them, had had the management of it for the last fifty years, it is conceivable that they might have succeeded better, but it is certain that they could not have done worse than the diplomatists. The vice of your ordinary diplomatist is that he is ignorant of his own ignorance, which is the very worst kind of ignorance. He thinks he knows everything about foreign politics, whereas his mind moves in a narrow groove of custom and is unable to look over the wall of his office into the world beyond. We all remember how a permanent Under-Secretary of long experience at the Foreign Office told Lord Granville on the eve of the Franco-German War that he had never known the political sky so free from any symptom of war. To ordinary mortals who were not Under-Secretaries the portents of the coming tempest were plainly visible above the horizon.

The fact is that, except in the case of superior and independent minds, official life has a tendency to confine the mental vision to the narrow routine of red-tape rules and formulas, and to incapacitate it for taking a larger view when a crisis arises. There are certain stereotyped maxims on the Eastern question which a Minister receives with the seals of his office, without examination, and which he regards as sacred rules which he must in no wise transgress. One of these is *Quieta non movere*. In the intervals between the massacres, which are periodical in Turkey as part of a regular policy, the rule of the Foreign Offices of Europe is to keep things quiet for fear of raising the bogey of the Eastern question. They might as well hope to prevent a volcanic eruption by sitting tightly on the crust of a crater while the incandescent gases beneath them were accumulating upwards. Their efforts to keep things quiet only serve to make the explosion more violent when it comes, as come it must and always does, hardly ever at an interval of more than ten years. This *dolce far niente* policy is not unlikely one day to issue in an explosion which will blow the rotten empire of the Sultan into the air, leaving the diplomatists sprawling about among the ruins, without anything to put into its place, and likely enough to quarrel among themselves about the distribution of the spoils.

CHAPTER XVIII.

THE ARGUMENT OF MASSACRE.

LORD ROSEBERY has laid such emphasis on the certainty of massacre, resulting in the extermination of the whole Armenian population, as the inevitable prelude or consequence of the use of force against the Sultan, that it is necessary to examine his premisses. I have already shown that the argument is a stale one, and that it has been invariably refuted by events,* and I will now give some more reasons in support of that conclusion.

It would be easy to fill pages with extracts from the Blue-books to show that a threat of massacre of Christians from Musulman fanaticism is one of the time-worn devices of the Sultan and his Ministers to frighten Europe from pressing reforms upon them. But three typical examples will suffice.

It is one of the immutable tenets of Islâm that a convert from it is subject to a barbarous death. After several executions of this sort in the end of 1843, Lord Aberdeen, who was then at the Foreign Office, wrote a despatch to Sir

* See pp. 31-35.

Stratford Canning, dated January 16, 1844, of which the drift will be seen from one extract :—

They (*i.e.* the Christian Powers) will not endure that the Porte should insult and trample on their faith by treating as a criminal any person who embraces it. Her Majesty's Government require the Porte to abandon once for all so revolting a principle.

Count Nesselrode, on behalf of Russia, knowing more accurately than Lord Aberdeen the theocratic basis of Ottoman legislation, 'perceived the difficulty, not to say impossibility, of discovering the suitable means of definitely paralysing the effect of the law of the Koran relating to apostasy.' He therefore contented himself with asking the Porte ' to comprehend the necessity of allowing to become obsolete ' a law ' which cannot be upheld but in disregard of the unanimous representation of all the Powers.' That was the wise course to take, if the Powers had added that they would hold the Sultan personally responsible for the next execution of a Muslim convert to Christianity. Short of that, remonstrances from the Powers and promises from the Sultan were alike useless, as the event has proved. For the law, belonging as it does to the category of sacred legislation, is irrepealable, and the Sultan has no power to let it become obsolete except under *force majeure*. A very simple truth, which explains all the difficulties of the Eastern question, if only statesmen would admit it into their minds.

But I am now dealing with the Porte's threats of massacre in case of any interference with the law of apostasy. Lord Stratford declared in a despatch to Lord Aberdeen (March 14, 1844) 'that there was in reality no such feeling,' and he attributed the alarming rumours of popular excitement 'to Rifaat Pasha (the Minister for Foreign Affairs) himself.' After much diplomatic pressure on this subject, Lord Stratford de Redcliffe wrote to Lord Aberdeen on March 23, 1844:—

I have the honour and satisfaction to inform your lordship that the question of religious executions is happily, and to all appearance conclusively, settled. . . He (*i.e.* the Sultan) gave me his royal word that henceforward neither should Christianity be insulted in his dominions, nor should Christians be in any way persecuted for their religion.

A great triumph for 'the Great Eltchi'? Let us see. On September 17, 1855, there is a despatch to Lord Stratford de Redcliffe from Lord Clarendon, then Secretary for Foreign Affairs, from which I quote a few sentences:—

The Turkish Government assured your Excellency some years ago that the Turkish law which inflicted the severest punishment upon Musulmans who might become Christians had been repealed. Great doubts are entertained as to the correctness of that assurance; and instances are proved to have happened since the date of those assurances, the one at Aleppo, the other at Adrianople, in which seceders from Islamism were punished by death. . . . This subject is one which must be pressed on the most serious and immediate attention of the Porte. The Turkish Government cannot expect that the great Christian Powers of Europe, who are making gigantic efforts [the Crimean War was then going on] and submitting to enormous sacrifices to save the Turkish Empire from ruin and destruction, can permit the continuance of a law in Turkey which is not only a standing insult to them, but a source of cruel persecution towards their co-religionists, which they never can consent to perpetuate by the successes of their fleets and armies. They are entitled to demand, and Her Majesty's Government do distinctly demand, that no punishment whatever shall attach to the Mohammedan who becomes Christian, whether originally a Mohammedan or originally a Christian, more than any punishment attaches to a Christian who embraces Mohammedanism. In all such cases the movements of human conscience must be left free, and the temporal arm must not interfere to coerce the spiritual decision.

So much for the 'royal word,' which the Ambassador told the Foreign Office eleven years before had settled the matter 'conclusively.' Now again 'the Great Eltchi' wields his diplomatic wand in his usual pompous manner, and assures a credulous Foreign Office that it is going to be all right this time:—

Objections and difficulties are to be expected in a later stage; but I am willing to believe that firmness and perseverance will ultimately prevail, if not to obtain the formal repeal of established laws, to remove all uncertainties from the intentions of the Porte, and to obtain the practical cessation of punishment and minor kinds of persecution in the case of any seceder from a religious creed.

That was on October 2, 1855. Exactly two months later he writes :—

> It has come round to me that the Turkish Ministers are very little disposed to meet the demands of Her Majesty's Government on the subject of religious persecution ; that they pretend to entertain apprehensions of popular discontent among the Musulmans if they were to give way. . . . What I am instructed to require is nothing more, in reality, than a frank and entire confirmation in practice of the promises virtually made to me ten years ago, as well by the Sultan himself as by the Porte. With respect to danger from popular discontent among the Musulman population, I do not believe it.*

Another promise was got from the Sultan and Porte that religious persecutions should cease, and this was confirmed by the Sultan's promises in the Treaties of Paris (1856) and of Berlin (1878), which not only promised entire religious liberty throughout the Ottoman Empire, but also perfect equality between Musulmans and Christians.

In 1880 a Parliamentary paper [*Turkey*, No. 6 (1880)] was published containing correspondence relating to the arrest of an English clergyman for employing a Turkish professor at Constantinople to revise a Turkish translation of the Book of Common Prayer. The professor was summarily condemned to death, and it took the Governments of the Great Powers more than three months to save the wretched man's life ;

---
* *Eastern Papers*, pt. xvii. pp. 15, 28, 32.

but in appearance only. For he was banished to a Greek island, in which he would certainly have been put to death if he had not managed to escape to England. But what I am now concerned with is the fact that, on that occasion also, as Sir Henry Layard, the Ambassador, declares, the Sultan and Porte raised the cry of Musulman fanaticism and massacre if the Musulman professor's life were spared. He had not become a convert to Christianity, be it observed; he had only revised the translation into Turkish of a Christian book. Sir Henry Layard says that the popular excitement on the subject was artificial; in fact, got up by the Palace, which inspired the fanatical articles in the Musulman press. And then, on looking back to Lord Stratford de Redcliffe's days, he says he finds nothing changed:—

In Lord Stratford's day, as at the present, the Ministers attempted to excite public opinion against the course pursued by the British Ambassador, and then alleged its existence as an excuse for declining to comply with his demands.*

The bugbear of massacre was paraded to frighten England from any action in Bulgaria in 1876–7. Mr. Forster referred to it as follows in his speech after his return from Constantinople in 1876:—

Men try to frighten you—men who are in favour of leaving things as they are—by saying that by your

---

* *Turkey*, No. 6 (1880), pp. 14 27-29.

expression of feeling we incurred the greatest possible danger to civilisation and to the Christians, and that it might result in a general massacre of the Christians. Nothing more completely proves the weakness of the Turkish Government than that that should be the argument. When driven into a corner, the advocates of Turkey always produce this massacre argument. I do not myself believe it.

I have already referred to the threat of the Porte that if France and England intervened by force of arms in Syria in 1860 there would be another massacre of Christians. A quiet intimation that the two Powers would hold the Sultan responsible sufficed, and a similar intimation would suffice now, and will always suffice. These massacres are always organised at the Palace and Porte, and can always be stopped by a stern message delivered there. Lord Rosebery has alarmed himself unnecessarily. There is no danger of a massacre of the Armenians in consequence of a policy of coercion. The danger is in a policy of inaction, or, what is even worse than inaction—diplomatic activity in futile representations and remonstrances. Let the Powers leave the Christians of Turkey alone, or let them adopt effective measures on their behalf. Paper reforms without practical security for their execution only provoke the Sultan to fresh cruelties.

One of the common fallacies about the Turkish Government is its supposed toleration towards other creeds. Let us see what that toleration means. By the unchangeable law of Islâm, Jews are forbidden to build synagogues and Christians churches. They may repair old buildings, but on the same site and of the same dimensions. And even for this they must obtain a firman from Constantinople, which means a series of bribes and a delay of months, perhaps of years. The churches must have no bells, for fear of offending the religious sensibilities of the Musulmans; and for the same reason there must be no loud singing inside churches or synagogues, or lamentation or singing at funerals. Apostasy from Islâm is death alike to converter and converted. On the other hand, it is a penal crime for a Jew or Christian to dissuade a relation or friend from becoming a Mohammedan. The most opprobrious language is applied in official documents and courts of justice to Christians and Jews. They are called 'dogs' and 'pigs,' and in burial certificates and other legal documents they are said to be not 'dead,' but 'damned.' I could fill pages with evidence of all this out of the reports of British Consuls and the despatches of British Ambassadors. Here is a burial certificate, attested by a British Ambassador:—

> We certify to the priest of the Church of Mary (in Armenia) that the impure, putrid, stinking carcase of ——, damned [*i.e.* deceased] this day, may be concealed under ground.

No wonder Lord Clarendon, then Secretary

for Foreign Affairs, denounced language of this sort as 'a standing insult to Christendom,' and sternly demanded that it should be discontinued. And it was discontinued in one of the numberless dishonoured promises of the Sultan and his Ministers, but not in fact. I saw one of those certificates quite lately. One of our Consuls reports as follows in 1867 :—

> The grossest and most galling terms of abuse are habitually addressed to the Christian with absolute impunity, the very authorities being in this respect the worst offenders. In the councils and seats of justice there is no form of abuse of which the Turkish language, so pre-eminently rich therein, is capable, however gross, disgusting, and insulting to his faith, which is not hourly and openly applied to the hated and despised 'Ghiaour' by the judges and authorities of the land.*

In a Blue-book on 'Religious Persecution in Turkey,' published in 1875, I find the following facts attested by her Majesty's Ambassador and Consuls in Turkey. The Porte 'definitely refused' to permit the establishment of Christian schools; prohibited the publication of the Bible in the Turkish language; and, in direct violation of the Hatt-i-Humaioun of 1856, the children, not only of Musulmans, but of Pagan parents as well, can never be recognised as Christians, even if they have been baptised in infancy. 'The law,' said the Grand Vizir, 'did not recognise such men as Christians at all, but as Moham-

---

* Consular Reports of 1867, p. 28.

medans.' The controversy arose out of the case of some young men, the sons of heathen converts to Christianity. These young men had been baptised in infancy, but when their parentage was found out they were imprisoned and put to the torture to force them to conform to Islâm. It was in vain that the British *Chargé d'Affaires* appealed to the promise of complete religious liberty solemnly given by the Sultan in the Hatt-i-Humaioun. The Grand Vizir merely wondered at the obtuseness which could not see the invalidity of promises extorted from the Sultan's necessity, and blandly explained that any interpretation of the Hatt-i-Humaioun which conflicted with the law of Islâm must be a wrong interpretation. By the law of Turkey the children of non-Christian parents can never become Christians.

But that was twenty years ago, and things may have improved since then? Things never improve in Turkey, except under coercion from one or more of the Great Powers. Left to itself, the progress is always from bad to worse. This could be proved in detail if space permitted; but it is not necessary. I will take official evidence, published last year in a document entitled: 'Violations of the Hatt-i-Humaioun, a Paper prepared at the request of Sir Philip Currie, British Ambassador to the Sublime Porte.'

Although the building of places for public

worship is by the sacred law of Islâm forbidden to Jews and Christians, the authorities, from 1856 to 1891, winked at meetings for worship in private houses. In the latter year the local authorities prohibited this scanty privilege; and in January, 1892, an Imperial Edict was published, 'decreeing the suppression of worship and schools, not formally authorised and found to be without permits, after a stipulated delay.' This decree, however, was not at once strictly enforced. It was a feeler to test the forbearance of the Powers. There being no protest from any quarter against this outrageous violation of the solemn promise of toleration given by the Porte in the Hatt-i-Humaioun, in 1894 the celebration of divine worship in private houses was peremptorily forbidden, on the ground that 'every place where a Christian says his prayers is reckoned as a church, and a church cannot exist without an Imperial firman.' One of the results of this decree is thus described in the document prepared under the auspices of the British Ambassador:—

At this moment congregations of from 150 to 300 Christians are prohibited from worship in places which have been recognised as their meeting-houses during ten to twenty years: at Fatza in the province of Trebizond, Inetzig, and Aghn in the province of Harpoot, Kir Shehir in the province of Angora, and Osmaniye in the province of Adana; to say nothing of the case of congregations in Sidon and Gedik Pasha in Constantinople.

The opening of Christian schools after the

Crimean War was also winked at till 1892, 'when the Government suddenly commenced to suppress Christian schools.' In the same year, 1892, another decree was issued closing all Government employment to all who are educated in other than Government schools—that is, virtually, to all but Muslims.

Having declared war against Christian schools, the next step was to destroy and exclude all but Islamic literature, in accordance with the dictum of Khalif Omar, the destroyer of the libraries of Alexandria and Persia—that literature which agreed with the Koran was superfluous, while literature that differed from it was pernicious, and must be destroyed.

It has become a usual thing for travellers to be stripped of their books at any guard station in the interior of Turkey. The fact of authorisation printed on the title-page in Turkish makes no difference. The book must be sent to the headquarters of the province, perhaps a hundred miles away, for examination. The owner of the book is happy if he is not detained under arrest until the result of the examination is made known. Of course he surrenders his books rather than wait several days for the examination to be made. In fact, the suspicion exhibited against Christians who possess books . . . has at last made the Christians of Asiatic Turkey almost as terrified at sight of a book as are the officials who are set over them. So complete is the destruction of Christian books in some districts through these causes, that the Christian children now growing up in those districts bid fair to be as ignorant as were their forefathers. The same causes operate to destroy the book trade.

The censorship of foreign religious and literary works is so stringent as to deprive the Christians in Turkey of the ordinary means of keeping in touch with the advancement of knowledge among their co-religionists abroad. Such classics of English literature, for instance, as Shakespeare, Byron, Milton, Scott, are refused authorisation. So with the higher literature of any language. No standard history, no encyclopædia, no treatise on metaphysics of any extended character, no full and extended theology or commentary on the Bible, can pass the censorship for introduction into the interior of Turkey. And if any minister or teacher, anxious to fill well his place, venture to smuggle such books through, or to possess the rudiments of a library, he is certain, sooner or later, to fall under the notice of the paid spy, and then must submit to condemnation for the crime which the authorities choose to consider to be 'incited' by the history or theological work concerned. The censorship of books published within the empire is still more rigorous.

I can bear personal testimony to the rigour of this censorship. In the year 1892 I could not find a single copy of Dante, Shakespeare, or even Murray's handbook, in any bookseller's shop in Constantinople. They used to keep such books, but are now forbidden. In the same year Mr. Brooke Lambert, Vicar of Greenwich, had even his Bible confiscated on passing the frontier between Bulgaria and Turkey. I reached Constantinople in a yacht, and thus avoided such inconveniences and indignities. Nor has the Porte the wretched excuse of pretending that this forbidden literature might undermine the faith of Musulmans, for it is written in languages of which the Musulmans, with very few exceptions, do not understand a single word. It is, in fact, a crescentade against freedom of thought and intellectual progress. And this intolerance extends to details which would be incredible without authentic evidence. Christians must not publish articles in their own religious newspapers, in any language, 'which contain the quotation of texts of Scripture,' because anarchical doctrines might thus be furtively insinuated. 'For instance, a text which alludes to rising from the dead may not be used because the verb "to rise" might suggest insurrection.'

Any passage from the Bible is prohibited which contains any of the following words: persecution, courage, liberty, strength, rights, union, equality, star* (in astronomy one has to use the word 'luminary' instead), king, palace, arms, bloodshed, tyranny, hero, &c., &c. These words are prohibited in religious articles in any context whatever. A Christian religious newspaper may not place before its readers a hymn or other poetry; and from the hymn-books used in Christian worship many of the grand old hymns of the Church have been expunged, and the suppression sustained after appeal to the highest authority of the Porte.

Such expressions as the following are also forbidden:—

'The guiding grace of God,' because Muslims do not admit that Christians can have this grace; 'good news or gospel,' because Muslims do not admit

---

* Because the Magi were led by a star to worship the Messiah, and this might encourage Jews and Christians to look for a Deliverer.

that the Gospel of Jesus Christ is 'good news'; 'apostle,' because the word implies that the Apostles of Jesus Christ were sent of God, which Muslims deny; references to our Saviour as 'the Saviour of the world,' or to His shedding His blood for the cleansing from sin.

Christian preachers are forbidden to recommend ' the virtues of manliness, of moral courage, of resignation under affliction, of hope in God under adversity.' Any transgression against these rules is severely punished.

Protestant pastors everywhere declare that they are compelled, in choosing texts from the Bible, and in framing their exhortations upon them, to hesitate, and paraphrase, and weigh words, through fear that if they speak of the consolations of Christianity they will be charged with encouraging discontent; if they urge resistance to sin, they will be condemned for suggesting resistance to the Turkish Government; or if they speak of the demand of Christianity for pure and noble character, they will be charged with inciting to unlawful aspirations. On complaint being made of such restrictions upon the legitimate instruction of Christians, officials in high positions have answered that while provincial Governors are constantly sending extracts from the Bible to prove the necessity of their suppressing that book, Christians should be grateful for the privilege of being allowed to have the Bible, instead of complaining at being restricted in making or publishing comments upon it.

I have already given some instances of the insults which, to quote again the language of a British Consul, are 'openly and hourly' flung at 'the hated and despised ghiaour' in official documents and by Turkish authorities, from pashas and judges to the ruffianly police. I have myself seen a Musulman judge in a Musulman court of so-called justice taking evidence against an accused Christian, and following the evidence with a running commentary of hard blows with his clenched fist on the face of the accused, who was then sentenced, without being allowed to say a word in self-defence. The attempt to do so was treated as a fresh offence, and punished accordingly. The following extract from the document, already quoted at some length, casts a lurid light on the 'humane' and 'tolerant' temper of the cruel and unscrupulous despot whose mild manners and humanitarian 'blarney' have so often imposed upon simple-minded British tourists.

In 1886 a book called the 'Mudafaa,' and in 1892 another called 'Resalei Hamidiê,' were published at Constantinople. Both of these books were full of the most scurrilous attacks on Christianity and of the most contemptuous epithets applied to those who profess that religion. *The authors of those works were decorated by H.I.M. the Sultan, and many efforts were made to give the books the widest possible circulation.* Since that time, especially in 1892 and 1893, the Turkish newspapers of the capital have contained article after article which have thrown opprobrium upon the Christian religion. These articles have been published with the approval of a censorship that by law must decide beforehand whether an article may be published. But at the same time Christians have been rigorously prohibited from making in Turkish any answer to statements maliciously false concerning Christianity, by which these works have sought to excite the contempt and hatred of the Mohammedan populace towards their Christian neighbours.

Let the reader carefully note the last sentence in this 'Paper, prepared at the request of Sir Philip Currie, British Ambassador to the Sublime Porte,' for the information of Lord Kimberley, in the spring of 1894. It exhibits the Sultan at the head of a crescentade against Christianity, fomenting and disseminating 'most scurrilous attacks on Christianity' and Christians, and decorating the authors of those attacks, which have for their object ' to excite the contempt and hatred of the Mohammedan populace towards their Christian neighbours.' It was part of the Sultan's careful preparations for the massacres which followed, and which are by no means ended if the Powers do not stop him.

I hope I have now made it clear that all danger of wholesale massacres of Christians in Turkey has its source and home in Yildiz Kiosk. So that the only effectual way to stop them is to deal sternly with the irresponsible tyrant who issues his sanguinary orders from that secure retreat; while the surest way to encourage the murderer in his bloody work is to assure him that the Powers will not permit any action that may imperil his throne. They have given him that assurance, and he feels safe while it lasts. What cares he for their squeamish objection to his carnival of horrors, so long as they proclaim in the face of Heaven that, do what he will, they will in their own interest save his empire from disruption? He feels no gratitude for their forbearance. Why should he, since he knows that it does not come from love of him, but from their sordid belief that the continued existence of the most incurably inhuman system of government that has ever existed is necessary to their own private ends? Secure in this belief, he has ceased to fear the Concert of Europe, and has learnt, as he well may, to despise it. How he must have laughed in his sleeve at Lord Rosebery's ingenuous trust in ' diplomatic action, strenuous, self-denying,' followed by the comforting assurance that, 'if that fails, nothing will succeed.' He has put diplomatic action to a crucial test before the eyes of the Ambassadors, and has proved its impotence by 'a deed of dreadful note,' which has gone unpunished. What has he to fear? Certainly not Lord Salisbury's Providence, for he believes, being a sincere Musulman, that Providence is on his side in his policy of exterminating Infidels whom he is pressed to place, in violation of his creed, on a footing of equality with ' True Believers.' Till the Powers recognise that fact, and its necessary corollary in the shape of coercion, they had better cease talking about reforms and diplomatic action, however ' strenuous ' and ' self-denying ' ; for their futile policy serves only to irritate the

Sultan and aggravate the lot of his Christian subjects. Let them do nothing at all, or let them agree on an effectual remedy, and demand its acceptance within a fixed time on pain of deposition. Anything between the two is purely mischievous.

I cannot agree with Lord Salisbury in acquitting the Concert of Europe of selfishness. The selfishness of the Powers during the last two years is only equalled by their folly. Any day within that period such an ultimatum as I have suggested would have secured, without the movement of a ship or regiment, the cringing submission of the puppet who enjoys his power of mischief solely through their sufferance. In one sense they are more guilty than he. For it is possible to credit him with belief in a God who approves of the extermination of the Armenians. But it is not possible to credit the Great Powers of Christendom with belief in a God who approves of their virtual complicity in the Sultan's fell design. That—as I have already shown—is the programme laid down for the Concert of Europe by Austria nearly a year ago. Admitting that it was a 'heartrending prospect,' the Austrian Government faced the situation with tranquil stoicism, and declared that no action must be taken by any of the Powers 'to put a stop to the extermination of the miserable Armenians.' I doubt whether the history of Christendom furnishes any parallel to so ghastly an exhibition of unmixed selfishness on the part of any Government calling itself Christian. How is it that a people so brave, and chivalrous, and attractive in private life should, as a Government, represent precisely the opposite of Aristotle's splendid description of the character of the 'high-souled man' (μεγαλόψυχος)? I am reminded thereby of a passage in the 'Life of the Prince Consort' on the funeral of the Duke of Wellington:—

> Every first-class State in Europe, except one, sent its representative to the funeral. That one was not France. On the contrary, its ruler, who might perhaps have been expected to hang back from joining in the last honour to 'the great World-Victor's victor,' was among the first to announce his intention to send a representative.

Who was the absent representative? The Queen supplies the answer in a touching letter to the King of the Belgians, descriptive of the scene:—

> There is but one feeling of indignation and surprise at the conduct of Austria in taking this opportunity to slight England in return for what happened to Haynau because of his own character.

If ever a man deserved to be called μεγαλόψυχος it was the Great Duke, and it was perhaps fitting that the State which has in its foreign policy always exhibite dthe opposite character should be the one which sought to avenge on the dead body of its deliverer the rough handling by

London working men of the flogger of Italian women. But I leave the biographer of the Prince Consort to furnish the appropriate comment :—

Some there were, however, who, remembering events yet recent, saw only a fitness in the absence of representatives from that country at the funeral of the Great General, whose campaigns were sullied by no cruelties, no crimes; and who, 'on his deathbed, might remember his victories among his good works.'*

* *Life of the Prince Consort*, ii. pp. 471-2.

CHAPTER XIX.

CYPRUS AND EGYPT.

It seems to be admitted on all hands and by all parties, that among the principal aims of our foreign policy should be the bringing about of a good understanding between our own country and Russia and France. We are perhaps the three countries in Europe which have most to gain by a friendly understanding, and most to lose by mutual suspicions and misunderstandings. Lord Salisbury's allusions to Russia in his recent speech at the Guildhall confirm what I have said in previous chapters about his feelings towards Russia. He dismissed with scorn 'the superstition of an antiquated diplomacy' on that subject. A disastrous superstition indeed it has been, costing us dear in treasure and in blood; and dearest of all in the misery which it has inflicted for half a century on the Christians of Turkey, and the desolation which it has wrought in the fairest lands on earth. But superstitions die hard, and although the number is rapidly diminishing, there are still men, able and honest, who seriously believe that it is a secular and persistent aim of Russian policy to invade and annex India. The history of mankind, however, and of the British Parliament not the least, proves abundantly that intellectual ability and moral integrity afford no security against the most monstrous delusions. To take one instance out of many. It is hardly credible that only a little more than fifty years ago theft of anything above five shillings in value should in this country be punishable with death. And not only so, but that the repeal of that law should have been strenuously resisted by nearly the whole of the propertied classes; by almost the entire body of lawyers; by the judicial bench—which was then adorned by some of the most illustrious luminaries of the law—without exception; by a number of the leading bishops; and by overwhelming majorities in the House of Lords. An extract from the speech of Lord Ellenborough (Chief Justice) in the House of Lords will show that I do not exaggerate the grossness of that superstition:—

I trust that your Lordships will pause before you assent to a measure pregnant with danger to the security of property. The learned judges are *unanimously* agreed that the expediency of justice and the public security require there should not be a remission of capital punishment in this part of the criminal law. My Lords, if we suffer this Bill to pass we shall not know where to stand; we shall not know whether we are on our heads or on our feet. My Lords, I think this, above all, is a law on which so much of the security of mankind depends on its execution, that I should deem myself neglectful of my duty to the public if I failed to let the law take its course.

We now know that the juries all over England, who compelled the repeal of that atrocious law by refusing to convict, deficient as they may have been in learning and mental power and trained statecraft, as compared with the galaxy of brilliant intellects and skilled statesmen to whom they were opposed, had nevertheless all the foresight and statesmanship on their side. I am not dismayed, therefore, by finding great names still supporting the superstition of a Russian invasion of India. I put the difficulty and danger of the enterprise—really amounting to an impossibility—out of the question, and merely ask what possible motive Russia could have for the invasion of India. That she will use her position in Central Asia to threaten and worry us in India is likely enough, so long as we threaten and worry her elsewhere. But if we do not worry her, why should she engage in the mad adventure of invading India? What use would India be to her even if, *per impossibile*, she succeeded? It would entail the annexation of Afghanistan and all the other intervening territories, and probably also the re-conquest of India after we were turned out of it. For even if some of the people of India should join Russia in expelling us, it would not be for the sake of riveting her yoke upon their own necks.

Again I ask what motive Russia could have for wantonly running so tremendous a risk. Would England, would any Power in Europe, willingly run such a risk? The loss of India would be a great blow to our prestige and pride; but it may be doubted whether it would affect us prejudicially in any other way. It offers an outlet for a certain portion of our educated population; but its possession adds considerably to our expenditure and greatly embarrasses our foreign policy; and it is certain that if we had not acquired the country piecemeal by the enterprise of traders, we should not have risked a war with a Great Power to possess it. Then why should Russia? It would be more likely to impoverish than to enrich her exchequer, even if she got possession of it without striking a blow. For India is not a rich country for its teeming population. Will the alarmists consider the rate of increase of the population of India? Let them reflect on the following extract from a speech delivered by Lord Lansdowne in Leeds on the 29th of last month (October):—

> While Lord Wenlock and I were in India a census was taken, and we found that in the decade which had passed no fewer than thirty-three millions of people had been added to the population for which the British Government had become responsible. That is a population equal to that of the whole of Great Britain.

An increase of thirty-three millions in ten

years, with an ever-advancing ratio! Where is it to end? And how is the problem to be met when the increase of population outstrips the means of subsistence, already circumscribed by periodical famines? Formerly the population was kept down by intestine wars, barbarous punishments, no organised attempts to cope with famine and disease, and all those checks on population which are incident to uncivilised life. We have given peace to India and have furnished her with all the incentives and means which tend to multiply population at so alarming a rate. But we are there, in possession of a great trust; and there we must abide. 'There we are placed by the Sovereign Disposer; and we must do the best we can in our situation. The situation of man is the preceptor of his duty.'*

But where would be Russia's inducement to take our place if we offered to clear out and invited her to succeed us? I am sure that she would decline the offer with thanks. Russia has no need of any outlet for a redundant population. On the contrary, her population, large as it is, is far too sparse for the vast area over which she rules. And that area is, moreover, full of undeveloped wealth, which it will take generations to develop. Yet men, otherwise sane, clear-headed, and perchance skilled and able in affairs, have succeeded in persuading themselves that the one consuming desire of

* Burke's Speech on Fox's India Bill: Works, iii. p. 689.

Russia is to turn her back on the undeveloped resources, which lie in rich abundance within her frontiers, for the sake of invading and conquering India! I am not crediting Russia with any transcendental unselfishness or any extraordinary freedom from political ambition. I am crediting her with nothing more than reasoning faculties and ordinary sanity. In order to credit the fears of the Russophobists, it would be necessary to assume that the Russians are a nation of lunatics. And that is an accusation which even their worst enemies will not make against them.

Dismissing this 'superstition of an antiquated diplomacy' from our relations with Russia, it is manifest that we have no motive to quarrel with her, and that she has none to quarrel with us if we leave her alone. The ownership of Constantinople concerns Austria and Germany, and they may be left henceforward to look after their own interests. We have played the part of watchdog for them a great deal too long. Prince Bismarck will try in vain to frighten either Power into the belief that the other is by an ordinance of Nature its antagonist. Constantinople concerns us not, except for its command of an outlet for our trade; and in that respect any owner would be more profitable for us than the Turk.* In trade, moreover, Germany is our dangerous rival, not Russia.

* In May, 1877, the Russian Government made the following

As a 'place of arms'—Lord Beaconsfield's description of it—Cyprus has been given up by all who now repudiate—and who does not?—our obligation to defend the Sultan against Russian attack. Why not give it up, then? Yes, but to whom? To restore it to the Sultan is out of the question. To whom, then, shall it go if we give it up? Either to Greece, or to autonomy, with a Prince reigning under the protection of the Great Powers. There seems to be no other alternative. But who is to pay the piper in either case? Who is to be responsible for the purchase money? I would answer that question very summarily. The Turkish Government—to quote the late Professor Freeman's favourite phrase—is in literal fact, and ever has been, 'an organised brigandage.' Now, to apply to such a barbarous Government any rule of rational policy derived from the law of nations would be absurd. The right of conquest is nothing but the right of

formal declaration to the British Government:—'As far as concerns Constantinople, without being able to prejudge the cause or issue of the war, the Imperial Cabinet repeats that the acquisition of Constantinople is excluded from the views of His Majesty the Emperor. They recognise that, in any case, the future of Constantinople is a question of common interest, which cannot be settled otherwise than by a general understanding; and that if the possession of that city were to be put in question, it could not be allowed to belong to any of the European Powers' (*Russia*, No. 2 (1877), p. 3). I believe that Constantinople presents no difficulty as far as Russia is concerned. And why should England object to Russia having free access to the Mediterranean and having a port there? Let us come to a friendly understanding with Russia, and then a Russian fleet in the Mediterranean would be more likely to be with us than against us. Our interests are the same in most places, and clash nowhere.

the sword, which is never legitimate except when sanctioned by justice. History presents us with many instances of nations who, after conquering their opponents by force of arms, have received from their captives the civilising yoke of literature and art. It was thus that

> Græcia capta ferum victorem cepit, et artes
> Intulit agresti Latio.

Nor have there been wanting examples of the introduction of the arts of peace by the conqueror himself, who has thus made amends, by the blessings of civilisation, for the havoc which he had caused by the sword. The Turk, on the contrary, has been a destroyer, and nothing but a destroyer, all through the long course of his calamitous rule; a destroyer of science, literature, art, human happiness, and even the very lands which his presence has blighted. Humanity owes him one long-drawn curse, unsoftened by a single memory of a good deed done.

I hold, therefore, that the Sultan, having broken all his pledges, has no more right in equity to any compensation for Cyprus than a brigand for his stolen booty. Time does not run against the inalienable rights of men, and length of tenure can never validate a brigand's rule. Let the private property of Turks in Cyprus be respected; but let the tribute to the Sultan cease. That would be the decision of a Court of Equity.

But if that should be thought too drastic, let

the Sultan be met on his own ground. He has practically repudiated a large debt, the interest of which Great Britain and France have guaranteed to the tune of nearly £100,000 a year. They have thus a clear legal lien on his property, and would be entitled alike by the law of nations and of equity to take Cyprus in payment. On that ground alone, therefore, we have an indisputable legal right, in union with France, to dispose of Cyprus as we please without consulting the Sultan. Anyhow, the Anglo-Turkish Convention, by the admission of Lord Salisbury and other members of the Government, has lapsed as a menace to Russia and a pledge of protection to the Sultan; and all that remains on that score is the final disposal of Cyprus. While the Convention lasts we have a right to call upon the Sultan to fulfil his engagements; but if we are not prepared to enforce our rights in that matter, ought we not formally to repudiate the Convention and retain Cyprus (to be disposed of hereafter as may seem best) in return for the Sultan's indebtedness to France and ourselves?

The case of Egypt is different. I have always endeavoured to consider it entirely on its merits, and I shall do so now. No Frenchman who may chance to do me the honour of reading these pages will suspect me of unfriendly feelings towards his country. While the Franco-German War was going on I engaged, under the *nom de plume* of 'Scrutator,' in a controversy in the *Times*, on behalf of France, with Professor Max Müller, the most chivalrous antagonist with whom I ever crossed pens. My letters were afterwards expanded into a volume, and passed through several editions in a French translation. When my name came out as the author of 'Who is Responsible for the War?' I received the thanks of the French Government through the Duc de Broglie, then Ambassador in London; and I have received many kindnesses in France at different times since then.

With these credentials, I think I may claim to speak my mind quite frankly on the Egyptian question without being suspected of any but the most friendly feelings towards France.

Let our good friends and neighbours, then, look facts fairly in the face. They declined our invitation to join us in restoring order in Egypt, and thereby with their own hands put an end to the *condominium*. That is the view which the French themselves took of it at the time; and it is notorious that they were surprised when, after the collapse of the rebellion, the British Government invited them back. For my own part, I think that the invitation was a mistake. France would have acquiesced more readily in a friendly notice to quit at that time—for which, indeed, she was fully prepared—than in an invitation to return on any other terms than the *status quo ante*.

That is the first fact which our French friends ought to take into their consideration. The next is, that we are in Egypt on much the same terms on which Austria is in Bosnia, and with quite as good a title as France is in Tunis. Our promises to leave Egypt are not more explicit—are they as explicit?—as the promises of France to leave Tunis and not to fortify Biserta. Yet France has practically annexed Tunis, as she has annexed Madagascar, without any menaces or reproaches from England, which has not even remonstrated against the fortification of Biserta. Now Britons who, like myself, earnestly desire unbroken friendship with France, have a right to feel aggrieved at the very different measures of justice which France metes out to us and to herself.

Yet I have no wish to see France evacuate Tunis; on the contrary, I hold that her abandonment of Tunis would be a crime against civilisation. But let France be just, and admit that our abandonment of Egypt would be not the less a crime against civilisation. To restore to Musulman rule any country once emancipated would be a wrong and a cruelty against humanity. I have spent two winters on the Nile, and have seen the wilderness 'blossom as the rose' under our benign sway, while justice and prosperity and happiness prevail where anarchy and cruelty were rampant. It warms one's blood to see British officers, well educated and brought up delicately, working hard among regiments of natives, whom they have not only trained into good soldiers, but whose confidence and affection they have won.

What would happen if we were to leave Egypt? Within a year our reforms would be a thing of the past. The automatic law of Islâm would gradually, but surely, resume its sway, and the last state would be worse than the first. I have written the preceding pages in vain if I have failed to prove that a Musulman ruler is, under the theocratic law of Islâm which dominates the civil as well as the spiritual sphere, powerless to do justice to his non-Musulman subjects, or to guarantee reforms which are contrary to the Sacred Law of Islâm. Hence the fallacy of our promises to leave Egypt when we have placed our reforms on a stable footing. Practically, that is to postpone our departure to the Greek Kalends; for our reforms, which are largely opposed to the Koranic law, can never be put on a stable footing while a Musulman, ruling independently, is at the top.

But why not place Egypt under the control of the Great Powers? To which I reply, God save Egypt from the Concert of Europe, after the exhibition which it has made of itself in Turkey during the last fifty years! Even M. Hanotaux deprecated, with something like alarm, the idea of putting Turkey under any form of *condo-*

minium. We may therefore dismiss European control as impracticable.

What guarantee, then, does France suggest against the relapse of Egypt into its former condition on the cessation of the British occupation? I see only one alternative to the British occupation—the creation of Egypt into an autonomous State under a Christian Prince, for whose independence the Great Powers should make themselves conjointly responsible. That might solve the difficulty; but I can think of no other solution outside the present arrangement. Let France produce her case in the dry light of reason and of facts, that we may examine it. This country, I presume, would have no objection to the neutralisation of the Suez Canal, for I do not suppose that any British Government would be so rash as to make use for military purposes of a canal which could so easily be blocked for weeks by the sinking of a steamer. I suppose that most naval officers who have examined the subject would agree with Lord Charles Beresford on that point. And the difference in point of time between the Suez Canal and the Cape route is so small that it would not be worth while to run any risk. The Suez Canal therefore presents no difficulty to a friendly understanding with France or Russia.

From a military point of view our occupation of Egypt is a serious embarrassment to us. It deprives us of the advantage of our insular position, and might subject us to the humiliation of scuttling out of it in an undignified manner in case of troubles elsewhere, as France was forced to leave Rome hurriedly in 1870. But there we are, and I do not see how we can go till we have provided an efficient substitute.

I am afraid I differ from most Liberals in being in favour of the Dongola expedition. The patient and industrious peasantry of Egypt suffered cruelly from the tyrannical domination of the Dervishes, and I sympathise with them as I do with the Armenians, though their skin is dark and their creed is Islâm. To break the power of the Dervishes is surely a service to humanity and civilisation. Mr. John Morley thinks that facts have refuted the two reasons given for the expedition to Dongola, namely, the relief of Kasala and the insecurity of the Egyptian frontier. Yet even so, I should hold the expedition justified by the recovery of a rich province from Dervish misrule. Nevertheless, I believe that there is more in the two reasons given for the expedition than Mr. Morley admits. The danger to Kasala after the disaster of Adowa is not disproved by Italy's subsequent half-formed intention of evacuating the place. I was in Rome at the time, and can testify that the danger was believed by the Italian Ministry to be a very real one. An attack on Kasala by the whole Dervish force at that critical moment might have succeeded, with the result of the massacre of the Italian garrison. If that had followed the defeat in Abyssinia, it is doubtful whether the monarchy would have survived the tragedy. I rejoiced, therefore, when it was announced that the order had been given for an expedition to Dongola. The diversion thus caused probably saved Kasala, and it is not logical to infer from that safety the inutility of what caused it. Nor does the feebleness of the Dervish resistance to the Egyptian force prove that the Dervishes were not a source of danger. True, they could make no head against the frontier force at Wady Halfa. They were too prudent to try. But the contiguity of their presence, their minute knowledge of the desert, and their occasional raids, diffused a general sense of insecurity among the peasantry. On all accounts, therefore, I believe the expedition has done good service, and I trust, for my part, that the malign power of the Khalifa will be destroyed by the capture of his stronghold, which I believe will not be a difficult matter. The impetuous rush of the desert warriors is useless against disciplined troops with quick-firing guns and led by officers whom they trust. Having seen a good deal of the Egyptian and black troops, I had no doubt as to the success of the expedition, and I have still less doubt of its success if it should advance on Khartum. Whatever may be settled about Egypt, I, for one, shall rejoice at the delivery of as large an area as possible from the cruel yoke of the Dervishes.

CHAPTER XX.

CONCLUDING OBSERVATIONS.

THERE are many aspects of the Eastern question on which I have not touched at all in the foregoing pages, for my object has been to confine my criticism to what is germane to the present situation. It remains only to notice a few points which escaped my memory when I was writing, or on which I touched too briefly.

The first is the following remark by the Duke of Argyll in the interesting letter which he published in the *Times* of October 28:—

> I have always held firmly to the great principle for which the Crimean War was waged—the principle, namely, that the fate of Turkey and the final disposal of her territories is a matter for Europe, as a whole, to determine, and not for any one of its Powers. If this principle was good against Russia in 1854–6, it is equally good against England now. If we were to attempt such a task alone—directly or indirectly—a great war would be inevitable.

I have already observed on the contention of the Duke of Argyll and Mr. Gladstone, that the Crimean War was waged to repel a violation of the public law of Europe, as explained in the passage just quoted from the Duke of Argyll.

Doubtless that was the impression at the time. It was the impression propagated so sedulously by the late Emperor of the French, by Lord Palmerston, and by Lord Stratford de Redcliffe. And it is the impression which has possessed the public mind. A careful study of the official and other evidence, some of it unavailable then, has convinced me that the impression is erroneous. I have already shown who the real authors of the Crimean War were, and their motives. Before the Crimean War the relations of the Great Powers towards the Christians of Turkey, *vis-à-vis* of the Porte, were these: with the tacit, if not formal, consent of Europe, Russia exercised a protectorate over the members of the Eastern Churches; France over those in communion of the Pope; and Great Britain over Anglicans and other Christian communions. The other Great Powers did not interfere unless their intervention was invited by one or more of the three Powers named. The result of this arrangement was that when any outrage took place, the Porte found itself confronted by one Great Power, with the acquiescence, if not active support, of one or two more. Its plan of playing the Powers against each other was thus frustrated, and it either yielded, or, if it proved recalcitrant, it might be coerced by a combination of Powers, and some of its territory wrested from it, as in the case of Greece. This was the *status quo ante* the Crimean War, and Napoleon was the first to disturb it, in order to fasten a quarrel on the Emperor Nicholas preparatory to the war on which he had set his heart, provided that he succeeded in manœuvring England into it. After sundry vexatious encroachments on the rights of Russia as protector of the Orthodox in Jerusalem and Bethlehem, Napoleon got a *firman* from the Sultan in favour of France, which ousted Russia from her traditional and acknowledged position. Nicholas, one of the ablest and most clear-sighted sovereigns of modern times, saw that Russia's whole position as protector of the Orthodox Christians of the East was at stake, and, on the principle of *principiis obsta*, he determined to make a stand at once. That was, in fact, the hinge on which the whole controversy turned, though the real issue was disguised by the subtle craft of the diplomatists of France, England, and Austria. Russia was asking nothing new. Here is her case as stated by Baron Jomini on behalf of the Russian Government years after the dust and bitterness of the controversy had passed away:—

> In effect our claims had for their aim to confirm the obligations which the Porte had contracted towards us as to the maintenance of the privileges and immunities of the Orthodox Church; and to guarantee the *status quo* without any prejudice to the other forms of worship, without any innovation arming us with new rights. In the situation which had been made for us this demand was nothing but equitable. It seemed to us just and necessary, since the ancient guarantees had just

been infringed by an act of bad faith and partiality on the part of the Turkish Government in favour of France.

The Porte was not substantially opposed to our views. Its own interest was evidently to reassure its Christian subjects against new infractions, and thus to calm a general discontent which might manifest itself in tumults and insurrections. It might expect even to find an advantage in fortifying itself against new pretensions on the part of the Latins, strangers to the country, and covered by a protection which threatened to become a source of serious embarrassment.

But it objected to the form. It was ready to give to its subjects the promises and guarantees desired. It gave them, in fact, explicitly in the various notes which it addressed to us, in those which it forwarded to the other Cabinets, and in a *firman* to the Patriarch of Constantinople. But it would not bind itself on the subject to a foreign Power. It was told that it would thus alienate its independence, and that Europe would not permit it.

Our adversaries went still further. The new guarantees which were demanded had, in our eyes, no other object than to set forth the ancient rights acquired by previous treaties, without adding anything to them. Not only did they oppose the granting of these new guarantees, but they attacked the very rights which we wished to have confirmed.

They maintained that none of the treaties concluded between the Porte and ourselves gave us the right to interfere in any manner on behalf of the Orthodox Church in Turkey. Article VII. of the Treaty of Kainardji recorded on the part of the Sultan a promise to *protect the Christian religion in his States*. From this was deduced for us merely the right to see to the religious protection of *Russian subjects residing in Turkey*, but in no way to that of the *Orthodox subjects of the Sultan*.

Evidently we could not keep silent before such pretensions. To contest the patronage which by right, and in fact, we exercised over our co-religionists in the East was to deny all our history. The Imperial Cabinet revindicated it firmly, while recalling the use we had made of it. It is impossible to deny that if the Christians of European Turkey, superior in number to their rulers, had given proofs of such constant resignation, that was due to their being convinced of our sympathetic support resting upon treaties. Without our conciliatory, essentially conservative, intervention, it was evident that the Musulmans would have passed all limits, and the Christians lost all patience. We desired nothing more than a continuation of this tutelary action ; the sole efficacious guarantee of the repose of the East, and of the existence of the Ottoman Empire. We were not, moreover, the only Power in Europe to exercise it in regard to the Christians of Turkey. At all times France had claimed the right of protecting the Latins. We recalled expressly the fact that in 1832, when the Hellenic Kingdom was constituted, the French Government had formally renounced in favour of the Greek Government the protectorate which it formerly exercised on behalf of the Catholics in the Peninsula, when it was under the Turkish *régime*. This right was no longer necessary from the moment that Greece was to live beneath a Christian Government. But since the French Government thought fit to transfer it so formally to the Hellenic Government, it must have considered it as legally existing; as constituting, indeed, an obligation imposed upon France by its religious conscience and its traditions.

England equally protected the Protestants residing in Turkey. On what grounds should the same rights and the same duties be contested in our case?

Was it, as some argued, because the protection

exercised by the other Powers extended only to a small number of Christians, most of them strangers to the country, whilst ours embraced the immense majority of the Sultan's subjects in European Turkey?

But it would have been absurd to pretend that the Catholics and Protestants ought to be protected because they were not numerous, while the Orthodox were to be delivered over without defence to Turkish fanaticism because their numbers reached several millions.

That is why we were called upon to defend our entire position in the East.

In these conditions, to retreat was to efface at one stroke all our traditions and all our history for more than a century past, and to abdicate for the benefit of Europe the rights we had acquired, and which we had so dearly paid for. Russia might be forced to this by an unfortunate war; she could not consent to it without drawing the sword.*

Anyone who will now read the diplomatic correspondence dispassionately must admit the entire accuracy of this summary of the case. The Treaty of Paris withdrew the Christian subjects of the Sultan from any special protectorate, and placed them under the protectorate of the Concert of Europe. That process was repeated in the Treaty of Berlin. The protectorate which Russia had secured for the Christians of Armenia and Macedonia was rescinded, and they were placed under the protection of the Concert of Europe. The result is before our eyes.

The experience of the last forty years proves

* *Diplomatic Study of the Crimean War*, i. 187-9.

to demonstration that the only rational policy is to revert to the *status quo ante* the Crimean War. Russia must be allowed to resume the right of protecting the Christians of the Eastern Churches; France, those in communion with the Holy See; and England the rest. These rights being mutually recognised, it will be the interest of the three Powers to support each other. It seems plain that the Concert of Europe can, as a rule, be depended on for nothing except the negation of its name. A concert implies harmonious action. The Concert of Europe has done nothing for two years but proclaim its own impotence, qualified by some discordant tuning of its instruments when the Sultan has startled it by some fresh horror into some temporary spasms of diplomatic activity.

While the naval demonstration at Dulcigno was in progress Lord Salisbury made a speech in which he treated the Concert of Europe with some sarcasm:—

It appears that when the ships of the six Powers were sent to the coast of Albania it was officially stipulated, if I read the telegraphic intelligence aright, that the crews of those ships should never land, and the guns which those ships carried should never fire. I do not say that those were the instructions given to all the ships of all the Powers; but they appear to have been given to some of them; and when Lord Granville promised that England should not act without the others, it became very clear why the Sultan did not care very much for the naval demonstration. . . .

Whether it ever will be possible to induce the six Powers to agree together to use, not diplomatic pressure, but naval and military force, I very much doubt. But whether that be possible or not, I am sure nothing can be gained by a compromise between the two—by an exhibition of a naval demonstration, which, in truth, is nothing but another form of diplomatic pressure, putting on the appearance and pretence of an exercise of naval force.*

This is obviously true. A naval demonstration with orders to do nothing would be as likely to frighten the Sultan—to quote Lord Salisbury's humorous comparison—as 'six washing-tubs with flags attached to them.' But the French papers had misled Lord Salisbury as to the facts. It is true, as Mr. Gladstone informed the public in his Liverpool speech, that some of the Powers had given orders that no guns should be fired on their ships. It is also true that the Sultan, knowing this, snapped his fingers at the demonstration. But the English admiral had no such orders, and when Austria, Germany, and France declined, after some vacillation, to join England in seizing Smyrna, and the Sultan heard that the British fleet would go notwithstanding, with the acquiescence of Russia, he yielded at once, even before the answer of Italy was received. Lord Granville spoke a month after Lord Salisbury and corrected the mistake:—

I see that it may be supposed from an expression in the French Yellow Book that I declared that we had

* *Times*, October 27, 1890.

no intention of firing a shot. This I never said; it would have been absolutely contrary to my argument. What I stated was, that the necessity for doing so was extremely unlikely.*

Of course. Let the Sultan learn that even one Power, with the acquiescence of the rest, *will* fire a shot if necessary, and the necessity will never arise. Hence the folly and the mischief of proclaiming aloud that none of the Powers will take isolated action—the only action which he fears, for the experience of two years has made him believe that no action will ever come from the Concert. To tell him that there will be no isolated action is, in fact, to give him a free hand for more massacres. Some massacres followed Lord Rosebery's speech. I rejoice to notice that Lord Salisbury avoided that fatal mistake in his Guildhall speech. There is a contingent menace of isolated action in the following extract :—

I never have pledged, I do not now pledge, the British Government to any isolated action. *I do not debar isolated action.* He would be a very imprudent man who did that; but I say that as matters stand now isolated action has been and would be most imprudent.

How rare is strict accuracy of quotation! A few days after the meeting at St. James's Hall, on the 19th of last October, the following appeared in the *Daily News* :—

Mr. Gladstone's apparent abandonment now of the

---

* *Times*, Nov. 29, 1880.

principle of the European Concert is involving him in some curious conflicts with himself. He was very severe in his last letter on the idea of England feeling bound to keep step with those laggards, the rest of the world. In 1880, however, this necessity was the very ground on which, through the mouth of his Foreign Secretary, he based and justified his policy. Lord Granville's statement of the case was put with his usual felicity in a homely and effective phrase. The contrast is so curious that we put the two passages in parallel columns:—

I remember many years ago joining the Staffordshire Yeomanry. The first lesson I received was that I must only charge according to the pace of the slowest horse under the heaviest farmer in the troop.—(Mr. Gladstone's Foreign Secretary, speech at Hanley, Nov. 27, 1880.)	To advertise beforehand, in the ears of the Great Assassin, that our action will, under all circumstances, be cut down to what the most backward of the Six may think sufficient, appears to me, after the experience we have had, to be an abandonment alike of duty and of prudence. —(Mr. Gladstone, 1896.)

The writer evidently copied his first extract from a commonplace book without verifying it. It is inaccurate in three respects. The place and date of Lord Granville's speech are wrong, and the quotation finishes before a sentence which reverses the writer's inference. The speech was delivered at Stoke, on November 29, 1880; and the two sentences following the quotation are:—

If some of the horses stopped altogether, it then was a question whether you would abandon the charge altogether, or go on with the rest. But I was assured that as long as the troop charged together, even at a slow pace, nothing could resist it but troops drawn up in square.

Lord Granville was describing precisely what had happened. The other Powers moved slowly—

much too slowly for Lord Granville's and Mr. Gladstone's pace. But as long as they moved at all it was thought wise 'to charge according to the pace of the slowest horse.' When, however, 'some of the horses stopped altogether,' Mr. Gladstone and Lord Granville, instead of 'abandoning the charge,' decided to 'go on with the rest.' And with entire success, for Lord Granville announced in that very speech that the charge of England alone, with Russia's acquiescence, had compelled the Sultan's submission. Lord Granville's speech is therefore in perfect harmony with Mr. Gladstone's letter to the St. James's Hall meeting. Mr. Gladstone praised the Concert of Europe when it was eager to charge against the enemy, and was obstructed by England. He blames it when it stands still and does its best to prevent any of the troop from galloping to the rescue of men, women, and children from the hands of ravishers and murderers. Where is the inconsistency?

I wish Mr. Gladstone and the Duke of Argyll could find time to revise their opinion of the cause and origin of the Crimean War, and, if they see cause to change it, do Russia that justice which I believe to be her due. Such an *amende* would come gracefully from the two sole survivors of the Cabinet which made the war. From that war and the treaty that followed it dates all the mischief. Having got rid of Russian interference on behalf of the Christians by the intervention of France and England, the Porte determined to get rid of *all* interference by means of the weapon which Lord Palmerston and Lord Stratford de Redcliffe had so maladroitly placed in its hands. The Grand Vizir, Fuad Pasha, formulated this new doctrine as follows while the Treaty of Paris was still under discussion :—

> It is not right that the Powers, friends and allies of the Sublime Porte, after having so far supported the Sultan in the legitimate defence of his sovereign authority as to have taken up arms for his cause, and sent their soldiers to die side by side with his, fighting gloriously for the consolidation of the moral and material integrity of an empire *declared to be for ever necessary for the balance of power in Europe*—it is not right that these very Powers should, in the name of friendship, demand from the Sublime Porte the same concession to foreign influence which they considered, and still consider, so dangerous in the hands of Russia. . . . Justice, reason, and prudence, then, unite in rejecting a demand which it would be dangerous to introduce into the public law of Europe.*

In the important Russian work from which I have quoted Russia protests as follows against a most mischievous doctrine which her own Government has unfortunately preached, with tragical effect, however little intended, during the last year :—

> For our part, while desiring its [Ottoman Empire's] preservation, we had never concealed our repugnance whenever there had been any question of guaranteeing

* *Eastern Papers* (1856), pp. 10, 11.

its integrity. This repugnance was founded, first, on the distance at which lay the countries forming part of this empire, beyond the reach of all material action on our part; secondly, on the consequences which might result from the feeling of security which the Porte would find in such a guarantee. Sure to lose none of its possessions, whatever might happen, it might give full play to the abuses of its administration. The representations of Europe would no longer have had any weight with it; and cases might occur in which the Powers would feel called upon to intervene, as in Greece, to put an end to sanguinary struggles produced by the despair of exasperated populations.*

How wise, and how prophetic! It is the continued assurance of the security of the *status quo*, coupled with his belief in his ability to baffle any united action, that has emboldened the Sultan to go on from one excess to another, till at last he stained the streets of the ancient metropolis of Eastern Christendom with the innocent blood of 5,000 Christians.

Another evil that followed from the Crimean War was the destruction of a number of feudal chieftainships which enjoyed a sort of semi-independence, thus keeping the Porte in check and protecting the Christians from many of the extortions and some of the worst excesses of the officials of the Sultan. The effect of the Crimean War was to enable the Sultans to gather into their own hands the reins not only of all military power, but of the whole of the civil administration also.

* *Diplomatic Study of the Crimean War*, i. 201.

What use the Sultans have made of this concentration of all the resources of the empire into their own hands has been related by Murad Bey in the *Times* of October 13. In explaining the cause of the dissolution of Midhat's short-lived Parliament he gives the following picture of Abdul Hamid's methods :—

> The fact is that Abdul Hamid had ordered large presents of money to be taken out of the State Treasury and given to different favourites. The Parliamentary Financial Commission objected that the amounts did not figure in the Budget, and refused their sanction. 'What!' exclaimed the Sultan, 'What is this about the Budget and Finance Commission? Am I not to dispose of the State funds myself? I will not put up with that.' Shortly afterwards the Constitution, the Parliament, and all the commissions connected with it were abolished by the Iradé of the Sultan. He took back the little freedom he had given us, and our constitutional system lived but for a day.
>
> Abdul Hamid began his reign with peculiar ideas. His conviction was that the Turkish Empire was approaching its dissolution. It was, therefore, desirable before all to secure for himself and his household resources for the future—in other words, to procure as much money as possible. The accumulation of wealth became the *mot d'ordre* at Yildiz Kiosk. The *camarilla* and the high State parasites did not require to be told twice. All interests of the Empire, of the army, and of the Administration were subjected to the craving for gold at the Palace. Everything was done to conceal this *régime* from the outside world. Officers and Government *employés* were made to wait months for their salaries, the people and the army were allowed to starve, *and*

fabulous sums found their way abroad to purchase the public opinion of Europe. This money-grabbing system at the Court of Stambul constitutes one of the principal causes of the hopeless and desperate state of things which characterises the present Administration and the entire public life of Turkey.

There is one aspect of this question which has been strangely forgotten through all the controversy. One factor has been left out with which those who are responsible for the horrors of the last two years will yet have to reckon. We have heard of sovereigns, and statesmen, and diplomatists; and all the while there has been One sitting silent 'above the waterfloods,' and watching the massacre of innocents by myriads; the cries of outraged maidens; tortures prolonged, untold, unspeakable; and all for bearing the name of the crucified Redeemer of Mankind; cries for help tossed about on the unheeding winds; despair of help from God or man forcing many—though few among the noble army of martyrs—to renounce the Saviour and own the false prophet; and all the while Christendom, which could stop it all by one stern word to the tyrant, looking calmly on, and going about its business and pleasure with less emotion than would be excited by the histrionic representation of some melodrama. And statesmen who call themselves Christians tell us that the cries of a martyred nation, whose safety we have guaranteed, concerns us less than a strip of territory in the depths of Asia; that while it would be a crime to risk a great war in defence of the former, it might be a duty to risk it in defence of the latter. Is it for that end that God has entrusted to the inhabitants of these small islands an empire and resources such as the world never saw before? Is this the way we show our gratitude to Him who has said, 'By Me kings reign and princes decree justice,' and who 'doeth according to His will in the armies of heaven and among the inhabitants of the earth'? When did ever a nation perish, or even suffer damage, from following the law of righteousness and doing the will of God? No; the ruin of nations comes from within. 'Jeshurun waxed fat and kicked: thou art waxen fat, thou art grown gross, thou art covered with fatness; then he forsook God who made him, and lightly esteemed the Rock of his salvation.' Are there not ominous symptoms among us of the degeneration of which the great Leader and Prophet of Israel warned his people before they possessed the 'land flowing with milk and honey' towards which he was leading them? We have been reminded lately of the vast additions which we have made within the last twelve years to our already huge empire, and of the alleged impossibility of our redeeming our pledged honour on account of these acquisitions. If that be true, then indeed Jeshurun—' the righteous nation' —is 'waxen fat,' 'forsaken God who made him, and lightly esteemed the Rock of his salvation.' Change a few expressions in the following passage from Burke, and would his description of the men who went out to make rapid fortunes in India, and returned to corrupt society and the press and legislature, be very inapplicable to some of the transactions of the last few years?—

Their prey is lodged in England; and the cries of India are given to seas and winds, to be blown about in every breaking-up of the monsoon over a remote and unhearing ocean. In India all the vices operate by which sudden fortune is acquired. In England are often displayed by the same persons the virtues which dispense hereditary wealth. Arrived in England, the destroyers of the nobility and gentry of a whole kingdom will find the best company in this nation at a board of elegance and hospitality. Here the manufacturer and husbandman will bless the just and punctual hand that in India has torn the cloth from the loom, or wrested the scanty portion of rice and salt from the peasant of Bengal; or wrung from him the very opium in which he forgot his oppressions and his oppressor. They marry into your families; they enter into your senate; they ease your estates by loans; they raise their value by demand; they cherish and protect your relations which lie heavy on your patronage; and there is scarcely a house in the kingdom that does not feel some concern and interest, that makes all reform of our Eastern Government appear officious and disgusting; and on the whole a most discouraging attempt. In such an attempt you hurt those who are able to return kindness, or to resent injury. If you succeed, you save those who cannot so much as give you thanks.*

* Speech on Fox's India Bill: Works, iii. p. 678.

Has not a good deal of the elements of national weakness and decadence which Burke here describes been at the root of our statesmanship and diplomacy for some time past? Have not Stock Exchange gamblers and financial adventurers been exercising far too much influence on both our domestic and foreign policy? Have not ideas of duty and obligations of honour been largely supplanted by lust of gain and vulgar pursuit of wealth? The nation that is willing to barter its honour and duty for gold is already on the slope that leads to ruin, though the catastrophe may yet be a long way off. It has received a poison into its blood of which the end is death. The nearest parallel to the British Empire in extent and, on the whole, in beneficent influence, is the old Empire of pagan Rome; and to the eye of him who penetrates beneath the fair surface of the magnificent picture are there not visible not a few of the ominous symptoms which fired the indignation of Juvenal, and revealed to his prescient eye the inevitable Decline and Fall which a British historian afterwards described in detail? The Roman satirist complained bitterly that 'Syrian Orontes had flowed into the Tiber,' and flooded the city on the Seven Hills with the effeminate luxury and pollutions of the East; so that it had ceased to be any advantage to the Roman youth to have in infancy inhaled the air of the Aventine and been nourished on the Sabine olive.* He reverts to the theme in another place, and contrasts the old Roman virtue, when Rome was poor, with the degeneracy which the spoils of a conquered world had engendered. 'In days of yore their humble fortune preserved the Latin women chaste, and their lowly roofs were kept from the contamination of vice by toil, by short slumbers, by hands galled and hardened with the Tuscan fleece, and Hannibal close to the city, and their husbands standing guard on the Colline tower. Now we suffer the evils of long peace; luxury, more cruel than war, broods over us and avenges a conquered world. No crime is wanting, or deed of lust, from the time that Roman poverty came to an end. Henceforth the Sybaris flowed to these hills, and Rhodes, and Miletus, and garlanded, saucy, drunken Tarentum.'†

Lord Lansdowne has lately assured us that if we are bent on succouring the Armenians we must make up our minds to have the conscription established among us, and Lord Salisbury has repeated the warning in his recent Guildhall speech. That may be a good reason for eschewing all foreign alliances and entanglements in

---

* Jam pridem Syrus in Tiberim defluxit Orontes,
Et linguam, et mores, et cum tibicine chordas
Obliquas, nec non gentilia tympana secum
Vexit, et ad circum jussas prostare puellas:
Ite quibus grata est picta lupa barbara mitra!
Rusticus ille tuus sumit trechedipna, Quirine,
Et ceremático fert niceteria collo!—*Juv.*, Sat. iii. 62-67.
† *Ibid.*, Sat. vi. 287-298.

future; and, for my part, I do not see what more we have to do with the politics of Continental Powers than America has. Let us have a navy strong enough to guard our interests—using that expression as embracing moral not less than material considerations—and let us cultivate the goodwill and friendship of our neighbours, and there seems to be no likelihood of our being obliged ever again to land troops on the Continent of Europe. The less we have to do with the quarrels of Continental Powers, the more likely are they not only to respect, but even to fear us. But we are unfortunately bound by the strongest obligations of honour to do our best for the Armenians. It is we who, above all others, have endamaged the Armenians, and it is we, consequently, who are especially bound to use our best endeavours to indemnify them for the wrong which we have done them.

But surely that can be done without need of the conscription. I am conscious of my presumption in criticising the opinions of such eminent men as I have had occasion to notice in these pages. I have criticised Lord Rosebery, and now I am going to venture on a criticism of a small portion of the Prime Minister's Guildhall speech. 'If,' he says, ' you desire, by force and against the will of the existing Government [of Turkey], to amend the government, and to protect the industry and security of the inhabitants of Turkish provinces, you can only do it by military occupation. Military occupation is a very large undertaking. It requires a great military force. No fleet in the world can do it. No fleet in the world can go upon the mountains of Taurus to protect the Armenians.' This argument reminds me of the boxer in Thucydides who, instead of parrying his opponent's blows and planting his own where they would be most effective, kept clapping his hands on every spot which his adversary hit. The troubles in Armenia have their root and cause in Yildiz Kiosk, and no great military force, or any military force at all, is needed to reach the author of the mischief. Any fleet in the world can do it, even the smallest; for it may be done even without passing the Dardanelles. There is no Government in the world so vulnerable by sea as the Ottoman Porte. It is exposed in scores of vital places to a naval occupation without any power of resistance, for the Sultan has no navy. But, indeed, no occupation, naval or military, would be necessary if the Powers, or even one of them, without opposition from the rest, would only formulate their demand, and bid the Sultan accept it in a few days on pain of having some portion of his territory occupied by a naval force. All that is needed is to convince the Sultan that the Powers are in earnest. Let him believe that, and his submission will follow without more ado. Let the useless reforms, about which such fuss was made eighteen months ago, and of which the basis has been purposely destroyed by the Sultan's massacres, be swept away, and let the Sultan be compelled to appoint European officials, in concert with the Powers, and irremovable without their consent, with a mixed gendarmerie of Christians and Muslims under their orders, and both Anatolia and Macedonia can be pacified without any fresh laws. The laws promulgated by Sultan Medjid in the Hatt-i-Humaioun of 1856 will suffice for all purposes, provided they are executed; and there will be no difficulty in executing them through the agency of officials not dependent for their orders, or pay, or tenure of office, on the Sultan. I think I have already proved sufficiently that there need be no serious apprehension of any opposition on the part of the local populations. They would all, Muslims and Christians alike, only be too glad to welcome an arrangement which, while delivering them from the rapacity and cruelty of the Sultan's rule, would guarantee the secure enjoyment of their religion and property. 'The fish rots from the head'—to quote again the Turkish proverb. The Sultan and his tribe of corrupt officials are the source of all the evil. Let him reign, but not rule, and the territorial framework of his empire may last till something better is ready to take its place. The difficulties of the question are hugely exaggerated by the mutual jealousies and irrational fears of the Powers. The Sultan would,

x

of course, be certain to endeavour to checkmate the Powers by stirring up local fanaticism. But that could easily be prevented by a notification from the Powers that they would hold him personally responsible.

Lord Salisbury has again warned the Sultan of the Providential Nemesis that ever dogs the footsteps of crime. But the Sultan is not likely to be much alarmed by the warning, since it is probable that he is not conscious of any sin in what he has done. But, in any case, what we as Christians have to consider is that the rule of Providence is to work through the means which He has Himself appointed for fulfilling His purposes. The rule is universal. It prevails in man's relations with the physical not less than with the moral world. The earth will not yield her fruits, or precious gems, or the warmth and light and motive powers that lie hidden and inert within her, unless the human will cooperates with the Divine to organise her latent forces and constrain her to give up her precious gifts. Nor will Providence develop our moral or intellectual faculties, or cure the ills that afflict our mortal frame, except through the intervention of our fellow-men. Why, then, should we lay upon Providence the responsibility of political and social evils which He has given us the means to cure? It is not irreverent to say that God condescends to need our help, for we have His own warrant for the statement.

'Curse ye Meroz,' said the Angel of the Lord, 'curse ye bitterly the inhabitants thereof, because they came not to the help of the Lord, to the help of the Lord against the mighty.' Where is Meroz now? The traveller and the archæologist will seek its site in vain. The curse of a neglected opportunity blighted it, and it has perished, without leaving 'a rack behind' to mark where it had been.

A fine story is told of Mohammed before prosperity and irresponsible power had corroded the finer elements of his character. While he was hiding with Abu Bakr in the cave of Mount Thaur, Abu Bakr expressed his fear that their pursuers would discover their hiding-place and make an end of the two fugitives. 'Nay,' said Mohammed, 'we are three, for God is with us.' Is there not something of an atheistic element in all this panic about 'separate action'? The true strength of a nation, after all, does not come from drilled battalions and lines of battleships, but from its faith in God and from loyal obedience to His will. If we could look below the surface of things, and trace effects to their causes, we should probably be able to put our finger on the critical decision which fixes the destiny alike of nations and of individuals, consolidating previous betrayals of duty into a choice which now has become final and irretrievable, although the individual or the nation may still go on for a time with no change visible to the naked eye.

It was not when he uttered his bitter but unavailing cry that the blessing departed from Esau, but when, years before, he profanely sold his birthright. Nations, too, may sell their birthright for a mess of pottage, and afterwards, like Esau, 'find no place of repentance,' though they seek it 'carefully with tears.'

Once to every man and nation comes the moment to decide,
In the strife of truth with falsehood, for the good or evil side:
Some great cause, God's new Messiah, offering each the bloom or blight,
Parts the goats upon the left hand, and the sheep upon the right;
And the choice goes by for ever 'twixt that darkness and that light.

A Classified Catalogue

OF WORKS IN

GENERAL LITERATURE

PUBLISHED BY

LONGMANS, GREEN, & CO.

39 PATERNOSTER ROW, LONDON, E.C.

91 AND 93 FIFTH AVENUE, NEW YORK, AND 32 HORNBY ROAD, BOMBAY.

CONTENTS.

	PAGE		PAGE
BADMINTON LIBRARY (THE)	10	MANUALS OF CATHOLIC PHILOSOPHY	16
BIOGRAPHY, PERSONAL MEMOIRS, &c.	7	MENTAL, MORAL, AND POLITICAL PHILOSOPHY	14
CHILDREN'S BOOKS	26	MISCELLANEOUS AND CRITICAL WORKS	29
CLASSICAL LITERATURE TRANSLATIONS, ETC.	18	MISCELLANEOUS THEOLOGICAL WORKS	31
COOKERY, DOMESTIC MANAGEMENT, &c.	28	POETRY AND THE DRAMA	18
EVOLUTION, ANTHROPOLOGY, &c.	17	POLITICAL ECONOMY AND ECONOMICS	16
FICTION, HUMOUR, &c.	21	POPULAR SCIENCE	24
FUR AND FEATHER SERIES	12	SILVER LIBRARY (THE)	27
HISTORY, POLITICS, POLITY, POLITICAL MEMOIRS, &c.	3	SPORT AND PASTIME	10
LANGUAGE, HISTORY AND SCIENCE OF	16	TRAVEL AND ADVENTURE, THE COLONIES, &c.	8
LONGMANS' SERIES OF BOOKS FOR GIRLS	26	VETERINARY MEDICINE, &c.	9
		WORKS OF REFERENCE	25

INDEX OF AUTHORS AND EDITORS.

	Page		Page		Page		Page
Abbott (Evelyn)	3, 18	Babington (W. D.)	17	Blackwell (Elizabeth)	7	Carmichael (J.)	19
—— (T. K.)	14, 15	Bacon	7, 14	Boase (Rev. C. W.)	4	Chesney (Sir G.)	3
—— (E. A.)	14	Bagehot (W.)	7, 16, 29	Boedder (B.)	16	Chisholm (G. G.)	25
Acland (A. H. D.)	3	Bagwell (R.)	3	Bolland (W. E.)	14	Cholmondeley-Pennell	
Acton (Eliza)	28	Bain (Alexander)	14	Bosanquet (B.)	14	(H.)	11
Acworth (H. A.)	18	Baker (James)	21	Boyd (Rev. A. K. H.)	7, 29, 31	Christie (Nimmo)	19
Æschylus	18	Baker (Sir S. W.)	8	Brassey (Lady)	8	Cicero	18
Ainger (A. C.)	12	Balfour (A. J.)	11, 31	—— (Lord)	3, 8, 12, 16	Clarke (Rev. R. F.)	16
Albemarle (Earl of)	10	Ball (J. T.)	3	Bray (C. and Mrs.)	14	Clodd (Edward)	17
Alden (W. L.)	21	Baring-Gould (Rev. S.)	27, 29	Bright (J. F.)	3	Clutterbuck (W. J.)	9
Allen (Grant)	24			Broadfoot (Major W.)	10	Cochrane (A.)	19
Allingham (W.)	18, 29	Barnett (Rev. S. A. & Mrs.)	16	Brögger (W. C.)	7	Comyn (L. N.)	26
Anstey (F.)	21			Brown (J. Moray)	11	Conington (John)	18
Aristophanes	18	Baynes (T. S.)	29	Browning (H. Ellen)	8	Conybeare (Rev. W. J.)	
Aristotle	14	Beaconsfield (Earl of)	21	Buck (H. A.)	12	& Howson (Dean)	27
Armstrong (E.)	3	Beaufort (Duke of)	10, 11	Buckle (H. T.)	3	Coventry (A.)	11
—— (G. F. Savage)	19	Becker (Prof.)	18	Bull (T.)	28	Cox (Harding)	10
—— (E. J.)	7, 19, 29	Beesly (A. H.)	19	Burke (U. R.)	3	Crake (Rev. A. D.)	26
Arnold (Sir Edwin)	8, 19	Bell (Mrs. Hugh)	19	Burrows (Montagu)	4	Creighton (Bishop)	3, 4
—— (Dr. T.)	3	Bent (J. Theodore)	8	Butler (E. A.)	24	Cuningham (G. C.)	3
Ashley (W. J.)	16	Besant (Sir Walter)	3	—— (Samuel)	29	Curzon (Hon. G. N.)	3
Astor (J. J.)	21	Bickerdyke (J.)	11, 13			Cutts (Rev. E. L.)	4
Atelier du Lys (Author of)	26	Bicknell (A. C.)	8	Cameron of Lochiel	12		
		Bird (R.)	31	Cannan (E.)	17	Davidson (W. L.)	14, 16

INDEX OF AUTHORS AND EDITORS—continued.

Name	Page
Davies (J. F.)	18
De la Saussaye (C.)	32
Deland (Mrs.)	26
Dent (C. T.)	11
Deploige	17
De Salis (Mrs.)	28, 29
De Tocqueville (A.)	3
Devas (C. S.)	16
Dickinson (G. L.)	3
Dougall (L.)	21
Dowell (S.)	16
Doyle (A. Conan)	6
Dufferin (Marquis of)	12
Dunbar (Mary F.)	20
Ebrington (Lord)	12
Ellis (J. H.)	13
Ewald (H.)	3
Falkener (E.)	13
Farnell (G. S.)	18
Farrar (Dean)	16, 21
Fitzwygram (Sir F.)	9
Florian	19
Follett (M. P.)	4
Ford (H.)	13
Fowler (Edith H.)	21
Francis (Francis)	13
Freeman (Edward A.)	4
Froude (James A.)	4, 7, 8, 21
Furneaux (W.)	24
Galton (W. F.)	17
Gardiner (Samuel R.)	4
Gerard (D.)	26
Gibbons (J. S.)	11, 12
Gibson (Hon. H.)	13
Gill (H. J.)	22
Gleig (Rev. G. R.)	8
Goethe	19
Graham (P. A.)	13
—— (G. F.)	16
Grant (Sir A.)	14
Granville (Countess)	7
Graves (R. P.)	7
Green (T. Hill)	14
Greville (C. C. F.)	4
Grey (Maria)	26
Grose (T. H.)	14
Grove (F. C.)	11
—— (Mrs. Lilly)	10
Gurney (Rev. A.)	19
Gwilt (J.)	30
Haggard (H. Rider)	21
Hake (O.)	12
Halliwell-Phillipps (J.)	7
Hamlin (A. D. F.)	30
Hart (Albert B.)	4
Harte (Bret)	22
Hartwig (G.)	24
Hassall (A.)	6
Haweis (Rev. H. R.)	7, 30
Hayward (Jane M.)	24
Hearn (W. E.)	4
Heathcote (J. M. and C. G.)	12
Helmholtz (Hermann von)	24
Henry (W.)	12
Herbert (Col. Kenney)	12
Hewins (W. A. S.)	17
Hillier (G. Lacy)	10
Hodgson (Shadworth H.)	14
Holroyd (Maria J.)	7
Hope (Anthony)	22
Hornung (E. W.)	22
Howell (G.)	16
Howitt (W.)	9
Hudson (W. H.)	24
Hueffer (F. M.)	7
Hume (David)	14
Hunt (Rev. W.)	4
Hutchinson (Horace G.)	11
Ingelow (Jean)	19, 26
Jefferies (Richard)	30
Jones (H. Bence)	25
Johnson (J. & J. H.)	30
Jowett (Dr. B.)	17
Joyce (P. W.)	4
Justinian	14
Kalisch (M. M.)	32
Kant (I.)	14, 15
Kaye (Sir J. W.)	4
Kerr (Rev. J.)	12
Killick (Rev. A. H.)	15
Kitchin (Dr. G. W.)	4
Knight (E. F.)	5, 9, 12
Köstlin (J.)	7
Ladd (G. T.)	15
Lang (Andrew)	5, 10, 11, 13, 14, 17, 18, 19, 20, 22, 26, 30
Lascelles (Hon. G.)	10, 12
Laurie (S. S.)	5
Leaf (Walter)	31
Lear (H. L. Sidney)	29
Lecky (W. E. H.)	5, 19
Lees (J. A.)	9
Lewes (G. H.)	15
Lindley (J.)	25
Lindsay (Lady)	19
Lodge (H. C.)	4
Loftie (Rev. W. J.)	4
Longman (C. J.)	10, 13, 30
—— (F. W.)	13
—— (G. H.)	11, 12
Lubbock (Sir John)	17
Lucan	18
Lyall (Edna)	22
Lyttelton (Hon. R. H.)	10
Lytton (Earl of)	19
MacArthur (Miss E. A.)	17
Macaulay (Lord)	5, 20
Macdonald (George)	20, 32
Macfarren (Sir G. A.)	30
Magruder (Julia)	22
Mackail (J. W.)	18
Mackinnon (J.)	5
Macleod (H. D.)	17
Macpherson (Rev. H. A.)	12
Maher (M.)	16
Malleson (Col. G. B.)	4
Mandello (J.)	17
Marbot (Baron de)	7
Marshman (J. C.)	7
Martineau (Dr. James)	32
Maskelyne (J. N.)	13
Matthews (Brander)	22
Maunder (S.)	25
Max Müller (F.)	15, 16, 30, 32
May (Sir T. Erskine)	5
Meade (L. T.)	26
Melville (G. J. Whyte)	22
Merivale (Dean)	5
Merriman (H. S.)	22
Mill (James)	15
—— (John Stuart)	15, 17
Milner (G.)	30
Miss Molly (Author of)	26
Molesworth (Mrs.)	26
Montague (F. C.)	6
Moore (T.)	25
—— (Rev. Ed.)	14
Morris (W.)	20, 22, 31
—— (Mowbray)	11
Mosso (A.)	15
Munk (W.)	7
Murdoch (W. G. Burn)	9
Murray (R. F.)	20
Nansen (F.)	9
Nesbit (E.)	20
Newman (Cardinal)	22
O'Brien (W.)	6
Oliphant (Mrs.)	22
Onslow (Earl of)	12
Orchard (T. N.)	31
Osbourne (L.)	23
Palmer (A. H.)	8
Park (W.)	13
Parr (Mrs. Louisa)	26
Payne-Gallwey (Sir R.)	11, 13
Peary (Mrs. Josephine)	9
Peek (H.)	20
Pembroke (Earl of)	12
Perring (Sir P.)	6
Phillips (M.)	32
Phillipps-Wolley (C.)	10, 22
Piatt (S. & J. J.)	20
Pleydell-Bouverie (E. O.)	12
Pole (W.)	13
Pollock (W. H.)	11
Poole (W. H. and Mrs.)	29
Poore (G. V.)	31
Potter (J.)	16
Prevost (C.)	11
Pritchett (R. T.)	12
Proctor (R. A.)	13, 24, 31
Quill (A. W.)	18
Quillinan (Mrs.)	9
Quintana (A.)	22
Raine (Rev. James)	4
Ransome (Cyril)	3
Rhoades (J.)	18, 20
Rhoscomyl (O.)	23
Rich (A.)	18
Richardson (Sir B. W.)	31
—— (C.)	12
Richman (I. B.)	6
Rickaby (John)	16
—— (Joseph)	16
Ridley (Annie E.)	7
Ridley (E.)	18
Riley (J. W.)	20
Robertson (A.)	23
Roget (Peter M.)	16, 25
Rokeby (C.)	23
Rolfsen (N.)	7
Romanes (G. J.)	15, 17, 32
—— (Mrs.)	7
Ronalds (A.)	13
Roosevelt (T.)	4
Rossetti (M. F.)	31
Saintsbury (G.)	12
Sandars (T. C.)	14
Scott-Montagu (Hon. J.)	12
Seebohm (F.)	6, 7
Selous (F. C.)	10
Selss (A. M.)	19
Sewell (Elizabeth M.)	23
Shakespeare	20
Shand (A. I.)	12
Sharpe (R. R.)	6
Shearman (M.)	10
Sheppard (Rev. Edgar)	6
Sinclair (A.)	12
Smith (R. Bosworth)	6
—— (W. P. Haskett)	9
Solovyoff (V. S.)	31
Sophocles	18
Soulsby (Lucy H.)	26
Spedding (J.)	7, 14
Stanley (Bishop)	24
Steel (A. G.)	10
Steel (J. H.)	9
Stephen (Sir James)	7
—— (Leslie)	9
Stephens (H. Morse)	6
—— (W. W.)	8
Stevens (R. W.)	31
Stevenson (R. L.)	23, 26
Stock (St. George)	15
'Stonehenge'	9
Storr (F.)	14
Stuart-Wortley (A. J.)	12
Stubbs (J. W.)	6
Sturdy (E. T.)	30
Sturgis (J.)	20
Suffolk & Berkshire (Earl of)	11
Sullivan (Sir E.)	12
Sully (James)	15
Sutherland (A. and G.)	6
Suttner (B. von)	23
Swinburne (A. J.)	15
Symes (J. E.)	17
Tacitus	18
Taylor (Meadows)	6
Tebbutt (C. G.)	12
Thornhill (W. J.)	18
Todd (A.)	6
Toynbee (A.)	17
Trevelyan (Sir G. O.)	7
—— (C. P.)	17
Trollope (Anthony)	23
Tyndall (J.)	9
Tyrrell (R. Y.)	18
Upton (F. K. and Bertha)	26
Verney (Frances P. and Margaret M.)	8
Vincent (J. E.)	6
Virgil	18
Vivekananda (Swami)	32
Wakeman (H. O.)	6
Walford (Mrs.)	23
Walker (Jane H.)	6
Walpole (Spencer)	6
Walrond (Col. H.)	10
Walsingham (Lord)	11
Walter (J.)	7
Watson (A. E. T.)	11, 13
Waylen (H. S. H.)	30
Webb (Mr. and Mrs. Sidney)	17
—— (T. E.)	19
Weber (A.)	15
Weir (Capt. R.)	11
West (B. B.)	23, 31
Weyman (Stanley)	23
Whately (Archbishop)	14, 15
—— (Jane E.)	16
Whishaw (F. J.)	9, 23
Whitelaw (R.)	18
Wilcocks (J. C.)	13
Wilkins (G.)	18
Willich (C. M.)	25
Witham (T. M.)	12
Wolff (H. W.)	6
Wood (Rev. J. G.)	25
Woodgate (W. B.)	10
Wood-Martin (W. G.)	6
Wordsworth (Eliz.)	26
Wylie (J. H.)	6
Youatt (W.)	9
Zeller (E.)	15

History, Politics, Polity, Political Memoirs, &c.

Abbott.—A HISTORY OF GREECE. By EVELYN ABBOTT, M.A., LL.D.
Part I.—From the Earliest Times to the Ionian Revolt. Crown 8vo., 10s. 6d.
Part II.—500-445 B.O. Crown 8vo., 10s. 6d.

Acland and Ransome.—A HANDBOOK IN OUTLINE OF THE POLITICAL HISTORY OF ENGLAND TO 1894. Chronologically Arranged. By A. H. DYKE ACLAND, M.P., and CYRIL RANSOME, M.A. Crown 8vo., 6s.

ANNUAL REGISTER (THE). A Review of Public Events at Home and Abroad, for the year 1895. 8vo., 18s.

Volumes of the ANNUAL REGISTER for the years 1863-1894 can still be had. 18s. each.

Armstrong.—ELIZABETH FARNESE; The Termagant of Spain. By EDWARD ARMSTRONG, M.A. 8vo., 16s.

Arnold (THOMAS, D.D.), formerly Head Master of Rugby School.

INTRODUCTORY LECTURES ON MODERN HISTORY. 8vo., 7s. 6d.

MISCELLANEOUS WORKS. 8vo., 7s. 6d.

Bagwell.—IRELAND UNDER THE TUDORS. By RICHARD BAGWELL, LL.D. (3 vols.) Vols. I. and II. From the first invasion of the Northmen to the year 1578. 8vo., 32s. Vol. III. 1578-1603. 8vo., 18s.

Ball.—HISTORICAL REVIEW OF THE LEGISLATIVE SYSTEMS OPERATIVE IN IRELAND, from the Invasion of Henry the Second to the Union (1172-1800). By the Rt. Hon. J. T. BALL. 8vo., 6s.

Besant.—THE HISTORY OF LONDON. By Sir WALTER BESANT. With 74 Illustrations. Crown 8vo., 1s. 9d. Or bound as a School Prize Book, 2s. 6d.

Brassey (LORD).—PAPERS AND ADDRESSES.

NAVAL AND MARITIME. 1872-1893. 2 vols. Crown 8vo., 10s.

MERCANTILE MARINE AND NAVIGATION, from 1871-1894. Crown 8vo., 5s.

IMPERIAL FEDERATION AND COLONISATION FROM 1880 to 1894. Cr. 8vo., 5s.

POLITICAL AND MISCELLANEOUS. 1861-1894. Crown 8vo 5s.

Bright.—A HISTORY OF ENGLAND. By the Rev. J. FRANCK BRIGHT, D.D.
Period I. MEDIÆVAL MONARCHY: A.D. 449 to 1485. Crown 8vo., 4s. 6d.
Period II. PERSONAL MONARCHY. 1485 to 1688. Crown 8vo., 5s.
Period III. CONSTITUTIONAL MONARCHY. 1689 to 1837. Crown 8vo., 7s. 6d.
Period IV. THE GROWTH OF DEMOCRACY. 1837 to 1880 Crown 8vo., 6s.

Buckle.—HISTORY OF CIVILISATION IN ENGLAND AND FRANCE, SPAIN AND SCOTLAND. By HENRY THOMAS BUCKLE. 3 vols. Crown 8vo., 24s.

Burke.—A HISTORY OF SPAIN from the Earliest Times to the Death of Ferdinand the Catholic. By ULICK RALPH BURKE, M.A. 2 vols. 8vo., 32s.

Chesney.—INDIAN POLITY: a View of the System of Administration in India. By General Sir GEORGE CHESNEY, K.C.B., With Map showing all the Administrative Divisions of British India. 8vo., 21s.

Creighton.—HISTORY OF THE PAPACY DURING THE REFORMATION. By MANDELL CREIGHTON, D.D., LL.D., Vols. I. and II., 1378-1464, 32s. Vols. III. and IV., 1464-1518, 24s. Vol. V., 1517-1527, 8vo., 15s.

Cuningham. — A SCHEME FOR IMPERIAL FEDERATION: a Senate for the Empire. By GRANVILLE C. CUNINGHAM, of Montreal, Canada. Crown 8vo., 3s. 6d.

Curzon.—PERSIA AND THE PERSIAN QUESTION. By the Right Hon. GEORGE N. CURZON, M.P. With 9 Maps, 96 Illustrations, Appendices, and an Index. 2 vols. 8vo., 42s.

De Tocqueville.—DEMOCRACY IN AMERICA. By ALEXIS DE TOCQUEVILLE. 2 vols. Crown 8vo., 16s.

Dickinson.—THE DEVELOPMENT OF PARLIAMENT DURING THE NINETEENTH CENTURY. By G. LOWES DICKINSON, M.A. 8vo., 7s. 6d.

Ewald.—THE HISTORY OF ISRAEL. By HEINRICH EWALD. 8 vols., 8vo., Vols. I. and II., 24s. Vols. III. and IV., 21s. Vol. V., 18s. Vol. VI., 16s. Vol. VII., 21s. Vol. VIII., 18s.

History, Politics, Polity, Political Memoirs, &c.—*continued*.

Follett.—THE SPEAKER OF THE HOUSE OF REPRESENTATIVES. By M. P. FOLLETT. With an Introduction by ALBERT BUSHNELL HART, Ph.D., of Harvard University. Crown 8vo, 6s.

Froude (JAMES A.).
THE HISTORY OF ENGLAND, from the Fall of Wolsey to the Defeat of the Spanish Armada.
Popular Edition. 12 vols. Crown 8vo. 3s. 6d. each.
'*Silver Library*' *Edition*. 12 vols. Crown 8vo., 3s. 6d. each.

THE DIVORCE OF CATHERINE OF ARAGON. Crown 8vo., 6s.

THE SPANISH STORY OF THE ARMADA, and other Essays. Cr. 8vo., 3s. 6d.

THE ENGLISH IN IRELAND IN THE EIGHTEENTH CENTURY.
Cabinet Edition. 3 vols. Cr. 8vo., 18s.
'*Silver Library*' *Edition*. 3 vols. Cr. 8vo., 10s. 6d.

ENGLISH SEAMEN IN THE SIXTEENTH CENTURY. Cr. 8vo., 6s.

THE COUNCIL OF TRENT. Crown 8vo., 6s.

SHORT STUDIES ON GREAT SUBJECTS. 4 vols. Cr. 8vo., 3s. 6d. each.

CÆSAR: a Sketch. Cr. 8vo, 3s. 6d.

Gardiner (SAMUEL RAWSON, D.C.L., LL.D.).
HISTORY OF ENGLAND, from the Accession of James I. to the Outbreak of the Civil War, 1603-1642. 10 vols. Crown 8vo., 6s. each.

A HISTORY OF THE GREAT CIVIL WAR, 1642-1649. 4 vols. Cr. 8vo., 6s. ea.

A HISTORY OF THE COMMONWEALTH AND THE PROTECTORATE. 1649-1660. Vol. I. 1649-1651. With 14 Maps. 8vo., 21s.

THE STUDENT'S HISTORY OF ENGLAND. With 378 Illustrations. Crown 8vo., 12s.
Also in Three Volumes, price 4s. each.
Vol. I. B.C. 55—A.D. 1509. 173 Illustrations.
Vol. II. 1509-1689. 96 Illustrations.
Vol. III. 1689-1885. 109 Illustrations.

Greville.—A JOURNAL OF THE REIGNS OF KING GEORGE IV., KING WILLIAM IV., AND QUEEN VICTORIA. By CHARLES C. F. GREVILLE, formerly Clerk of the Council.
Cabinet Edition. 8 vols. Crown 8vo., 6s. each.
'*Silver Library*' *Edition*. 8 vols. Crown 8vo., 3s 6d. each.

Hearn.—THE GOVERNMENT OF ENGLAND: its Structure and its Development. By W. EDWARD HEARN. 8vo., 16s.

Historic Towns.—Edited by E. A. FREEMAN, D.C.L., and Rev. WILLIAM HUNT, M.A. With Maps and Plans. Crown 8vo., 3s. 6d. each.

Bristol. By Rev. W. Hunt.	Oxford. By Rev. C. W. Boase.
Carlisle. By Mandell Creighton, D.D., Bishop of Peterborough.	Winchester. By G. W. Kitchin, D.D.
Cinque Ports. By Montague Burrows.	York. By Rev. James Raine.
Colchester. By Rev. E. L. Cutts.	New York. By Theodore Roosevelt.
Exeter. By E. A. Freeman.	
London. By Rev. W. J. Loftie.	Boston (U.S.) By Henry Cabot Lodge.

Joyce.—A SHORT HISTORY OF IRELAND, from the Earliest Times to 1608. By P. W. JOYCE, LL.D. Crown 8vo., 10s. 6d.

Kaye (SIR JOHN W.) **and Malleson** (COLONEL G. B.).
HISTORY OF THE SEPOY WAR IN INDIA, 1857-1858. By Sir JOHN W. KAYE, K.C.S.I., F.R.S. 3 vols. 8vo. Vol. I., 18s.; Vol. II., 20s.; Vol. III., 20s.

HISTORY OF THE INDIAN MUTINY, 1857-1858. Commencing from the close of the Second Volume of Sir John W. Kaye's "History of the Sepoy War". By Colonel G. B. MALLESON, C.S.I. 3 vols. 8vo. Vol. I. with Map, 20s.; Vol. II. with 4 Maps and Plans, 20s.; Vol. III. with 4 Maps, 20s.

ANALYTICAL INDEX TO SIR JOHN W. KAYE'S "HISTORY OF THE SEPOY WAR" AND COL. G. B. MALLESON'S "HISTORY OF THE INDIAN MUTINY". (Combined in One Volume.) By FREDERIC PINCOTT, Member of the Royal Asiatic Society. 8vo, 10s. 6d.

KAYE AND MALLESON'S 'HISTORY OF THE INDIAN MUTINY, 1857-1858'. (Being a Cabinet Edition of the above Works.) Edited by Colonel G. B. MALLESON. With Analytical Index by FREDERIC PINCOTT, and Maps and Plans. 6 vols. Crown 8vo., 6s. each.

History, Politics, Polity, Political Memoirs, &c.—*continued.*

Knight.—*Madagascar in War Time: The Experiences of 'The Times' Special Correspondent with the Hovas during the French Invasion of 1895.* By E. F. Knight. With 16 Illustrations and a Map. 8vo., 12s. 6d.

Lang (Andrew).
Pickle the Spy. Disclosing the Treasons of A—— M——, Esq., of G——; also of James Mohr Macgregor, and Macallester, an Irishman. With the Secret Amours and Misfortunes of H.R.H. Charles P—— of W——. Drawn from the Cabinets of the late Elector of Hanover, and of their French and Prussian Majesties. With Portraits and Illustrations. 8vo., 18s. (and for Crown 8vo. Edition also.
St. Andrews. With 8 Plates and 24 Illustrations in the Text by T. Hodge. 8vo., 15s. net.

Laurie. — *Historical Survey of Pre-Christian Education.* By S. S. Laurie, A.M., LL.D. Crown 8vo., 12s.

Lecky (William Edward Hartpole).
History of England in the Eighteenth Century.
Library Edition. 8 vols. 8vo., £7 4s.
Cabinet Edition. England. 7 vols. Crown 8vo., 6s. each. Ireland. 5 vols. Crown 8vo., 6s. each.
History of European Morals from Augustus to Charlemagne. 2 vols. Crown 8vo., 16s.
History of the Rise and Influence of the Spirit of Rationalism in Europe. 2 vols. Crown 8vo., 16s.
Democracy and Liberty. 2 vols. 8vo., 36s.
The Empire: its value and its Growth. An Inaugural Address delivered at the Imperial Institute, November 20, 1893. Cr. 8vo., 1s. 6d.

Macaulay (Lord).
Complete Works.
Cabinet Edition. 16 vols. Post 8vo., £4 16s.
Library Edition. 8 vols. 8vo., £5 5s.
'Edinburgh' Edition. 8 vols. 8vo., 6s. each.
History of England from the Accession of James the Second.
Popular Edition. 2 vols. Cr. 8vo., 5s.
Student's Edition. 2 vols. Cr. 8vo., 12s.
People's Edition. 4 vols. Cr. 8vo., 16s.
Cabinet Edition. 8 vols. Post 8vo., 48s.
Library Edition. 5 vols. 8vo., £4.

Macaulay (Lord)—*continued.*
Critical and Historical Essays, with Lays of Ancient Rome, in 1 volume.
Popular Edition. Crown 8vo., 2s. 6d.
Authorised Edition. Crown 8vo., 2s. 6d., or 3s. 6d., gilt edges.
Silver Library Edition. Cr. 8vo., 3s. 6d.
Critical and Historical Essays.
Student's Edition. 1 vol. Cr. 8vo., 6s.
People's Edition. 2 vols. Cr. 8vo., 8s.
Trevelyan Edition. 2 vols. Cr. 8vo., 9s.
Cabinet Edition. 4 vols. Post 8vo., 24s.
Library Edition. 3 vols. 8vo., 36s.
Essays which may be had separately price 6d. each sewed, 1s. each cloth.

Addison and Walpole.	Ranke and Gladstone.
Croker's Boswell's Johnson.	Milton and Machiavelli.
Hallam's Constitutional History.	Lord Byron.
Warren Hastings.	Lord Clive.
The Earl of Chatham (Two Essays).	Lord Byron, and The Comic Dramatists of the Restoration.
Frederick the Great.	

Miscellaneous Writings.
People's Edition. 1 vol. Cr. 8vo., 4s. 6d.
Library Edition. 2 vols. 8vo., 21s.
Miscellaneous Writings and Speeches.
Popular Edition. Crown 8vo., 2s. 6d.
Cabinet Edition. Including Indian Penal Code, Lays of Ancient Rome, and Miscellaneous Poems. 4 vols. Post 8vo., 24s.
Selections from the Writings of Lord Macaulay. Edited, with Occasional Notes, by the Right Hon. Sir G. O. Trevelyan, Bart. Crown 8vo., 6s.

Mackinnon.—*The Union of England and Scotland: a Study of International History.* By James Mackinnon, Ph.D. Examiner in History to the University of Edinburgh. 8vo., 16s.

May.—*The Constitutional History of England* since the Accession of George III. 1760-1870. By Sir Thomas Erskine May, K.C.B. (Lord Farnborough). 3 vols. Cr. 8vo., 18s.

Merivale (the late Dean).
History of the Romans under the Empire. 8 vols. Crown 8vo., 3s. 6d. each.
The Fall of the Roman Republic: a Short History of the Last Century of the Commonwealth. 12mo., 7s. 6d.

History, Politics, Polity, Political Memoirs, &c.—*continued.*

Montague.—THE ELEMENTS OF ENGLISH CONSTITUTIONAL HISTORY. By F. C. MONTAGUE, M.A. Crown 8vo., 3s. 6d.

O'Brien.—IRISH IDEAS. REPRINTED ADDRESSES. By WILLIAM O'BRIEN. Cr. 8vo. 2s. 6d.

Richman.—APPENZELL: PURE DEMOCRACY AND PASTORAL LIFE IN INNER-RHODEN. A Swiss Study. By IRVING B. RICHMAN, Consul-General of the United States to Switzerland. With Maps. Crown 8vo., 5s.

Seebohm (FREDERIC).

THE ENGLISH VILLAGE COMMUNITY Examined in its Relations to the Manorial and Tribal Systems, &c. With 13 Maps and Plates. 8vo., 16s.

THE TRIBAL SYSTEM IN WALES: Being Part of an Inquiry into the Structure and Methods of Tribal Society. With 3 Maps. 8vo., 12s.

Sharpe.—LONDON AND THE KINGDOM: a History derived mainly from the Archives at Guildhall in the custody of the Corporation of the City of London. By REGINALD R. SHARPE, D.C.L., Records Clerk in the Office of the Town Clerk of the City of London. 3 vols. 8vo. 10s. 6d. each.

Sheppard.—MEMORIALS OF ST. JAMES'S PALACE. By the Rev. EDGAR SHEPPARD, M.A., Sub-Dean of H.M. Chapels Royal. With 41 Full-page Plates (8 Photo-Intaglio) and 32 Illustrations in the Text. 2 vols. 8vo., 36s. net.

Smith.—CARTHAGE AND THE CARTHAGINIANS. By R. BOSWORTH SMITH, M.A., With Maps, Plans, &c. Cr. 8vo., 3s. 6d.

Stephens.—A HISTORY OF THE FRENCH REVOLUTION. By H. MORSE STEPHENS. 3 vols. 8vo. Vols. I. and II. 18s. each.

Stubbs.—HISTORY OF THE UNIVERSITY OF DUBLIN, from its Foundation to the End of the Eighteenth Century. By J. W. STUBBS. 8vo., 12s. 6d.

Sutherland.—THE HISTORY OF AUSTRALIA AND NEW ZEALAND, from 1606 to 1890. By ALEXANDER SUTHERLAND, M.A., and GEORGE SUTHERLAND, M.A. Crown 8vo., 2s. 6d.

Taylor.—A STUDENT'S MANUAL OF THE HISTORY OF INDIA. By Colonel MEADOWS TAYLOR, C.S.I., &c. Cr. 8vo., 7s. 6d.

Todd.—PARLIAMENTARY GOVERNMENT IN THE BRITISH COLONIES. By ALPHEUS TODD, LL.D. 8vo., 30s. net.

Vincent.—THE LAND QUESTION IN NORTH WALES: being a Brief Survey of the History, Origin, and Character of the Agrarian Agitation, and of the Nature and Effect of the Proceedings of the Welsh Land Commission. By J. E. VINCENT, Barrister-at-Law. 8vo., 5s.

Wakeman and Hassall.—ESSAYS INTRODUCTORY TO THE STUDY OF ENGLISH CONSTITUTIONAL HISTORY. By Resident Members of the University of Oxford. Edited by HENRY OFFLEY WAKEMAN, M.A., and ARTHUR HASSALL, M.A. Crown 8vo., 6s.

Walpole.—HISTORY OF ENGLAND FROM THE CONCLUSION OF THE GREAT WAR IN 1815 TO 1858. By SPENCER WALPOLE. 6 vols. Crown 8vo., 6s. each.

Wolff.—ODD BITS OF HISTORY: being Short Chapters intended to Fill Some Blanks. By HENRY W. WOLFF. 8vo., 8s. 6d.

Wood-Martin.—PAGAN IRELAND: AN ARCHÆOLOGICAL SKETCH. A Handbook of Irish Pre-Christian Antiquities. By W. G. WOOD-MARTIN, M.R.I.A. With 512 Illustrations. Crown 8vo., 15s.

Wylie.—HISTORY OF ENGLAND UNDER HENRY IV. By JAMES HAMILTON WYLIE, M.A., one of H. M. Inspectors of Schools. 3 vols. Crown 8vo. Vol. I., 1399-1404, 10s. 6d. Vol. II., 15s. Vol. III., 15s.
[Vol. IV. *In the press.*

Biography, Personal Memoirs, &c.

Armstrong.—THE LIFE AND LETTERS OF EDMUND J. ARMSTRONG. Edited by G. F. ARMSTRONG. Fcp. 8vo., 7s. 6d.

Bacon.—THE LETTERS AND LIFE OF FRANCIS BACON, INCLUDING ALL HIS OCCASIONAL WORKS. Edited by JAMES SPEDDING. 7 vols. 8vo., £4 4s.

Bagehot.—BIOGRAPHICAL STUDIES. By WALTER BAGEHOT. Crown 8vo., 3s. 6d.

Blackwell. — PIONEER WORK IN OPENING THE MEDICAL PROFESSION TO WOMEN: Autobiographical Sketches. By Dr. ELIZABETH BLACKWELL. Cr. 8vo., 6s.

Boyd (A. K. H.) ('A.K.H.B.').
TWENTY-FIVE YEARS OF ST. ANDREWS. 1865-1890. 2 vols. 8vo. Vol. I. 12s. Vol. II. 15s.

ST. ANDREWS AND ELSEWHERE: Glimpses of Some Gone and of Things Left. 8vo., 15s.

THE LAST YEARS OF ST. ANDREWS: SEPTEMBER 1890 TO SEPTEMBER 1895. 8vo., 15s.

Brown.—THE LIFE OF FORD MADOX BROWN. By FORD MADOX HUEFFER, With 49 Plates and 7 Illustrations in the Text, being reproductions of the Artist's Pictures.

Buss.—FRANCES MARY BUSS AND HER WORK FOR EDUCATION. By ANNIE E. RIDLEY. With 5 Portraits and 4 Illustrations. Crown 8vo, 7s. 6d.

Carlyle.—THOMAS CARLYLE: A History of his Life. By JAMES ANTHONY FROUDE.
1795-1835. 2 vols. Crown 8vo., 7s.
1834-1881. 2 vols. Crown 8vo., 7s.

Digby.—THE LIFE OF SIR KENELM DIGBY, by one of his Descendants. By the Author of 'The Life of a Conspirator,' 'A Life of Archbishop Laud,' etc. With Illustration. 8vo.

Erasmus.—LIFE AND LETTERS OF ERASMUS. By JAMES ANTHONY FROUDE. Crown 8vo., 6s.

Fox.— THE EARLY HISTORY OF CHARLES JAMES FOX. By the Right Hon. Sir G. O. TREVELYAN, Bart.
Library Edition. 8vo., 18s.
Cabinet Edition. Crown 8vo., 6s.

Granville.—LETTERS OF HARRIET, COUNTESS GRANVILLE, 1810-1845. Edited by her son, the Hon. F. LEVESON GOWER. With Portrait. 2 Vols. 8vo., 32s.

Halford.—THE LIFE OF SIR HENRY HALFORD, BART., G.C.H., M.D., F.R.S., By WILLIAM MUNK, M.D., F.S.A. 8vo., 12s. 6d.

Hamilton.—LIFE OF SIR WILLIAM HAMILTON. By R. P. GRAVES. 8vo. 3 vols. 15s. each. ADDENDUM. 8vo., 6d. sewed.

Haweis.—MY MUSICAL LIFE. By the Rev. H. R. HAWEIS. With Portrait of Richard Wagner and 3 Illustrations. Crown 8vo., 7s. 6d.

Havelock.—MEMOIRS OF SIR HENRY HAVELOCK, K.C.B. By JOHN CLARK MARSHMAN. Crown 8vo., 3s. 6d.

Holroyd.—THE GIRLHOOD OF MARIA JOSEPHA HOLROYD (Lady Stanley of Alderley), as told in Letters of a Hundred Years Ago, from 1776 to 1796.

Luther. — LIFE OF LUTHER. By JULIUS KÖSTLIN. With Illustrations from Authentic Sources. Translated from the German. Crown 8vo., 7s. 6d.

Macaulay.—THE LIFE AND LETTERS OF LORD MACAULAY. By the Right Hon. Sir G. O. TREVELYAN, Bart., M.P.
Popular Edition. 1 vol. Cr. 8vo., 2s. 6d.
Student's Edition. 1 vol. Cr. 8vo., 6s.
Cabinet Edition. 2 vols. Post 8vo., 12s.
Library Edition. 2 vols. 8vo., 36s.
Edinburgh Edition. 2 vols. 8vo., 6s. each.

Marbot. — THE MEMOIRS OF THE BARON DE MARBOT. Translated from the French. Crown 8vo., 7s. 6d.

Nansen.—FRIDTIOF NANSEN, 1861-1893. By W. C. BRÖGGER and NORDAHL ROLFSEN. With an Introductory Poem by BJÖRNSTJERN BJÖRNSON. Translated by WILLIAM ARCHER. With numerous Illustrations, Portraits, and Maps.

Romanes.—THE LIFE AND LETTERS OF GEORGE JOHN ROMANES, M.A., LL.D., F.R.S. Written and Edited by his WIFE. With Portrait and 2 Illustrations. 8vo., 15s.

Seebohm.—THE OXFORD REFORMERS—JOHN COLET, ERASMUS AND THOMAS MORE: a History of their Fellow-Work. By FREDERIC SEEBOHM. 8vo., 14s.

Shakespeare. — OUTLINES OF THE LIFE OF SHAKESPEARE. By J. O. HALLIWELL-PHILLIPPS. With Illustrations and Fac-similes. 2 vols. Royal 8vo., £1 1s.

Shakespeare's TRUE LIFE. By JAMES WALTER. With 500 Illustrations by GERALD E. MOIRA. Imp. 8vo., 21s.

Stephen.—ESSAYS IN ECCLESIASTICAL BIOGRAPHY. By Sir JAMES STEPHEN. Crown 8vo., 7s. 6d.

Biography, Personal Memoirs, &c.—continued.

Turgot.—THE LIFE AND WRITINGS OF TURGOT, Comptroller-General of France, 1774-1776. Edited for English Readers by W. WALKER STEPHENS. 8vo., 12s. 6d.

Verney.—MEMOIRS OF THE VERNEY FAMILY.
Vols. I. & II., DURING THE CIVIL WAR. By FRANCES PARTHENOPE VERNEY. With 38 Portraits, Woodcuts and Fac-simile. Royal 8vo., 42s.
Vol. III., DURING THE COMMONWEALTH. 1650-1660. By MARGARET M. VERNEY. With 10 Portraits, &c. Royal 8vo., 21s.

Wellington.—LIFE OF THE DUKE OF WELLINGTON. By the Rev. G. R. GLEIG, M.A. Crown 8vo., 3s. 6d.

Wolf.—THE LIFE OF JOSEPH WOLF, ANIMAL PAINTER. By A. H. PALMER. With 53 Plates and 14 Illustrations in the Text. 8vo., 21s.

Travel and Adventure, the Colonies, &c.

Arnold (SIR EDWIN).
SEAS AND LANDS. With 71 Illustrations. Cr. 8vo., 3s. 6d.
WANDERING WORDS. With 45 Illustrations. 8vo., 18s.
EAST AND WEST: With 14 Illustrations by R. T. PRITCHETT. 8vo., 18s.

AUSTRALIA AS IT IS, or Facts and Features, Sketches, and Incidents of Australia and Australian Life with Notices of New Zealand. By A CLERGYMAN, thirteen years resident in the interior of New South Wales. Crown 8vo., 5s.

Baker (SIR S. W.).
EIGHT YEARS IN CEYLON. With 6 Illustrations. Crown 8vo., 3s. 6d.
THE RIFLE AND THE HOUND IN CEYLON. With 6 Illustrations. Crown 8vo., 3s. 6d.

Bent (J. THEODORE).
THE RUINED CITIES OF MASHONALAND: being a Record of Excavation and Exploration in 1891. With 117 Illustrations. Crown 8vo., 3s. 6d.
THE SACRED CITY OF THE ETHIOPIANS: being a Record of Travel and Research in Abyssinia in 1893. With 8 Plates and 65 Illustrations in the Text. 8vo., 10s. 6d.

Bicknell.—TRAVEL AND ADVENTURE IN NORTHERN QUEENSLAND. By ARTHUR C. BICKNELL. With 24 Plates and 22 Illustrations in the Text. 8vo., 15s.

Brassey.—VOYAGES AND TRAVELS OF LORD BRASSEY, K.C.B., D.C.L., 1862-1894. Arranged and Edited by Captain S. EARDLEY-WILMOT. 2 vols. Cr. 8vo., 10s.

Brassey (THE LATE LADY).
A VOYAGE IN THE 'SUNBEAM;' OUR HOME ON THE OCEAN FOR ELEVEN MONTHS.
Library Edition. With 8 Maps and Charts, and 118 Illustrations. 8vo. 21s.
Cabinet Edition. With Map and 66 Illustrations. Crown 8vo., 7s. 6d.
Silver Library Edition. With 66 Illustrations. Crown 8vo., 3s. 6d.
Popular Edition. With 60 Illustrations. 4to., 6d. sewed, 1s. cloth.
School Edition. With 37 Illustrations. Fcp., 2s. cloth, or 3s. white parchment.

SUNSHINE AND STORM IN THE EAST.
Library Edition. With 2 Maps and 141 Illustrations. 8vo., 21s.
Cabinet Edition. With 2 Maps and 114 Illustrations. Crown 8vo., 7s. 6d.
Popular Edition. With 103 Illustrations. 4to., 6d. sewed, 1s. cloth.

IN THE TRADES, THE TROPICS, AND THE 'ROARING FORTIES.'
Cabinet Edition. With Map and 220 Illustrations. Crown 8vo., 7s. 6d.
Popular Edition. With 183 Illustrations. 4to., 6d. sewed, 1s. cloth.

THREE VOYAGES IN THE 'SUNBEAM'. Popular Ed. With 346 Illust. 4to., 2s. 6d.

Browning.—A GIRL'S WANDERINGS IN HUNGARY. By H. ELLEN BROWNING. With Illustrations. 8vo.

Froude (JAMES A.).
OCEANA: or England and her Colonies. With 9 Illustrations. Crown 8vo., 2s. boards, 2s. 6d. cloth.

THE ENGLISH IN THE WEST INDIES: or, the Bow of Ulysses. With 9 Illustrations. Crown 8vo., 2s. boards, 2s. 6d. cloth.

Travel and Adventure, the Colonies, &c.—*continued.*

Howitt.—VISITS TO REMARKABLE PLACES. Old Halls, Battle-Fields, Scenes, illustrative of Striking Passages in English History and Poetry. By WILLIAM HOWITT. With 80 Illustrations. Crown 8vo., 3s. 6d.

Knight (E. F.).
THE CRUISE OF THE '*ALERTE*' : the Narrative of a Search for Treasure on the Desert Island of Trinidad. With 2 Maps and 23 Illustrations. Crown 8vo., 3s. 6d.

WHERE THREE EMPIRES MEET : a Narrative of Recent Travel in Kashmir, Western Tibet, Baltistan, Ladak, Gilgit, and the adjoining Countries. With a Map and 54 Illustrations. Cr. 8vo., 3s. 6d.

THE '*FALCON*' ON THE BALTIC: a Voyage from London to Copenhagen in a Three-Tonner. With 10 Full-page Illustrations. Crown 8vo., 3s. 6d.

Lees and Clutterbuck.—B.C. 1887 : A RAMBLE IN BRITISH COLUMBIA. By J. A. LEES and W. J. CLUTTERBUCK. With Map and 75 Illustrations. Crown 8vo., 3s. 6d.

Murdoch. — FROM EDINBURGH TO THE ANTARCTIC: an Artist's Notes and Sketches during the Dundee Antarctic Expedition of 1892-93. By W. G. BURN-MURDOCH. With 2 Maps and numerous Illustrations. 8vo., 18s.

Nansen (FRIDTJOF).
THE FIRST CROSSING OF GREENLAND. With numerous Illustrations and a Map. Crown 8vo., 3s. 6d.

ESKIMO LIFE. With 31 Illustrations. 8vo., 16s.

Peary. — MY ARCTIC JOURNAL : a year among Ice-Fields and Eskimos. By JOSEPHINE DIEBITSCH-PEARY. With 19 Plates, 3 Sketch Maps, and 44 Illustrations in the Text. 8vo., 12s.

Quillinan.—JOURNAL OF A FEW MONTHS' RESIDENCE IN PORTUGAL, and Glimpses of the South of Spain. By Mrs. QUILLINAN (Dora Wordsworth). New Edition. Edited, with Memoir, by EDMUND LEE, Author of "Dorothy Wordsworth," &c. Crown 8vo., 6s.

Smith.—CLIMBING IN THE BRITISH ISLES. By W. P. HASKETT SMITH. With Illustrations by ELLIS CARR, and Numerous Plans.

Part I. ENGLAND. 16mo., 3s. 6d.

Part II. WALES AND IRELAND. 16mo., 3s. 6d.

Part III. SCOTLAND. [*In preparation.*

Stephen. — THE PLAY-GROUND OF EUROPE. By LESLIE STEPHEN. New Edition, with Additions and 4 Illustrations. Crown 8vo., 6s. net.

THREE IN NORWAY. By Two of Them. With a Map and 59 Illustrations. Crown 8vo., 2s. boards, 2s. 6d. cloth.

Tyndall.—THE GLACIERS OF THE ALPS: being a Narrative of Excursions and Ascents. An Account of the Origin and Phenomena of Glaciers, and an Exposition of the Physical Principles to which they are related. By JOHN TYNDALL, F.R.S. With numerous Illustrations. Crown 8vo., 6s. 6d. net.

Whishaw.—THE ROMANCE OF THE WOODS: Reprinted Articles and Sketches. By FRED. J. WHISHAW. Crown 8vo., 6s.

Veterinary Medicine, &c.

Steel (JOHN HENRY).

A TREATISE ON THE DISEASES OF THE DOG. With 88 Illustrations. 8vo., 10s. 6d.

A TREATISE ON THE DISEASES OF THE OX. With 119 Illustrations. 8vo., 15s.

A TREATISE ON THE DISEASES OF THE SHEEP. With 100 Illustrations. 8vo., 12s.

OUTLINES OF EQUINE ANATOMY : a Manual for the use of Veterinary Students in the Dissecting Room. Cr. 8vo., 7s. 6d.

Fitzwygram. — HORSES AND STABLES. By Major-General Sir F. FITZWYGRAM, Bart. With 56 pages of Illustrations. 8vo., 2s. 6d. net.

'Stonehenge.' — THE DOG IN HEALTH AND DISEASE. By 'STONEHENGE'. With 78 Wood Engravings. 8vo., 7s. 6d.

Youatt (WILLIAM).
THE HORSE. Revised and Enlarged by W. WATSON, M.R.C.V.S. With 52 Wood Engravings. 8vo., 7s. 6d.

THE DOG. Revised and Enlarged With 33 Wood Engravings. 8vo., 6s.

Sport and Pastime.

THE BADMINTON LIBRARY.

Edited by HIS GRACE THE DUKE OF BEAUFORT, K.G.
Assisted by ALFRED E. T. WATSON.

Crown 8vo., Price 10s. 6d. each Volume, Cloth.

*** *The Volumes are also issued half-bound in Leather, with gilt top. The price can be had from all Booksellers.*

ARCHERY. By C. J. LONGMAN and Col. H. WALROND. With Contributions by Miss LEGH, Viscount DILLON, Major C. HAWKINS FISHER, Rev. EYRE W. HUSSEY, Rev. W. K. R. BEDFORD, J. BALFOUR PAUL, and L. W. MAXSON. With 2 Maps, 23 Plates and 172 Illustrations in the Text. Crown 8vo., 10s. 6d.

ATHLETICS AND FOOTBALL. By MONTAGUE SHEARMAN. With an Introduction by Sir RICHARD WEBSTER, Q.C., M.P., and a contribution on Paper-chasing by WALTER RYE. With 6 Plates and 52 Illustrations in the Text from Drawings by STANLEY BERKELEY, and from Instantaneous Photographs by G. MITCHELL. Crown 8vo., 10s. 6d.

BIG GAME SHOOTING. By CLIVE PHILLIPPS-WOLLEY.

Vol. I. AFRICA AND AMERICA. With Contributions by Sir SAMUEL W. BAKER, W. C. OSWELL, F. J. JACKSON, WARBURTON PIKE, and F. C. SELOUS. With 20 Plates and 57 Illustrations in the Text by CHARLES WHYMPER, J. WOLF, and H. WILLINK, and from Photographs. Crown 8vo., 10s. 6d.

Vol. II. EUROPE, ASIA, AND THE ARCTIC REGIONS. With Contributions by Lieut.-Colonel R. HEBER PERCY, ARNOLD PIKE, Major ALGERNON C. HEBER PERCY, W. A. BAILLIE-GROHMAN, Sir HENRY POTTINGER, Bart., Lord KILMOREY, ABEL CHAPMAN, WALTER J. BUCK, and ST. GEORGE LITTLEDALE. With 17 Plates and 56 Illustrations in the Text by CHAS. WHYMPER, and from Photographs. Cr. 8vo., 10s. 6d.

BILLIARDS. By Major W. BROADFOOT, R.E. With Contributions by A. H. BOYD, SYDENHAM DIXON, W. J. FORD, DUDLEY D. PONTIFEX, RUSSELL D. WALKER, and REGINALD H. R. RIMINGTON-WILSON. With 11 Plates by LUCIEN DAVIS, R.I., 19 Illustrations in the Text from Photographs, and numerous Diagrams and Figures. Cr. 8vo., 10s. 6d.

BOATING. By W. B. WOODGATE. With an Introduction by the Rev. EDMOND WARRE, D.D., and a Chapter on 'Rowing at Eton' by R. HARVEY MASON. With 10 Plates, 39 Illustrations in the Text, after Drawings by FRANK DADD, and from Instantaneous Photographs, and 4 Maps of the Rowing Courses at Oxford, Cambridge Henley, and Putney. Crown 8vo., 10s. 6d.

COURSING AND FALCONRY.
COURSING. By HARDING COX.
FALCONRY. By the Hon. GERALD LASCELLES.
With 20 Plates and 56 Illustrations in the Text by JOHN CHARLTON, R. H. MOORE, G. E. LODGE, and L. SPEED. Crown 8vo., 10s. 6d.

CRICKET. By A. G. STEEL and the Hon. R. H. LYTTELTON. With Contributions by ANDREW LANG, R. A. H. MITCHELL, W. G. GRACE, and F. GALE. With 12 Plates and 52 Illustrations in the Text, after Drawings by LUCIEN DAVIS, and from Photographs. Crown 8vo., 10s. 6d.

CYCLING. By the EARL OF ALBEMARLE and G. LACY HILLIER. With 19 Plates and 44 Illustrations in the Text by the EARL OF ALBEMARLE, JOSEPH PENNELL, S. T. DADD, and GEORGE MOORE. Crown 8vo., 10s. 6d.

DANCING. By Mrs. LILLY GROVE, F.R.G.S. With Contributions by Miss MIDDLETON, The Hon. Mrs. ARMYTAGE, The COUNTESS OF ANCASTER, and Mrs. WORDSWORTH. With Musical Examples, and 38 Full-page Plates and 93 Illustrations in the Text. Crown 8vo., 10s. 6d.

DRIVING. By His Grace the DUKE of BEAUFORT, K.G. With Contributions by other Authorities. With Photogravure Intaglio Portrait of His Grace the DUKE OF BEAUFORT, and 11 Plates and 54 Illustrations in the Text, after Drawings by G. D. GILES and J. STURGESS, and from Photographs. Crown 8vo., 10s. 6d.

Sport and Pastime—*continued.*
THE BADMINTON LIBRARY—*continued.*

FENCING, BOXING, AND WRESTLING. By WALTER H. POLLOCK, F. C. GROVE, C. PREVOST, E. B. MITCHELL, and WALTER ARMSTRONG. With 18 Intaglio Plates and 24 Illustrations in the Text. Crown 8vo., 10s. 6d.

FISHING. By H. CHOLMONDELEY-PENNELL, Late Her Majesty's Inspector of Sea Fisheries.

Vol. I. SALMON AND TROUT. With Contributions by H. R. FRANCIS, Major JOHN P. TRAHERNE, FREDERIC M. HALFORD, H. S. HALL, and THOMAS ANDREWS. With Frontispiece, 8 Full-page Illustrations of Fishing Subjects by C. H. WHYMPER and CONWAY LLOYD-JONES, and very numerous Illustrations of Tackle, &c. Crown 8vo., 10s. 6d.

Vol. II. PIKE AND OTHER COARSE FISH. With Contributions by the MARQUIS OF EXETER, WILLIAM SENIOR, G. CHRISTOPHER DAVIS, H. R. FRANCIS, and R. B. MARSTON. With Frontispiece, 6 Full-page Illustrations of Fishing Subjects by C. H. WHYMPER and CONWAY LLOYD-JONES, and very numerous Illustrations of Tackle, &c. Crown 8vo., 10s. 6d.

GOLF. By HORACE G. HUTCHINSON. With Contributions by the Rt. Hon. A. J. BALFOUR, M.P., Sir WALTER SIMPSON, Bart., LORD WELLWOOD, H. S. C. EVERARD, ANDREW LANG, and other. With 25 Plates and 65 Illustrations in the Text, by THOMAS HODGE and HARRY FURNISS, and from Photographs. Crown 8vo., 10s. 6d.

HUNTING. By His Grace the DUKE OF BEAUFORT, K.G., and MOWBRAY MORRIS. With Contributions by the EARL OF SUFFOLK AND BERKSHIRE, Rev. E. W. L. DAVIES, DIGBY COLLINS, ALFRED E. T. WATSON, Sir MARTEINE LLOYD, GEORGE H. LONGMAN, and J. S. GIBBONS. With 5 Plates and 54 Illustrations in the Text by J. STURGESS, J. CHARLTON, G. D. GILES, and A. C. SEALY. Crown 8vo., 10s. 6d.

MOUNTAINEERING. By C. T. DENT. With Contributions by Sir W. M. CONWAY, D. W. FRESHFIELD, C. E. MATTHEWS, C. PILKINGTON, Sir F. POLLOCK, H. G. WILLINK, and an Introduction by Mr. JUSTICE WILLS. With 13 Plates and 95 Illustrations in the Text by H. G. WILLINK, and others. Crown 8vo., 10s. 6d.

RACING AND STEEPLE-CHASING.

RACING. By the EARL OF SUFFOLK AND BERKSHIRE, and W. G. CRAVEN. With a Contribution by the Hon. F. LAWLEY.

STEEPLE-CHASING. By ARTHUR COVENTRY and ALFRED E. T. WATSON. With Coloured Frontispiece and 56 Illustrations in the Text by J. STURGESS. Crown 8vo., 10s. 6d.

RIDING AND POLO.

RIDING. By Captain ROBERT WEIR. Riding-Master, R.H.G. With Contributions by the DUKE OF BEAUFORT, the EARL OF SUFFOLK AND BERKSHIRE, the EARL OF ONSLOW, E. L. ANDERSON, and ALFRED E. T. WATSON.

POLO. By J. MURRAY BROWN. With 18 Plates and 41 Illustrations in the Text, by G. D. GILES, FRANK DADD, and F. STUART ALLAN. Crown 8vo., 10s. 6d.

SEA FISHING. By JOHN BICKERDYKE. With Contributions on WHALING, by Sir H. W. GORE-BOOTH; TARPON, by ALFRED C. HARMSWORTH; ANTIPODEAN and FOREIGN FISH, by W. SENIOR. With 22 Full-page Plates and 175 Illustrations in the Text, by C. NAPIER HEMY, R. T. PRITCHETT, W. W. MAY, and others. Crown 8vo., 10s. 6d.

SHOOTING.

Vol. I. FIELD AND COVERT. By LORD WALSINGHAM and Sir RALPH PAYNE-GALLWEY, Bart. With Contributions by the Hon. GERALD LASCELLES and A. J. STUART-WORTLEY. With 11 Full-page Illustrations and 94 Illustrations in the Text by A. J. STUART-WORTLEY, HARPER PENNINGTON, C. WHYMPER, G. E. LODGE, J. M. OSWALD BROWN, Sir R. FRANKLAND, and from Photographs. Cr. 8vo., 10s. 6d.

Vol. II. MOOR AND MARSH. By LORD WALSINGHAM and Sir RALPH PAYNE-GALLWEY, Bart. With Contributions by LORD LOVAT and LORD CHARLES LENNOX KERR. With 8 Full-page Illustrations and 57 Illustrations in the Text by A. J. STUART-WORTLEY, HARPER PENNINGTON, C. WHYMPER, J. G. MILLAIS, G. E. LODGE, and from Photographs. Crown 8vo., 10s. 6d.

Sport and Pastime—*continued.*

THE BADMINTON LIBRARY—*continued.*

SKATING. By J. M. HEATHCOTE and C. G. TEBBUTT. FIGURE SKATING. By T. MAXWELL WITHAM. With Contributions on CURLING (Rev. JOHN KERR), TOBOGGANING (ORMOND HAKE), ICE-SAILING (HENRY A. BUCK), BANDY (C. G. TEBBUTT). With 12 Plates and 272 Illustrations and Diagrams in the Text by C. WHYMPER and K. WHYMPER and Capt. R. M. ALEXANDER. Crown 8vo., 10s. 6d.

SWIMMING. By ARCHIBALD SINCLAIR and WILLIAM HENRY, Hon. Secs. of the Life-Saving Society. With 13 Plates and 106 Illustrations in the Text by S. T. DADD and from Photographs by G. MITCHELL. Crown 8vo., 10s. 6d.

TENNIS, LAWN TENNIS, RACKETS AND FIVES. By J. M. and C. G. HEATHCOTE, E. O. PLEYDELL-BOUVERIE, and A.C. AINGER. With Contributions by the Hon. A. LYTTELTON, W. C. MARSHALL, Miss L. DOD, H. W. W. WILBERFORCE, H. F. LAWFORD, SPENCER W. GORE, R. D. SEARS, and HERBERT CHIPP. With 12 Plates and 67 Illustrations in the Text by LUCIEN DAVIS, C. M. NEWTON, and from Photographs. Crown 8vo., 10s. 6d.

YACHTING.
Vol. I. CRUISING, CONSTRUCTION OF YACHTS, YACHT RACING RULES, FITTING-OUT,&c. By Sir EDWARD SULLIVAN, Bart., LORD BRASSEY, K.C.B., C. E. SETH-SMITH, C.B., G. L. WATSON, R. T. PRITCHETT, Sir GEORGE LEACH, K.C.B., Vice-President Y.R.A., 'THALASSA,' The EARL OF PEMBROKE AND MONTGOMERY, E. F. KNIGHT, and Rev. G. L. BLAKE. With 21 Plates and 93 Illustrations in the Text by R. T. PRITCHETT, G. L. WATSON, J. M. SOPER, &c., and from Photographs. Crown 8vo., 10s. 6d.

Vol. II. YACHT CLUBS, YACHTING IN AMERICA AND THE COLONIES, YACHT RACING, &c. By R. T. PRITCHETT, The MARQUIS OF DUFFERIN AND AVA, K.P., JAMES MCFERRAN, Rev. G. L. BLAKE, T. B. MIDDLETON, EDWARD WALTER CASTLE and ROBERT CASTLE, G. CHRISTOPHER DAVIES, LEWIS HERRESHOFF, The EARL OF ONSLOW, G.C.M.G., H. HORN, and Sir GEORGE LEACH, K.C.B. Vice-President Y.R.A. With 35 Plates and 160 Illustrations in the Text by R. T. PRITCHETT, G. L. WATSON, J. M. SOPER, &c., and from Photographs. Crown 8vo., 10s. 6d.

FUR AND FEATHER SERIES.

Edited by A. E. T. WATSON.

Crown 8vo., price 5s. each Volume. Cloth.

*** *The Volumes are also issued half-bound in Leather, with gilt top. The price can be had from all Booksellers.*

THE PARTRIDGE. Natural History by the Rev. H. A. MACPHERSON; Shooting, by A. J. STUART-WORTLEY; Cookery, by GEORGE SAINTSBURY. With 11 Illustrations and various Diagrams in the Text. Crown 8vo., 5s.

THE GROUSE. Natural History by the Rev. H. A. MACPHERSON; Shooting, by A. J. STUART-WORTLEY; Cookery, by GEORGE SAINTSBURY. With 13 Illustrations and various Diagrams in the Text. Crown 8vo., 5s.

THE PHEASANT. Natural History by the Rev. H. A. MACPHERSON; Shooting, by A. J. STUART-WORTLEY; Cookery, by ALEXANDER INNES SHAND. With 10 Illustrations and various Diagrams. Crown 8vo., 5s.

THE HARE. Natural History by the Rev. H. A. MACPHERSON; Shooting, by the Hon. GERALD LASCELLES; Coursing, by CHARLES RICHARDSON; Hunting, by J. S. GIBBONS and G. H. LONGMAN; Cookery, by Col. KENNEY HERBERT. With 9 Illustrations. Crown 8vo, 5s.

WILD FOWL. By the Hon. JOHN SCOTT-MONTAGU, M.P., &c. [*In preparation.*

THE RED DEER. By CAMERON OF LOCHIEL, LORD EBRINGTON, &c. [*In preparation.*

Sport and Pastime—*continued.*

BADMINTON MAGAZINE (THE) OF SPORTS AND PASTIMES. Edited by ALFRED E. T. WATSON ("Rapier"). With numerous Illustrations. Price 1s. monthly.
Vol. I., August to December, 1895. 6s.
Vol. II., January to June, 1896. 6s.

Bickerdyke.—*DAYS OF MY LIFE ON WATERS FRESH AND SALT*; and other Papers. By JOHN BICKERDYKE. With Photo-Etched Frontispiece and 8 Full-page Illustrations. Crown 8vo., 6s.

DEAD SHOT (THE): or, Sportsman's Complete Guide. Being a Treatise on the Use of the Gun, with Rudimentary and Finishing Lessons on the Art of Shooting Game of all kinds. Also Game-driving, Wildfowl and Pigeon-shooting, Dog-breaking, etc. By MARKSMAN. Illustrated. Cr. 8vo., 10s. 6d.

Ellis.—*CHESS SPARKS;* or, Short and Bright Games of Chess. Collected and Arranged by J. H. ELLIS, M.A. 8vo., 4s. 6d.

Falkener.—*GAMES, ANCIENT AND ORIENTAL, AND HOW TO PLAY THEM.* By EDWARD FALKENER. With numerous Photographs, Diagrams, &c. 8vo., 21s.

Ford.—*THE THEORY AND PRACTICE OF ARCHERY.* By HORACE FORD. New Edition, thoroughly Revised and Re-written by W. BUTT, M.A. With a Preface by C. J. LONGMAN, M.A. 8vo., 14s.

Francis.—*A BOOK ON ANGLING:* or, Treatise on the Art of Fishing in every Branch; including full Illustrated List of Salmon Flies. By FRANCIS FRANCIS. With Portrait and Coloured Plates. Crown 8vo., 15s.

Gibson.—*TOBOGGANING ON CROOKED RUNS.* By the Hon. HARRY GIBSON. With Contributions by F. DE B. STRICKLAND and 'LADY-TOBOGANNER'. With 40 Illustrations. Crown 8vo., 6s.

Graham.—*COUNTRY PASTIMES FOR BOYS.* By P. ANDERSON GRAHAM. With 252 Illustrations from Drawings and Photographs. Crown 8vo. 6s.

Lang.—*ANGLING SKETCHES.* By ANDREW LANG. With 20 Illustrations. Crown 8vo., 3s. 6d.

Longman.—*CHESS OPENINGS.* By FREDERICK W. LONGMAN. Fcp. 8vo., 2s. 6d.

Maskelyne.—*SHARPS AND FLATS:* a Complete Revelation of the Secrets of Cheating at Games of Chance and Skill. By JOHN NEVIL MASKELYNE, of the Egyptian Hall. With 62 Illustrations. Crown 8vo., 6s.

Park.—*THE GAME OF GOLF.* By WILLIAM PARK, Jun., Champion Golfer, 1887-89. With 17 Plates and 26 Illustrations in the Text. Crown 8vo., 7s. 6d.

Payne-Gallwey (SIR RALPH, Bart.).

LETTERS TO YOUNG SHOOTERS (First Series). On the Choice and use of a Gun. With 41 Illustrations. Crown 8vo., 7s. 6d.

LETTERS TO YOUNG SHOOTERS (Second Series). On the Production, Preservation, and Killing of Game. With Directions in Shooting Wood-Pigeons and Breaking-in Retrievers. With Portrait and 103 Illustrations. Crown 8vo., 12s. 6d.

Pole (WILLIAM).

THE THEORY OF THE MODERN SCIENTIFIC GAME OF WHIST. Fcp. 8vo., 2s. 6d.

THE EVOLUTION OF WHIST: a Study of the Progressive Changes which the Game has undergone. Cr. 8vo., 6s.

Proctor.—*HOW TO PLAY WHIST: WITH THE LAWS AND ETIQUETTE OF WHIST.* By RICHARD A. PROCTOR. Crown 8vo., 3s. 6d.

Ronalds.—*THE FLY-FISHER'S ENTOMOLOGY.* By ALFRED RONALDS. With 20 coloured Plates. 8vo., 14s.

Wilcocks.—*THE SEA FISHERMAN:* Comprising the Chief Methods of Hook and Line Fishing in the British and other Seas, and Remarks on Nets, Boats, and Boating. By J. C. WILCOCKS. Illustrated. Cr. 8vo., 6s.

Mental, Moral, and Political Philosophy.

LOGIC, RHETORIC, PSYCHOLOGY, &c.

Abbott.—THE ELEMENTS OF LOGIC. By T. K. ABBOTT, B.D. 12mo., 3s.

Aristotle.

THE POLITICS: G. Bekker's Greek Text of Books I., III., IV. (VII.), with an English Translation by W. E. BOLLAND, M.A.; and short Introductory Essays by A. LANG, M.A. Crown 8vo., 7s. 6d.

THE POLITICS: Introductory Essays. By ANDREW LANG (from Bolland and Lang's 'Politics'). Crown 8vo, 2s. 6d.

THE ETHICS: Greek Text, Illustrated with Essay and Notes. By Sir ALEXANDER GRANT, Bart. 2 vols. 8vo., 32s.

AN INTRODUCTION TO ARISTOTLE'S ETHICS. Books I.-IV. (Book X. c. vi.-ix. in an Appendix). With a continuous Analysis and Notes. By the Rev. EDW. MOORE, D.D., Cr. 8vo. 10s. 6d.

Bacon (FRANCIS).

COMPLETE WORKS. Edited by R. L. ELLIS, JAMES SPEDDING and D. D. HEATH. 7 vols. 8vo., £3 13s. 6d.

LETTERS AND LIFE, including all his occasional Works. Edited by JAMES SPEDDING. 7 vols. 8vo., £4 4s.

THE ESSAYS: with Annotations. By RICHARD WHATELY, D.D. 8vo., 10s. 6d.

THE ESSAYS. Edited, with Notes, by F. STORR and C. H. GIBSON. Crown 8vo, 3s. 6d.

THE ESSAYS: with Introduction, Notes, and Index. By E. A. ABBOTT, D.D. 2 Vols. Fcp. 8vo., 6s. The Text and Index only, without Introduction and Notes, in One Volume. Fcp. 8vo., 2s. 6d.

Bain (ALEXANDER).

MENTAL SCIENCE. Cr. 8vo., 6s. 6d.

MORAL SCIENCE. Cr. 8vo., 4s. 6d.

The two works as above can be had in one volume, price 10s. 6d.

SENSES AND THE INTELLECT. 8vo., 15s.

EMOTIONS AND THE WILL. 8vo., 15s.

Bain (ALEXANDER)—continued.

LOGIC, DEDUCTIVE AND INDUCTIVE. Part I. 4s. Part II. 6s. 6d.

PRACTICAL ESSAYS. Cr. 8vo., 2s.

Bray (CHARLES).

THE PHILOSOPHY OF NECESSITY: or, Law in Mind as in Matter. Cr. 8vo,, 5s.

THE EDUCATION OF THE FEELINGS: a Moral System for Schools. Cr. 8vo., 2s. 6d.

Bray.—ELEMENTS OF MORALITY, in Easy Lessons for Home and School Teaching. By Mrs. CHARLES BRAY. Crown 8vo., 1s. 6d.

Davidson.—THE LOGIC OF DEFINITION, Explained and Applied. By WILLIAM L. DAVIDSON, M.A. Crown 8vo., 6s.

Green (THOMAS HILL).—THE WORKS OF. Edited by R. L. NETTLESHIP.

Vols. I. and II. Philosophical Works. 8vo., 16s. each.

Vol. III. Miscellanies. With Index to the three Volumes, and Memoir. 8vo., 21s.

LECTURES ON THE PRINCIPLES OF POLITICAL OBLIGATION. With Preface by BERNARD BOSANQUET. 8vo., 5s.

Hodgson (SHADWORTH H.).

TIME AND SPACE: A Metaphysical Essay. 8vo., 16s.

THE THEORY OF PRACTICE: an Ethical Inquiry. 2 vols. 8vo., 24s.

THE PHILOSOPHY OF REFLECTION. 2 vols. 8vo., 21s.

Hume.—THE PHILOSOPHICAL WORKS OF DAVID HUME. Edited by T. H. GREEN and T. H. GROSE. 4 vols. 8vo., 56s. Or separately, Essays. 2 vols. 28s. Treatise of Human Nature. 2 vols. 28s.

Justinian.—THE INSTITUTES OF JUSTINIAN: Latin Text, chiefly that of Huschke, with English Introduction, Translation, Notes, and Summary. By THOMAS C. SANDARS, M.A. 8vo., 18s.

Kant (IMMANUEL).

CRITIQUE OF PRACTICAL REASON, AND OTHER WORKS ON THE THEORY OF ETHICS.. Translated by T. K. ABBOTT, B.D. With Memoir. 8vo., 12s. 6d.

Mental, Moral and Political Philosophy—*continued.*

Kant (IMMANUEL)—*continued.*
 FUNDAMENTAL PRINCIPLES OF THE METAPHYSIC OF ETHICS. Translated by T. K. ABBOTT, B.D. (Extracted from 'Kant's Critique of Practical Reason and other Works on the Theory of Ethics.') Crown 8vo, 3s.

 INTRODUCTION TO LOGIC, AND HIS ESSAY ON THE MISTAKEN SUBTILTY OF THE FOUR FIGURES.. Translated by T. K. ABBOTT. 8vo., 6s.

Killick.—HANDBOOK TO MILL'S SYSTEM OF LOGIC. By Rev. A. H. KILLICK, M.A. Crown 8vo., 3s. 6d.

Ladd (GEORGE TRUMBULL).
 PHILOSOPHY OF MIND : An Essay on the Metaphysics of Psychology. 8vo., 16s.
 ELEMENTS OF PHYSIOLOGICAL PSYCHOLOGY. 8vo., 21s.
 OUTLINES OF PHYSIOLOGICAL PSYCHOLOGY. A Text-book of Mental Science for Academies and Colleges. 8vo., 12s.
 PSYCHOLOGY, DESCRIPTIVE AND EXPLANATORY : a Treatise of the Phenomena, Laws, and Development of Human Mental Life. 8vo., 21s.
 PRIMER OF PSYCHOLOGY. Cr. 8vo., 5s. 6d.

Lewes.—THE HISTORY OF PHILOSOPHY, from Thales to Comte. By GEORGE HENRY LEWES. 2 vols. 8vo., 32s.

Max Müller (F.).
 THE SCIENCE OF THOUGHT. 8vo., 21s.
 THREE INTRODUCTORY LECTURES ON THE SCIENCE OF THOUGHT. 8vo., 2s. 6d.

Mill.—ANALYSIS OF THE PHENOMENA OF THE HUMAN MIND. By JAMES MILL. 2 vols. 8vo., 28s.

Mill (JOHN STUART).
 A SYSTEM OF LOGIC. Cr. 8vo., 3s. 6d.
 ON LIBERTY. Crown 8vo., 1s. 4d.
 ON REPRESENTATIVE GOVERNMENT. Crown 8vo., 2s.
 UTILITARIANISM. 8vo., 2s. 6d.
 EXAMINATION OF SIR WILLIAM HAMILTON'S PHILOSOPHY. 8vo., 16s.
 NATURE, THE UTILITY OF RELIGION, AND THEISM. Three Essays. 8vo., 5s.

Mosso.—FEAR. By ANGELO MOSSO. Translated from the Italian by E. LOUGH and F. KIESOW. With 8 Illustrations. Cr. 8vo., 7s. 6d.

Romanes.—MIND AND MOTION AND MONISM. By GEORGE JOHN ROMANES, LL.D., F.R.S. Cr. 8vo., 4s. 6d.

Stock.—DEDUCTIVE LOGIC. By ST. GEORGE STOCK. Fcp. 8vo., 3s. 6d.

Sully (JAMES).
 THE HUMAN MIND: a Text-book of Psychology. 2 vols. 8vo., 21s.
 OUTLINES OF PSYCHOLOGY. 8vo., 9s.
 THE TEACHER'S HANDBOOK OF PSYCHOLOGY. Crown 8vo., 5s.
 STUDIES OF CHILDHOOD. 8vo, 10s. 6d.

Swinburne.—PICTURE LOGIC: an Attempt to Popularise the Science of Reasoning. By ALFRED JAMES SWINBURNE, M.A. With 23 Woodcuts. Crown 8vo., 5s.

Weber.—HISTORY OF PHILOSOPHY. By ALFRED WEBER, Professor in the University of Strasburg. Translated by FRANK THILLY, Ph.D. 8vo., 16s.

Whately (ARCHBISHOP).
 BACON'S ESSAYS. With Annotations. 8vo., 10s. 6d.
 ELEMENTS OF LOGIC. Cr. 8vo., 4s. 6d.
 ELEMENTS OF RHETORIC. Cr. 8vo., 4s. 6d.
 LESSONS ON REASONING. Fcp. 8vo., 1s. 6d.

Zeller (Dr. EDWARD, Professor in the University of Berlin).
 THE STOICS, EPICUREANS, AND SCEPTICS. Translated by the Rev. O. J. REICHEL, M.A. Crown 8vo., 15s.
 OUTLINES OF THE HISTORY OF GREEK PHILOSOPHY. Translated by SARAH F. ALLEYNE and EVELYN ABBOTT. Crown 8vo., 10s. 6d.
 PLATO AND THE OLDER ACADEMY. Translated by SARAH F. ALLEYNE and ALFRED GOODWIN, B.A. Crown 8vo. 18s.
 SOCRATES AND THE SOCRATIC SCHOOLS. Translated by the Rev. O. J. REICHEL, M.A. Crown 8vo., 10s. 6d.

Mental, Moral, and Political Philosophy—*continued.*

MANUALS OF CATHOLIC PHILOSOPHY.
(Stonyhurst Series).

A MANUAL OF POLITICAL ECONOMY. By C. S. DEVAS, M.A. Crown 8vo., 6s. 6d.

FIRST PRINCIPLES OF KNOWLEDGE. By JOHN RICKABY, S.J. Crown 8vo., 5s.

GENERAL METAPHYSICS. By JOHN RICKABY, S.J. Crown 8vo., 5s.

LOGIC. By RICHARD F. CLARKE, S.J. Crown 8vo., 5s.

MORAL PHILOSOPHY (ETHICS AND NATURAL LAW). By JOSEPH RICKABY, S.J. Crown 8vo., 5s.

NATURAL THEOLOGY. By BERNARD BOEDDER, S.J. Crown 8vo., 6s. 6d.

PSYCHOLOGY. BY MICHAEL MAHER, S.J. Crown 8vo., 6s. 6d.

History and Science of Language, &c.

Davidson.—LEADING AND IMPORTANT ENGLISH WORDS: Explained and Exemplified. By WILLIAM L. DAVIDSON, M.A. Fcp. 8vo., 3s. 6d.

Farrar.—LANGUAGE AND LANGUAGES: By F. W. FARRAR, D.D., F.R.S. Crown 8vo., 6s.

Graham.—ENGLISH SYNONYMS, Classified and Explained: with Practical Exercises. By G. F. GRAHAM. Fcp. 8vo., 6s.

Max Müller (F.).

THE SCIENCE OF LANGUAGE.—Founded on Lectures delivered at the Royal Institution in 1861 and 1863. 2 vols. Crown 8vo., 21s.

Max Müller (F.)—*continued.*

BIOGRAPHIES OF WORDS, AND THE HOME OF THE ARYAS. Crown 8vo., 7s. 6d.

THREE LECTURES ON THE SCIENCE OF LANGUAGE, AND ITS PLACE IN GENERAL EDUCATION, delivered at Oxford, 1889. Crown 8vo., 3s.

Roget.—THESAURUS OF ENGLISH WORDS AND PHRASES. Classified and Arranged so as to Facilitate the Expression of Ideas and assist in Literary Composition. By PETER MARK ROGET, M.D., F.R.S. Recomposed throughout, enlarged and improved, partly from the Author's Notes, and with a full Index, by the Author's Son, JOHN LEWIS ROGET. Crown 8vo. 10s. 6d.

Whately.—ENGLISH SYNONYMS. By E. JANE WHATELY. Fcp. 8vo., 3s.

Political Economy and Economics.

Ashley.—ENGLISH ECONOMIC HISTORY AND THEORY. By W. J. ASHLEY, M.A. Crown 8vo., Part I., 5s. Part II. 10s. 6d.

Bagehot.—ECONOMIC STUDIES. By WALTER BAGEHOT. Crown 8vo., 3s. 6d.

Barnett.—PRACTICABLE SOCIALISM. Essays on Social Reform. By the Rev. S. A. and Mrs. BARNETT. Crown 8vo., 6s.

Brassey.—PAPERS AND ADDRESSES ON WORK AND WAGES. By Lord BRASSEY. Edited by J. POTTER, and with Introduction by GEORGE HOWELL, M.P. Crown 8vo., 5s.

Devas.—A MANUAL OF POLITICAL ECONOMY. By C. S. DEVAS, M.A. Cr. 8vo., 6s. 6d. (Manuals of Catholic Philosophy.)

Dowell.—A HISTORY OF TAXATION AND TAXES IN ENGLAND, from the Earliest Times to the Year 1885. By STEPHEN DOWELL, (4 vols. 8vo). Vols. I. and II. The History of Taxation, 21s. Vols. III. and IV. The History of Taxes, 21s.

Political Economy and Economics—*continued*.

Macleod (HENRY DUNNING).
BIMETALISM. 8vo., 5s. net.
THE ELEMENTS OF BANKING. Cr. 8vo., 3s. 6d.
THE THEORY AND PRACTICE OF BANKING. Vol. I. 8vo., 12s. Vol. II. 14s.
THE THEORY OF CREDIT. 8vo. Vol. I., 10s. net. Vol. II., Part I., 10s. net. Vol. II., Part II., 10s. 6d.
A DIGEST OF THE LAW OF BILLS OF EXCHANGE, BANK-NOTES, &c.
[*In the press.*

Mill.—*POLITICAL ECONOMY.* By JOHN STUART MILL.
Popular Edition. Crown 8vo., 3s. 6d.
Library Edition. 2 vols. 8vo., 30s.

Symes.—*POLITICAL ECONOMY*: a Short Text-book of Political Economy. With Problems for Solution, and Hints for Supplementary Reading; also a Supplementary Chapter on Socialism. By Professor J. E. SYMES, M.A., of University College, Nottingham. Crown 8vo., 2s. 6d.

Toynbee.—*LECTURES ON THE INDUSTRIAL REVOLUTION OF THE 18TH CENTURY IN ENGLAND*: Popular Addresses, Notes and other Fragments. By ARNOLD TOYNBEE. With a Memoir of the Author by BENJAMIN JOWETT, D.D. 8vo., 10s. 6d.

Webb.—*THE HISTORY OF TRADE UNIONISM.* By SIDNEY and BEATRICE WEBB. With Map and full Bibliography of the Subject. 8vo., 18s.

STUDIES IN ECONOMICS AND POLITICAL SCIENCE.

Issued under the auspices of the London School of Economics and Political Science.

THE HISTORY OF LOCAL RATES IN ENGLAND: Five Lectures. By EDWIN CANNAN, M.A., Balliol College, Oxford. Crown 8vo., 2s. 6d.

SELECT DOCUMENTS ILLUSTRATING THE HISTORY OF TRADE UNIONISM.
1. The Tailoring Trade. Edited by W. F. GALTON. With a Preface by SIDNEY WEBB, LL.B. Crown 8vo., 5s.

DEPLOIGE'S REFERENDUM EN SUISSE. Translated, with Introduction and Notes, by C. P. TREVELYAN, M.A. [*In preparation.*

SELECT DOCUMENTS ILLUSTRATING THE STATE REGULATION OF WAGES. Edited, with Introduction and Notes, by W. A. S. HEWINS, M.A., Pembroke College, Oxford; Director of the London School of Economics and Political Science.
[*In preparation.*

HUNGARIAN GILD RECORDS. Edited by Dr. JULIUS MANDELLO, of Budapest.
[*In preparation.*

THE RELATIONS BETWEEN ENGLAND AND THE HANSEATIC LEAGUE. By Miss E. A. MACARTHUR, Vice-Mistress of Girton College, Cambridge. [*In preparation.*

Evolution, Anthropology, &c.

Babington.—*FALLACIES OF RACE THEORIES AS APPLIED TO NATIONAL CHARACTERISTICS.* Essays by WILLIAM DALTON BABINGTON, M.A. Crown 8vo., 6s.

Clodd (EDWARD).
THE STORY OF CREATION: a Plain Account of Evolution. With 77 Illustrations. Crown 8vo., 3s. 6d.

A PRIMER OF EVOLUTION: being a Popular Abridged Edition of 'The Story of Creation'. With Illustrations. Fcp. 8vo., 1s. 6d.

Lang.—*CUSTOM AND MYTH*: Studies of Early Usage and Belief. By ANDREW LANG. With 15 Illustrations. Crown 8vo., 3s. 6d.

Lubbock.—*THE ORIGIN OF CIVILISATION,* and the Primitive Condition of Man. By Sir J. LUBBOCK, Bart., M.P. With 5 Plates and 20 Illustrations in the Text. 8vo., 18s.

Romanes (GEORGE JOHN).
DARWIN, AND AFTER DARWIN: an Exposition of the Darwinian Theory, and a Discussion on Post-Darwinian Questions.
Part I. THE DARWINIAN THEORY. With Portrait of Darwin and 125 Illustrations. Crown 8vo., 10s. 6d.
Part II. POST-DARWINIAN QUESTIONS: Heredity and Utility. With Portrait of the Author and 5 Illustrations. Cr. 8vo., 10s. 6d.

AN EXAMINATION OF WEISMANNISM. Crown 8vo., 6s.

Classical Literature, Translations, &c.

Abbott.—*HELLENICA.* A Collection of Essays on Greek Poetry, Philosophy, History, and Religion. Edited by EVELYN ABBOTT, M.A., LL.D. 8vo., 16s.

Æschylus.—*EUMENIDES OF ÆSCHYLUS.* With Metrical English Translation. By J. F. DAVIES. 8vo., 7s.

Aristophanes. — *THE ACHARNIANS OF ARISTOPHANES,* translated into English Verse. By R. Y. TYRRELL. Crown 8vo., 1s.

Becker (PROFESSOR).
GALLUS: or, Roman Scenes in the Time of Augustus. Illustrated. Post 8vo., 3s. 6d.
CHARICLES: or, Illustrations of the Private Life of the Ancient Greeks. Illustrated. Post 8vo., 3s. 6d.

Cicero.—*CICERO'S CORRESPONDENCE.* By R. Y. TYRRELL. Vols. I., II., III., 8vo., each 12s. Vol. IV., 15s.

Farnell.—*GREEK LYRIC POETRY:* a Complete Collection of the Surviving Passages from the Greek Song-Writing. Arranged with Prefatory Articles, Introductory Matter and Commentary. By GEORGE S. FARNELL, M.A. With 5 Plates. 8vo., 16s.

Lang.—*HOMER AND THE EPIC.* By ANDREW LANG. Crown 8vo., 9s. net.

Lucan.—*THE PHARSALIA OF LUCAN.* Translated into blank Verse, with some Notes. By EDWARD RIDLEY, Q.C., sometime Fellow of All Souls College, Oxford.

Mackail.—*SELECT EPIGRAMS FROM THE GREEK ANTHOLOGY.* By J. W. MACKAIL, Fellow of Balliol College, Oxford. Edited with a Revised Text, Introduction, Translation, and Notes. 8vo., 16s.

Rich.—*A DICTIONARY OF ROMAN AND GREEK ANTIQUITIES.* By A. RICH, B.A. With 2000 Woodcuts. Crown 8vo., 7s. 6d.

Sophocles.—Translated into English Verse. By ROBERT WHITELAW, M.A., Assistant Master in Rugby School; late Fellow of Trinity College, Cambridge. Crown 8vo., 8s. 6d.

Tacitus. — *THE HISTORY OF P. CORNELIUS TACITUS.* Translated into English, with an Introduction and Notes, Critical and Explanatory, by ALBERT WILLIAM QUILL, M.A., T.C.D., sometime Scholar of Trinity College, Dublin. 2 vols. Vol. I. 8vo., 7s. 6d. Vol. II. 8vo., 12s. 6d.

Tyrrell.—*TRANSLATIONS INTO GREEK AND LATIN VERSE.* Edited by R. Y. TYRRELL. 8vo., 6s.

Virgil.
THE ÆNEID OF VIRGIL. Translated into English Verse by JOHN CONINGTON. Crown 8vo., 6s.

THE POEMS OF VIRGIL. Translated into English Prose by JOHN CONINGTON. Crown 8vo., 6s.

THE ÆNEID OF VIRGIL, freely translated into English Blank Verse. By W. J. THORNHILL. Crown 8vo., 7s. 6d.

THE ÆNEID OF VIRGIL. Books I. to VI. Translated into English Verse by JAMES RHOADES. Crown 8vo., 5s.

Wilkins.—*THE GROWTH OF THE HOMERIC POEMS.* By G. WILKINS. 8vo., 6s.

Poetry and the Drama.

Acworth.—*BALLADS OF THE MARATHAS.* Rendered into English Verse from the Marathi Originals. By HARRY ARBUTHNOT ACWORTH. 8vo., 5s.

Allingham (WILLIAM).
IRISH SONGS AND POEMS. With Frontispiece of the Waterfall of Asaroe. Fcp. 8vo., 6s.
LAURENCE BLOOMFIELD. With Portrait of the Author. Fcp. 8vo., 3s. 6d.
FLOWER PIECES; DAY AND NIGHT SONGS; BALLADS. With 2 Designs by D. G. ROSSETTI. Fcp. 8vo., 6s. large paper edition, 12s.

Allingham (WILLIAM)—*continued.*

LIFE AND PHANTASY: with Frontispiece by Sir J. E. MILLAIS, Bart., and Design by ARTHUR HUGHES. Fcp. 8vo., 6s.; large paper edition, 12s.

THOUGHT AND WORD, AND ASHBY MANOR: a Play. Fcp. 8vo., 6s.; large paper edition, 12s.

BLACKBERRIES. Imperial 16mo., 6s.

Sets of the above 6 vols. may be had in uniform Half-parchment binding, price 30s.

Poetry and the Drama—*continued*.

Armstrong (G. F. SAVAGE).
POEMS: Lyrical and Dramatic. Fcp. 8vo., 6s.
KING SAUL. (The Tragedy of Israel, Part I.) Fcp. 8vo., 5s.
KING DAVID. (The Tragedy of Israel, Part II.) Fcp. 8vo., 6s.
KING SOLOMON. (The Tragedy of Israel, Part III.) Fcp. 8vo., 6s.
UGONE: a Tragedy. Fcp. 8vo., 6s.
A GARLAND FROM GREECE: Poems. Fcp. 8vo., 7s. 6d.
STORIES OF WICKLOW: Poems. Fcp. 8vo., 7s. 6d.
MEPHISTOPHELES IN BROADCLOTH: a Satire. Fcp. 8vo., 4s.
ONE IN THE INFINITE: a Poem. Crown 8vo., 7s. 6d.

Armstrong.—THE POETICAL WORKS OF EDMUND J. ARMSTRONG Fcp. 8vo., 5s.

Arnold (Sir EDWIN).
THE LIGHT OF THE WORLD: or the Great Consummation. Cr. 8vo., 7s. 6d. net.
POTIPHAR'S WIFE, and other Poems. Crown 8vo., 5s. net.
ADZUMA: or the Japanese Wife. A Play. Crown 8vo., 6s. 6d. net.
THE TENTH MUSE, and other Poems. Crown 8vo., 5s. net.

Beesly. — BALLADS AND OTHER VERSE. By A. H. BEESLY. Fcp. 8vo., 5s.

Bell (Mrs. HUGH).
CHAMBER COMEDIES: a Collection of Plays and Monologues for the Drawing Room. Crown 8vo., 6s.
FAIRY TALE PLAYS, AND HOW TO ACT THEM. With numerous Illustrations by LANCELOT SPEED. Crown 8vo.

Carmichael.—POEMS. By JENNINGS CARMICHAEL (Mrs. FRANCIS MULLIS). Crown 8vo, 6s. net.

Christie.—LAYS AND VERSES. By NIMMO CHRISTIE. Crown 8vo., 3s. 6d.

Cochrane (ALFRED).
THE KESTREL'S NEST, and other Verses. Fcp. 8vo., 3s. 6d.
LEVIORE PLECTRO: Occasional Verses. Fcap. 8vo., 3s. 6d.

Florian's Fables.—THE FABLES OF FLORIAN. Done into English Verse by Sir PHILIP PERRING, Bart. Cr. 8vo., 3s. 6d.

Goethe.
FAUST, Part I., the German Text, with Introduction and Notes. By ALBERT M. SELSS, Ph.D., M.A. Crown 8vo., 5s.
FAUST. Translated, with Notes. By T. E. WEBB. 8vo., 12s. 6d.

Gurney.—DAY-DREAMS: Poems. By Rev. ALFRED GURNEY, M.A. Crown 8vo., 3s. 6d.

Ingelow (JEAN).
POETICAL WORKS. 2 vols. Fcp. 8vo., 12s.
LYRICAL AND OTHER POEMS. Selected from the Writings of JEAN INGELOW. Fcp. 8vo., 2s. 6d. cloth plain, 3s. cl. gilt.

Lang (ANDREW).
BAN AND ARRIÈRE BAN: a Rally of Fugitive Rhymes. Fcp. 8vo., 5s. net.
GRASS OF PARNASSUS. Fcp. 8vo. 2s. 6d. net.
BALLADS OF BOOKS. Edited by ANDREW LANG. Fcp. 8vo., 6s.
THE BLUE POETRY BOOK. Edited by ANDREW LANG. With 100 Illustrations. Crown 8vo., 6s.

Lecky.—POEMS. By W. E. H. LECKY. Fcp. 8vo., 5s.

Lindsay.—THE FLOWER SELLER, and other Poems. By LADY LINDSAY. Crown 8vo., 5s.

Lytton (THE EARL OF), (OWEN MEREDITH).
MARAH. Fcp. 8vo., 6s. 6d.
KING POPPY: a Fantasia. With 1 Plate and Design on Title-Page by ED. BURNE-JONES, A.R.A. Cr. 8vo., 10s. 6d.
THE WANDERER. Cr. 8vo., 10s. 6d.
LUCILE. Crown 8vo., 10s. 6d.
SELECTED POEMS. Cr. 8vo., 10s. 6d.

Poetry and the Drama—*continued*.

Macaulay.—LAYS OF ANCIENT ROME, &c. By Lord MACAULAY.
Illustrated by G. SCHARF. Fcp. 4to., 10s. 6d.
—————————— Bijou Edition. 18mo., 2s. 6d. gilt top.
—————————— Popular Edition. Fcp. 4to., 6d. sewed, 1s. cloth.
Illustrated by J. R. WEGUELIN. Crown 8vo., 3s. 6d.
Annotated Edition. Fcp. 8vo., 1s. sewed, 1s. 6d. cloth.

Macdonald.—A BOOK OF STRIFE, IN THE FORM OF THE DIARY OF AN OLD SOUL: Poems. By GEORGE MACDONALD, LL.D. 18mo., 6s.

Morris (WILLIAM).
POETICAL WORKS—LIBRARY EDITION. Complete in Ten Volumes. Crown 8vo., price 6s. each.
THE EARTHLY PARADISE. 4 vols. 6s. each.
THE LIFE AND DEATH OF JASON. 6s.
THE DEFENCE OF GUENEVERE, and other Poems. 6s.
THE STORY OF SIGURD THE VOLSUNG, AND THE FALL OF THE NIBLUNGS. 6s.
LOVE IS ENOUGH; or, the Freeing of Pharamond: A Morality; and POEMS BY THE WAY. 6s.
THE ODYSSEY OF HOMER. Done into English Verse. 6s.
THE ÆNEIDS OF VIRGIL. Done into English Verse. 6s.

Certain of the POETICAL WORKS may also be had in the following Editions:—
THE EARTHLY PARADISE.
Popular Edition. 5 vols. 12mo., 25s.; or 5s. each, sold separately.
The same in Ten Parts, 25s.; or 2s. 6d. each, sold separately.
Cheap Edition, in 1 vol. Crown 8vo., 7s. 6d.
LOVE IS ENOUGH; or, the Freeing of Pharamond: A Morality. Square crown 8vo., 7s. 6d.
POEMS BY THE WAY. Square crown 8vo., 6s.

⁎ For Mr. William Morris's Prose Works, see p. 31.

Murray (ROBERT F.).—Author of 'The Scarlet Gown'. His Poems, with a Memoir by ANDREW LANG. Fcp. 8vo., 5s. net.

Nesbit.—LAYS AND LEGENDS. By E. NESBIT (Mrs. HUBERT BLAND). First Series. Crown 8vo., 3s. 6d. Second Series. With Portrait. Crown 8vo., 5s.

Peek (HEDLEY) (FRANK LEYTON).
SKELETON LEAVES: Poems. With a Dedicatory Poem to the late Hon. Roden Noel. Fcp. 8vo., 2s. 6d. net.
THE SHADOWS OF THE LAKE, and other Poems. Fcp. 8vo., 2s. 6d. net.

Piatt (SARAH).
AN ENCHANTED CASTLE, AND OTHER POEMS: Pictures, Portraits, and People in Ireland. Crown 8vo., 3s. 6d.
POEMS: With Portrait of the Author. 2 vols. Crown 8vo., 10s.

Piatt (JOHN JAMES).
IDYLS AND LYRICS OF THE OHIO VALLEY. Crown 8vo., 5s.
LITTLE NEW WORLD IDYLS. Cr. 8vo., 5s.

Rhoades.—TERESA AND OTHER POEMS. By JAMES RHOADES. Crown 8vo., 3s. 6d.

Riley (JAMES WHITCOMB).
OLD FASHIONED ROSES: Poems. 12mo., 5s.
POEMS: Here at Home. Fcp. 8vo., 6s. net.

Shakespeare.—BOWDLER'S FAMILY SHAKESPEARE. With 36 Woodcuts. 1 vol. 8vo., 14s. Or in 6 vols. Fcp. 8vo., 21s.
THE SHAKESPEARE BIRTHDAY BOOK. By MARY F. DUNBAR. 32mo., 1s. 6d.

Sturgis.—A BOOK OF SONG. By JULIAN STURGIS. 16mo. 5s.

Works of Fiction, Humour, &c.

Alden.—*AMONG THE FREAKS.* By W. L. ALDEN. With 55 Illustrations by J. F. SULLIVAN and FLORENCE K. UPTON. Crown 8vo., 3s. 6d.

Anstey (F., Author of 'Vice Versâ').

VOCES POPULI. Reprinted from 'Punch'. First Series. With 20 Illustrations by J. BERNARD PARTRIDGE. Crown 8vo., 3s. 6d.

THE TRAVELLING COMPANIONS. Reprinted from 'Punch'. With 25 Illustrations by J. BERNARD PARTRIDGE. Post 4to., 5s.

THE MAN FROM BLANKLEY'S: a Story in Scenes, and other Sketches. With 24 Illustrations by J. BERNARD PARTRIDGE. Post 4to., 6s.

Astor.—*A JOURNEY IN OTHER WORLDS:* a Romance of the Future. By JOHN JACOB ASTOR. With 10 Illustrations. Cr. 8vo., 6s.

Baker.—*BY THE WESTERN SEA.* By JAMES BAKER, Author of 'John Westacott'. Crown 8vo., 3s. 6d.

Beaconsfield (THE EARL OF).

NOVELS AND TALES. Complete in 11 vols. Crown 8vo., 1s. 6d. each.

Vivian Grey.	Sybil.
The Young Duke, &c.	Henrietta Temple.
Alroy, Ixion, &c.	Venetia.
Contarini Fleming, &c.	Coningsby.
	Lothair.
Tancred.	Endymion.

NOVELS AND TALES. The Hughenden Edition. With 2 Portraits and 11 Vignettes. 11 vols. Crown 8vo., 42s.

Dougall (L.).

BEGGARS ALL. Cr. 8vo., 3s. 6d.

WHAT NECESSITY KNOWS. Crown 8vo., 6s.

Doyle (A. CONAN).

MICAH CLARKE: A Tale of Monmouth's Rebellion. With 10 Illustrations. Cr. 8vo., 3s. 6d.

THE CAPTAIN OF THE POLESTAR, and other Tales. Cr. 8vo., 3s. 6d.

THE REFUGEES: A Tale of Two Continents. With 25 Illustrations. Cr. 8vo., 3s. 6d.

THE STARK MUNRO LETTERS. Cr. 8vo, 6s.

Farrar (F. W., DEAN OF CANTERBURY).

DARKNESS AND DAWN: or, Scenes in the Days of Nero. An Historic Tale. Cr. 8vo., 7s. 6d.

GATHERING CLOUDS: a Tale of the Days of St. Chrysostom. Cr. 8vo., 7s. 6d.

Fowler.—*THE YOUNG PRETENDERS.* A Story of Child Life. By EDITH H. FOWLER. With 12 Illustrations by PHILIP BURNE-JONES. Crown 8vo., 6s.

Froude.—*THE TWO CHIEFS OF DUNBOY:* an Irish Romance of the Last Century. By JAMES A. FROUDE. Cr. 8vo., 3s. 6d.

Haggard (H. RIDER).

HEART OF THE WORLD. With 15 Illustrations. Crown 8vo., 6s.

JOAN HASTE. With 20 Illustrations. Crown 8vo., 6s.

THE PEOPLE OF THE MIST. With 16 Illustrations. Crown 8vo., 6s.

MONTEZUMA'S DAUGHTER. With 24 Illustrations. Crown 8vo., 3s. 6d.

SHE. With 32 Illustrations. Crown 8vo., 3s. 6d.

ALLAN QUATERMAIN. With 31 Illustrations. Crown 8vo., 3s. 6d.

MAIWA'S REVENGE: Crown 8vo., 1s. boards, 1s. 6d. cloth.

COLONEL QUARITCH, V.C. Cr. 8vo. 3s. 6d.

CLEOPATRA. With 29 Illustrations. Crown 8vo., 3s. 6d.

Works of Fiction, Humour, &c.—*continued.*

Haggard (H. RIDER)—*continued.*

BEATRICE. Cr. 8vo., 3s. 6d.

ERIC BRIGHTEYES. With 51 Illustrations. Crown 8vo., 3s. 6d.

NADA THE LILY. With 23 Illustrations. Crown 8vo., 3s. 6d.

ALLAN'S WIFE. With 34 Illustrations. Crown 8vo., 3s. 6d.

THE WITCH'S HEAD. With 16 Illustrations. Crown 8vo., 3s. 6d.

MR. MEESON'S WILL. With 16 Illustrations. Crown 8vo., 3s. 6d.

DAWN. With 16 Illustrations. Cr. 8vo., 3s. 6d.

Haggard and Lang.—*THE WORLD'S DESIRE.* By H. RIDER HAGGARD and ANDREW LANG. With 27 Illustrations. Crown 8vo., 3s. 6d.

Harte.—*IN THE CARQUINEZ WOODS* and other stories. By BRET HARTE. Cr. 8vo., 3s. 6d.

Hope.—*THE HEART OF PRINCESS OSRA.* By ANTHONY HOPE. With 9 Illustrations by JOHN WILLIAMSON. Crown 8vo., 6s.

Hornung.—*THE UNBIDDEN GUEST.* By E. W. HORNUNG. Crown 8vo., 3s. 6d.

Lang.—*A MONK OF FIFE;* being the Chronicle written by NORMAN LESLIE of Pitcullo, concerning Marvellous Deeds that befel in the Realm of France, 1429-31. By ANDREW LANG. With 13 Illustrations by SELWYN IMAGE. Cr. 8vo., 6s.

Lyall (EDNA).

THE AUTOBIOGRAPHY OF A SLANDER. Fcp. 8vo., 1s., sewed.

Presentation Edition. With 20 Illustrations by LANCELOT SPEED. Crown 8vo., 2s. 6d. net.

THE AUTOBIOGRAPHY OF A TRUTH. Fcp. 8vo., 1s., sewed; 1s. 6d., cloth.

DOREEN. The Story of a Singer. Crown 8vo., 6s.

Magruder.—*THE VIOLET.* By JULIA MAGRUDER. With Illustrations by C. D. GIBSON. Crown 8vo.

Matthews.—*HIS FATHER'S SON:* a Novel of the New York Stock Exchange. By BRANDER MATTHEWS. With 13 Illustrations. Cr. 8vo. 6s.

Melville (G. J. WHYTE).

The Gladiators.	Holmby House.
The Interpreter.	Kate Coventry.
Good for Nothing.	Digby Grand.
The Queen's Maries.	General Bounce.

Crown 8vo., 1s. 6d. each.

Merriman.—*FLOTSAM:* The Study of a Life. By HENRY SETON MERRIMAN. With Frontispiece and Vignette by H. G. MASSEY, A.R.E. Crown 8vo., 6s.

Morris (WILLIAM).

THE WELL AT THE WORLD'S END. 2 vols. 8vo., 24s.

THE STORY OF THE GLITTERING PLAIN, which has been also called The Land of the Living Men, or The Acre of the Undying. Square post 8vo., 5s. net.

THE ROOTS OF THE MOUNTAINS, wherein is told somewhat of the Lives of the Men of Burgdale, their Friends, their Neighbours, their Foemen, and their Fellows-in-Arms. Written in Prose and Verse. Square crown 8vo., 8s.

A TALE OF THE HOUSE OF THE WOLFINGS, and all the Kindreds of the Mark. Written in Prose and Verse. Second Edition. Square crown 8vo., 6s.

A DREAM OF JOHN BALL, AND A KING'S LESSON. 12mo., 1s. 6d.

NEWS FROM NOWHERE; or, An Epoch of Rest. Being some Chapters from an Utopian Romance. Post 8vo., 1s. 6d.

*** For Mr. William Morris's Poetical Works, see p. 20.

Newman (CARDINAL).

LOSS AND GAIN: The Story of a Convert. Crown 8vo. Cabinet Edition, 6s.; Popular Edition, 3s. 6d.

CALLISTA: A Tale of the Third Century. Crown 8vo. Cabinet Edition, 6s.; Popular Edition, 3s. 6d.

Oliphant.—*OLD MR. TREDGOLD.* By Mrs. OLIPHANT. Crown 8vo., 6s.

Phillipps-Wolley.—*SNAP:* a Legend of the Lone Mountain. By C. PHILLIPPS-WOLLEY. With 13 Illustrations. Crown 8vo., 3s. 6d.

Quintana.—*THE CID CAMPEADOR:* an Historical Romance. By D. ANTONIO DE TRUEBA Y LA QUINTANA. Translated from the Spanish by HENRY J. GILL, M.A., T.C.D. Crown 8vo, 6s.

Works of Fiction, Humour, &c.—*continued.*

Rhoscomyl (OWEN).

THE JEWEL OF YNYS GALON: being a hitherto unprinted Chapter in the History of the Sea Rovers. With 12 Illustrations by LANCELOT SPEED. Cr. 8vo., 6s.

BATTLEMENT AND TOWER : a Romance. With Frontispiece by R. CATON WOODVILLE. Crown 8vo., 6s.

Robertson.—*NUGGETS IN THE DEVIL'S PUNCH BOWL,* and other Australian Tales. By ANDREW ROBERTSON. Cr. 8vo., 3s. 6d.

Rokeby.—*DORCAS HOBDAY.* By CHARLES ROKEBY.

Sewell (ELIZABETH M.).

A Glimpse of the World.	Amy Herbert.
Laneton Parsonage.	Cleve Hall.
Margaret Percival.	Gertrude.
Katharine Ashton.	Home Life.
The Earl's Daughter.	After Life.
The Experience of Life.	Ursula. Ivors.

Cr. 8vo., 1s. 6d. each cloth plain. 2s. 6d each cloth extra, gilt edges.

Stevenson (ROBERT LOUIS).

THE STRANGE CASE OF DR. JEKYLL AND MR. HYDE. Fcp. 8vo., 1s. sewed. 1s. 6d. cloth.

THE STRANGE CASE OF DR. JEKYLL AND MR. HYDE; WITH OTHER FABLES. Crown 8vo., 3s. 6d.

MORE NEW ARABIAN NIGHTS—THE DYNAMITER. By ROBERT LOUIS STEVENSON and FANNY VAN DE GRIFT STEVENSON. Crown 8vo., 3s. 6d.

THE WRONG BOX. By ROBERT LOUIS STEVENSON and LLOYD OSBOURNE. Crown 8vo., 3s. 6d.

Suttner.—*LAY DOWN YOUR ARMS (Die Waffen Nieder)*: The Autobiography of Martha Tilling. By BERTHA VON SUTTNER. Translated by T. HOLMES. Cr. 8vo., 1s. 6d.

Trollope (ANTHONY).

THE WARDEN. Cr. 8vo., 1s. 6d.

BARCHESTER TOWERS. Cr. 8vo., 1s. 6d.

TRUE (A) RELATION OF THE TRAVELS AND PERILOUS ADVENTURES OF MATHEW DUDGEON, GENTLEMAN: Wherein is truly set down the Manner of his Taking, the Long Time of his Slavery in Algiers, and Means of his Delivery. Written by Himself, and now for the first time printed. Cr. 8vo., 5s.

Walford (L. B.).

MR. SMITH: a Part of his Life. Crown 8vo., 2s. 6d.

THE BABY'S GRANDMOTHER. Cr. 8vo., 2s. 6d.

COUSINS. Crown 8vo., 2s. 6d.

TROUBLESOME DAUGHTERS. Cr. 8vo., 2s. 6d.

PAULINE. Crown. 8vo., 2s. 6d.

DICK NETHERBY. Cr. 8vo., 2s. 6d.

THE HISTORY OF A WEEK. Cr. 8vo. 2s. 6d.

A STIFF-NECKED GENERATION. Cr. 8vo. 2s. 6d.

NAN, and other Stories. Cr. 8vo., 2s. 6d.

THE MISCHIEF OF MONICA. Cr. 8vo., 2s. 6d.

THE ONE GOOD GUEST. Cr. 8vo. 2s. 6d.

'PLOUGHED,' and other Stories. Crown 8vo., 6s.

THE MATCHMAKER. Cr. 8vo., 6s.

West (B. B.).

HALF-HOURS WITH THE MILLIONAIRES: Showing how much harder it is to spend a million than to make it. Cr. 8vo., 6s.

SIR SIMON VANDERPETTER, and *MINDING HIS ANCESTORS.* Cr. 8vo., 5s.

A FINANCIAL ATONEMENT. Cr. 8vo., 6s.

Weyman (STANLEY).

THE HOUSE OF THE WOLF. Cr. 8vo., 3s. 6d.

A GENTLEMAN OF FRANCE. Cr. 8vo., 6s.

THE RED COCKADE. Cr. 8vo., 6s.

Whishaw.—*A BOYAR OF THE TERRIBLE:* a Romance of the Court of Ivan the Cruel, First Tzar of Russia. By FRED. WHISHAW. With 12 Illustrations by H. G. MASSEY, A.R.E. Crown 8vo., 6s.

Popular Science (Natural History, &c.).

Butler.—*Our Household Insects.* An Account of the Insect-Pests found in Dwelling-Houses. By Edward A. Butler, B.A., B.Sc. (Lond.). With 113 Illustrations. Crown 8vo., 3s. 6d.

Furneaux (W.).

The Outdoor World; or The Young Collector's Handbook. With 18 Plates 16 of which are coloured, and 549 Illustrations in the Text. Crown 8vo., 7s. 6d.

Butterflies and Moths (British). With 12 coloured Plates and 241 Illustrations in the Text. Crown 8vo., 12s. 6d.

Hartwig (Dr. George).

The Sea and its Living Wonders. With 12 Plates and 303 Woodcuts. 8vo., 7s. net.

The Tropical World. With 8 Plates and 172 Woodcuts. 8vo., 7s. net.

The Polar World. With 3 Maps, 8 Plates and 85 Woodcuts. 8vo., 7s. net.

The Subterranean World. With 3 Maps and 80 Woodcuts. 8vo., 7s. net.

The Aerial World. With Map, 8 Plates and 60 Woodcuts. 8vo., 7s. net.

Heroes of the Polar World. 19 Illustrations. Cr. 8vo., 2s.

Wonders of the Tropical Forests. 40 Illustrations. Cr. 8vo., 2s.

Workers under the Ground. 29 Illustrations. Cr. 8vo., 2s.

Marvels Over our Heads. 29 Illustrations. Cr. 8vo., 2s.

Sea Monsters and Sea Birds. 75 Illustrations. Cr. 8vo., 2s. 6d.

Denizens of the Deep. 117 Illustrations. Cr. 8vo., 2s. 6d.

Hartwig (Dr. George)—*continued.*

Volcanoes and Earthquakes. 30 Illustrations. Cr. 8vo., 2s. 6d.

Wild Animals of the Tropics. 66 Illustrations. Cr. 8vo., 3s. 6d.

Hayward.—*Bird Notes.* By the late Jane Mary Hayward. Edited by Emma Hubbard. With Frontispiece and 15 Illustrations by G. E. Lodge. Cr. 8vo., 6s.

Helmholtz.—*Popular Lectures on Scientific Subjects.* By Hermann von Helmholtz. With 68 Woodcuts. 2 vols. Cr. 8vo., 3s. 6d. each.

Hudson.—*British Birds.* By W. H. Hudson, C.M.Z.S. With a Chapter on Structure and Classification by Frank E. Beddard, F.R.S. With 16 Plates (8 of which are Coloured), and over 100 Illustrations in the Text. Crown 8vo., 12s. 6d.

Proctor (Richard A.).

Light Science for Leisure Hours. Familiar Essays on Scientific Subjects. 3 vols. Cr. 8vo., 5s. each.

Rough Ways made Smooth. Familiar Essays on Scientific Subjects. Crown 8vo., 3s. 6d.

Pleasant Ways in Science. Crown 8vo., 3s. 6d.

Nature Studies. By R. A. Proctor, Grant Allen, A. Wilson, T. Foster and E. Clodd. Crown 8vo., 3s. 6d.

Leisure Readings. By R. A. Proctor, E. Clodd, A. Wilson, T. Foster and A. C. Ranyard. Cr. 8vo., 3s. 6d.

*** *For Mr. Proctor's other books see Messrs. Longmans & Co.'s Catalogue of Scientific Works.*

Stanley.—*A Familiar History of Birds.* By E. Stanley, D.D., formerly Bishop of Norwich. With Illustrations. Cr. 8vo., 3s. 6d.

Popular Science (Natural History, &c.)—*continued.*

Wood (REV. J. G.).

HOMES WITHOUT HANDS: A Description of the Habitation of Animals, classed according to the Principle of Construction. With 140 Illustrations. 8vo., 7s., net.

INSECTS AT HOME: A Popular Account of British Insects, their Structure, Habits and Transformations. With 700 Illustrations. 8vo., 7s. net.

INSECTS ABROAD: a Popular Account of Foreign Insects, their Structure, Habits and Transformations. With 600 Illustrations. 8vo., 7s. net.

BIBLE ANIMALS: a Description of every Living Creature mentioned in the Scriptures. With 112 Illustrations. 8vo., 7s. net.

PETLAND REVISITED. With 33 Illustrations. Cr. 8vo., 3s. 6d.

OUT OF DOORS; a Selection of Original Articles on Practical Natural History. With 11 Illustrations. Cr. 8vo., 3s. 6d.

Wood (REV. J. G.)—*continued.*

STRANGE DWELLINGS: a Description of the Habitations of Animals, abridged from 'Homes without Hands'. With 60 Illustrations. Cr. 8vo., 3s. 6d.

BIRD LIFE OF THE BIBLE. 32 Illustrations. Cr. 8vo., 3s. 6d.

WONDERFUL NESTS. 30 Illustrations. Cr. 8vo., 3s. 6d.

HOMES UNDER THE GROUND. 28 Illustrations. Cr. 8vo., 3s. 6d.

WILD ANIMALS OF THE BIBLE. 29 Illustrations. Cr. 8vo., 3s. 6d.

DOMESTIC ANIMALS OF THE BIBLE. 23 Illustrations. Cr. 8vo., 3s. 6d.

THE BRANCH BUILDERS. 28 Illustrations. Cr. 8vo., 2s. 6d.

SOCIAL HABITATIONS AND PARASITIC NESTS. 18 Illustrations. Cr. 8vo., 2s.

Works of Reference.

Longmans' *GAZETTEER OF THE WORLD.* Edited by GEORGE G. CHISHOLM, M.A., B.Sc. Imp. 8vo., £2 2s. cloth, £2 12s. 6d. half-morocco.

Maunder (Samuel).

BIOGRAPHICAL TREASURY. With Supplement brought down to 1889. By Rev. JAMES WOOD. Fcp. 8vo., 6s.

TREASURY OF NATURAL HISTORY: or, Popular Dictionary of Zoology. With 900 Woodcuts. Fcp. 8vo., 6s.

TREASURY OF GEOGRAPHY, Physical, Historical, Descriptive, and Political. With 7 Maps and 16 Plates. Fcp. 8vo., 6s.

THE TREASURY OF BIBLE KNOWLEDGE. By the Rev. J. AYRE, M.A. With 5 Maps, 15 Plates, and 300 Woodcuts. Fcp. 8vo., 6s.

TREASURY OF KNOWLEDGE AND LIBRARY OF REFERENCE. Fcp. 8vo., 6s.

Maunder (Samuel)—*continued.*

HISTORICAL TREASURY. Fcp. 8vo., 6s.

SCIENTIFIC AND LITERARY TREASURY. Fcp. 8vo., 6s.

THE TREASURY OF BOTANY. Edited by J. LINDLEY, F.R.S., and T. MOORE, F.L.S. With 274 Woodcuts and 20 Steel Plates. 2 vols. Fcp. 8vo., 12s.

Roget. — *THESAURUS OF ENGLISH WORDS AND PHRASES.* Classified and Arranged so as to Facilitate the Expression of Ideas and assist in Literary Composition. By PETER MARK ROGET, M.D., F.R.S. Recomposed throughout, enlarged and improved, partly from the Author's Notes, and with a full Index, by the Author's Son, JOHN LEWIS ROGET. Crown 8vo., 10s. 6d.

Willich.--*POPULAR TABLES* for giving information for ascertaining the value of Lifehold, Leasehold, and Church Property, the Public Funds, &c. By CHARLES M. WILLICH. Edited by H. BENCE JONES. Crown 8vo., 10s. 6d.

Children's Books.

Crake (REV. A. D.).
- *EDWY THE FAIR;* or, The First Chronicle of Æscendune. Cr. 8vo., 2s. 6d.
- *ALFGAR THE DANE;* or, The Second Chronicle of Æscendune. Cr. 8vo. 2s. 6d.
- *THE RIVAL HEIRS:* being the Third and Last Chronicle of Æscendune. Cr. 8vo., 2s. 6d.
- *THE HOUSE OF WALDERNE.* A Tale of the Cloister and the Forest in the Days of the Barons' Wars. Crown 8vo., 2s. 6d.
- *BRIAN FITZ-COUNT.* A Story of Wallingford Castle and Dorchester Abbey. Cr. 8vo., 2s. 6d.

Lang (ANDREW).—EDITED BY.
- *THE BLUE FAIRY BOOK.* With 138 Illustrations. Crown 8vo., 6s.
- *THE RED FAIRY BOOK.* With 100 Illustrations. Crown 8vo., 6s.
- *THE GREEN FAIRY BOOK.* With 99 Illustrations. Crown 8vo., 6s.
- *THE YELLOW FAIRY BOOK.* With 104 Illustrations. Crown 8vo., 6s.
- *THE BLUE POETRY BOOK.* With 100 Illustrations. Crown 8vo., 6s.
- *THE BLUE POETRY BOOK.* School Edition, without Illustrations. Fcp. 8vo., 2s. 6d.
- *THE TRUE STORY BOOK.* With 66 Illustrations. Crown 8vo., 6s.
- *THE RED TRUE STORY BOOK.* With 100 Illustrations. Crown 8vo., 6s.
- *THE ANIMAL STORY BOOK.* With 67 Illustrations. Crown 8vo., 6s.

Meade (L. T.).
- *DADDY'S BOY.* With Illustrations. Crown 8vo., 3s. 6d.
- *DEB AND THE DUCHESS.* With Illustrations. Crown 8vo., 3s. 6d.
- *THE BERESFORD PRIZE.* With Illustrations. Crown 8vo., 3s. 6d.
- *THE HOUSE OF SURPRISES.* With Illustrations. Crown 8vo. 3s. 6d.

Molesworth—*SILVERTHORNS.* By Mrs. MOLESWORTH. With Illustrations. Cr. 8vo., 5s.

Stevenson.—*A CHILD'S GARDEN OF VERSES.* By ROBERT LOUIS STEVENSON. Fcp. 8vo., 5s.

Upton (FLORENCE K. AND BERTHA).
- *THE ADVENTURES OF TWO DUTCH DOLLS AND A 'GOLLIWOGG'.* Illustrated by FLORENCE K. UPTON, with Words by BERTHA UPTON. With 31 Coloured Plates and numerous Illustrations in the Text. Oblong 4to., 6s.
- *THE GOLLIWOGG'S BICYCLE CLUB.* Illustrated by FLORENCE K. UPTON, with words by BERTHA UPTON. With Coloured Plates and numerous Illustrations in the Text. Oblong 4to., 6s.

Wordsworth.—*THE SNOW GARDEN, AND OTHER FAIRY TALES FOR CHILDREN.* By ELIZABETH WORDSWORTH. With 10 Illustrations by TREVOR HADDON. Crown 8vo., 5s.

Longmans' Series of Books for Girls.
Price 2s. 6d. each.

- *ATELIER (THE) DU LYS:* or, an Art Student in the Reign of Terror.
- BY THE SAME AUTHOR.
- *MADEMOISELLE MORI:* a Tale of Modern Rome.
- *IN THE OLDEN TIME:* a Tale of the Peasant War in Germany.
- *THE YOUNGER SISTER.*
- *THAT CHILD.*
- *UNDER A CLOUD.*
- *HESTER'S VENTURE.*
- *THE FIDDLER OF LUGAU.*
- *A CHILD OF THE REVOLUTION.*

- *ATHERSTONE PRIORY.* By L. N. COMYN.
- *THE STORY OF A SPRING MORNING,* etc. By Mrs. MOLESWORTH. Illustrated.
- *THE PALACE IN THE GARDEN.* By Mrs. MOLESWORTH. Illustrated.
- *NEIGHBOURS.* By Mrs. MOLESWORTH.
- *THE THIRD MISS ST. QUENTIN.* By Mrs. MOLESWORTH.
- *VERY YOUNG; AND QUITE ANOTHER STORY.* Two Stories. By JEAN INGELOW.
- *CAN THIS BE LOVE?* By LOUISA PARR.
- *KEITH DERAMORE.* By the Author of 'Miss Molly'.
- *SIDNEY.* By MARGARET DELAND.
- *AN ARRANGED MARRIAGE.* By DOROTHEA GERARD.
- *LAST WORDS TO GIRLS ON LIFE AT SCHOOL AND AFTER SCHOOL.* By MARIA GREY.

STRAY THOUGHTS FOR GIRLS. By LUCY H. M. SOULSBY, Head Mistress of Oxford High School. 16mo., 1s. 6d. net.

The Silver Library.

CROWN 8VO. 3s. 6d. EACH VOLUME.

Arnold's (Sir Edwin) Seas and Lands. With 71 Illustrations. 3s. 6d.

Bagehot's (W.) Biographical Studies. 3s. 6d.
Bagehot's (W.) Economic Studies. 3s. 6d.
Bagehot's (W.) Literary Studies. With Portrait. 3 vols. 3s. 6d. each.

Baker's (Sir S. W.) Eight Years in Ceylon. With 6 Illustrations. 3s. 6d.

Baker's (Sir S. W.) Rifle and Hound in Ceylon. With 6 Illustrations. 3s. 6d.

Baring-Gould's (Rev. S.) Curious Myths of the Middle Ages. 3s. 6d.

Baring-Gould's (Rev. S.) Origin and Development of Religious Belief. 2 vols. 3s. 6d. each.

Becker's (Prof.) Gallus: or, Roman Scenes in the Time of Augustus. Illustrated. 3s. 6d.

Becker's (Prof.) Charicles: or, Illustrations of the Private Life of the Ancient Greeks. Illustrated. 3s. 6d.

Bent's (J. T.) The Ruined Cities of Mashonaland. With 117 Illustrations. 3s. 6d.

Brassey's (Lady) A Voyage in the 'Sunbeam'. With 66 Illustrations. 3s. 6d.

Butler's (Edward A.) Our Household Insects. With 7 Plates and 113 Illustrations in the Text. 3s. 6d.

Clodd's (E.) Story of Creation: a Plain Account of Evolution. With 77 Illustrations. 3s. 6d.

Conybeare (Rev. W. J.) and Howson's (Very Rev. J. S.) Life and Epistles of St. Paul. 46 Illustrations. 3s. 6d.

Dougall's (L.) Beggars All: a Novel. 3s. 6d.

Doyle's (A. Conan) Micah Clarke. A Tale of Monmouth's Rebellion. 10 Illusts. 3s. 6d.

Doyle's (A. Conan) The Captain of the Polestar, and other Tales. 3s. 6d.

Doyle's (A. Conan) The Refugees: A Tale of Two Continents. With 25 Illustrations. 3s. 6d.

Froude's (J. A.) Short Studies on Great Subjects. 4 vols. 3s. 6d. each.

Froude's (J. A.) Thomas Carlyle: a History of his Life.
1795-1835. 2 vols. 7s.
1834-1881. 2 vols. 7s.

Froude's (J. A.) Cæsar: a Sketch. 3s. 6d.

Froude's (J. A.) The Spanish Story of the Armada, and other Essays. 3s. 6d.

Froude's (J. A.) The Two Chiefs of Dunboy: an Irish Romance of the Last Century. 3s. 6d.

Froude's (J. A.) The History of England, from the Fall of Wolsey to the Defeat of the Spanish Armada. 12 vols. 3s. 6d. each.

Froude's (J. A.) The English in Ireland. 3 vols. 10s. 6d.

Gleig's (Rev. G. R.) Life of the Duke of Wellington. With Portrait. 3s. 6d.

Greville's (C. C. F.) Journal of the Reigns of King George IV., King William IV., and Queen Victoria. 8 vols., 3s. 6d. each.

Haggard's (H. R.) She: A History of Adventure. 32 Illustrations. 3s. 6d.

Haggard's (H. R.) Allan Quatermain. With 20 Illustrations. 3s. 6d.

Haggard's (H. R.) Colonel Quaritch, V.C.: a Tale of Country Life. 3s. 6d.

Haggard's (H. R.) Cleopatra. With 29 Illustrations. 3s. 6d.

Haggard's (H. R.) Eric Brighteyes. With 51 Illustrations. 3s. 6d.

Haggard's (H. R.) Beatrice. 3s. 6d.

Haggard's (H. R.) Allan's Wife. With 34 Illustrations. 3s. 6d.

Haggard's (H. R.) Montezuma's Daughter. With 25 Illustrations. 3s. 6d.

Haggard's (H. R.) The Witch's Head. With 16 Illustrations. 3s. 6d.

Haggard's (H. R.) Mr. Meeson's Will. With 16 Illustrations. 3s. 6d.

Haggard's (H. R.) Nada the Lily. With 23 Illustrations. 3s. 6d.

Haggard's (H. R.) Dawn. With 16 Illusts. 3s. 6d.

Haggard (H. R.) and Lang's (A.) The World's Desire. With 27 Illustrations. 3s. 6d.

Harte's (Bret) In the Carquinez Woods and other Stories. 3s. 6d.

Helmholtz's (Hermann von) Popular Lectures on Scientific Subjects. With 68 Illustrations. 2 vols. 3s. 6d. each.

Hornung's (E. W.) The Unbidden Guest. 3s. 6d.

Howitt's (W.) Visits to Remarkable Places 80 Illustrations. 3s. 6d.

Jefferies' (R.) The Story of My Heart: My Autobiography. With Portrait. 3s. 6d.

Jefferies' (R.) Field and Hedgerow. With Portrait. 3s. 6d.

Jefferies' (R.) Red Deer. 17 Illustrations. 3s. 6d.

Jefferies' (R.) Wood Magic: a Fable. With Frontispiece and Vignette by E. V. B. 3s. 6d.

Jefferies (R.) The Toilers of the Field. With Portrait from the Bust in Salisbury Cathedral. 3s. 6d.

Knight's (E. F.) The Cruise of the 'Alerte': the Narrative of a Search for Treasure on the Desert Island of Trinidad. With 2 Maps and 23 Illustrations. 3s. 6d.

Knight's (E. F.) Where Three Empires Meet: a Narrative of Recent Travel in Kashmir, Western Tibet, Baltistan, Gilgit. With a Map and 54 Illustrations. 3s. 6d.

Knight's (E. F.) The 'Falcon' on the Baltic: a Coasting Voyage from Hammersmith to Copenhagen in a Three-Ton Yacht. With Map and 11 Illustrations. 3s. 6d.

Lang's (A.) Angling Sketches. 20 Illustrations. 3s. 6d.

Lang's (A.) Custom and Myth: Studies of Early Usage and Belief. 3s. 6d.

Lang's (Andrew) Cock Lane and Common-Sense. With a New Preface. 3s. 6d.

The Silver Library—*continued.*

Lees (J. A.) and Clutterbuck's (W. J.) B. C. 1887, A Ramble in British Columbia. With Maps and 75 Illustrations. 3s. 6d.

Macaulay's (Lord) Essays and Lays of Ancient Rome. With Portrait and Illustration. 3s. 6d.

Macleod's (H. D.) Elements of Banking. 3s. 6d.

Marshman's (J. C.) Memoirs of Sir Henry Havelock. 3s. 6d.

Max Müller's (F.) India, what can it teach us? 3s. 6d.

Max Müller's (F.) Introduction to the Science of Religion. 3s. 6d.

Merivale's (Dean) History of the Romans under the Empire. 8 vols. 3s. 6d. each.

Mill's (J. S.) Political Economy. 3s. 6d.

Mill's (J. S.) System of Logic. 3s. 6d.

Milner's (Geo.) Country Pleasures: the Chronicle of a Year chiefly in a Garden. 3s. 6d.

Nansen's (F.) The First Crossing of Greenland. With Illustrations and a Map. 3s. 6d.

Phillipps-Wolley's (C.) Snap: a Legend of the Lone Mountain. 13 Illustrations. 3s. 6d.

Proctor's (R. A.) The Orbs Around Us. 3s. 6d.

Proctor's (R. A.) The Expanse of Heaven. 3s. 6d.

Proctor's (R. A.) Other Worlds than Ours. 3s. 6d.

Proctor's (R. A.) Other Suns than Ours. 3s. 6d.

Proctor's (R. A.) Rough Ways made Smooth. 3s. 6d.

Proctor's (R. A.) Pleasant Ways in Science. 3s. 6d.

Proctor's (R. A.) Myths and Marvels of Astronomy. 3s. 6d.

Proctor's (R. A.) Nature Studies. 3s. 6d.

Proctor's (R. A,) Leisure Readings. By R. A. PROCTOR, EDWARD CLODD, ANDREW WILSON, THOMAS FOSTER, and A. C. RANYARD. With Illustrations. 3s. 6d.

Rossetti's (Maria F.) A Shadow of Dante. 3s. 6d.

Smith's (R. Bosworth) Carthage and the Carthaginians. With Maps, Plans, &c. 3s. 6d.

Stanley's (Bishop) Familiar History of Birds. 160 Illustrations. 3s. 6d.

Stevenson's (R. L.) The Strange Case of Dr. Jekyll and Mr. Hyde; with other Fables. 3s. 6d.

Stevenson (R. L.) and Osbourne's (Ll.) The Wrong Box. 3s. 6d.

Stevenson (Robert Louis) and Stevenson's (Fanny van de Grift) More New Arabian Nights.—The Dynamiter. 3s. 6d.

Weyman's (Stanley J.) The House of the Wolf: a Romance. 3s. 6d.

Wood's (Rev. J. G.) Petland Revisited. With 33 Illustrations. 3s. 6d.

Wood's (Rev. J. G.) Strange Dwellings. With 60 Illustrations. 3s. 6d.

Wood's (Rev. J. G.) Out of Doors. With 11 Illustrations. 3s. 6d.

Cookery, Domestic Management, Gardening, &c.

Acton.— *MODERN COOKERY.* By ELIZA ACTON. With 150 Woodcuts. Fcp. 8vo., 4s. 6d.

Bull (THOMAS, M.D.).

HINTS TO MOTHERS ON THE MANAGEMENT OF THEIR HEALTH DURING THE PERIOD OF PREGNANCY. Fcp. 8vo., 1s. 6d.

THE MATERNAL MANAGEMENT OF CHILDREN IN HEALTH AND DISEASE. Fcp. 8vo., 1s. 6d.

De Salis (MRS.).

CAKES AND CONFECTIONS À LA MODE. Fcp. 8vo., 1s. 6d.

DOGS: A Manual for Amateurs. Fcp. 8vo., 1s. 6d.

DRESSED GAME AND POULTRY À LA MODE. Fcp. 8vo., 1s. 6d.

De Salis (MRS.).—*continued.*

DRESSED VEGETABLES À LA MODE. Fcp. 8vo., 1s. 6d.

DRINKS À LA MODE. Fcp. 8vo., 1s. 6d.

ENTRÉES À LA MODE. Fcp. 8vo., 1s. 6d.

FLORAL DECORATIONS. Fcp. 8vo., 1s. 6d.

GARDENING À LA MODE. Fcp. 8vo. Part I., Vegetables, 1s. 6d. Part II., Fruits, 1s. 6d.

NATIONAL VIANDS À LA MODE. Fcp. 8vo., 1s. 6d.

NEW-LAID EGGS. Fcp. 8vo., 1s. 6d.

OYSTERS À LA MODE. Fcp. 8vo., 1s. 6d.

Cookery, Domestic Management, &c.—*continued.*

De Salis (Mrs.).—*continued.*

Puddings and Pastry à la Mode. Fcp. 8vo., 1s. 6d.

Savouries à la Mode. Fcp. 8vo., 1s. 6d.

Soups and Dressed Fish à la Mode. Fcp. 8vo., 1s. 6d.

Sweets and Supper Dishes à la Mode. Fcp. 8vo., 1s. 6d.

Tempting Dishes for Small Incomes. Fcp. 8vo., 1s. 6d.

Wrinkles and Notions for Every Household. Crown 8vo., 1s. 6d.

Lear.—*Maigre Cookery.* By H. L. Sidney Lear. 16mo., 2s.

Poole.—*Cookery for the Diabetic.* By W. H. and Mrs. Poole. With Preface by Dr. Pavy. Fcp. 8vo., 2s. 6d.

Walker (Jane H.).

A Book for Every Woman. Part I., The Management of Children in Health and out of Health. Crown 8vo., 2s. 6d.

A Handbook for Mothers: being being Simple Hints to Women on the Management of their Health during Pregnancy and Confinement, together with Plain Directions as to the Care of Infants. Crown 8vo., 2s. 6d.

Miscellaneous and Critical Works.

Allingham.—*Varieties in Prose.* By William Allingham. 3 vols. Cr. 8vo., 18s. (Vols. 1 and 2, Rambles, by Patricius Walker. Vol. 3, Irish Sketches, etc.)

Armstrong.—*Essays and Sketches.* By Edmund J. Armstrong. Fcp. 8vo., 5s.

Bagehot.—*Literary Studies.* By Walter Bagehot. With Portrait. 3 vols. Crown 8vo., 3s. 6d. each.

Baring-Gould.—*Curious Myths of the Middle Ages.* By Rev. S. Baring-Gould. Crown 8vo., 3s. 6d.

Baynes.—*Shakespeare Studies,* and other Essays. By the late Thomas Spencer Baynes, LL.B., LL.D. With a Biographical Preface by Professor Lewis Campbell. Crown 8vo., 7s. 6d.

Boyd (A. K. H.) ('A.K.H.B.').

And see MISCELLANEOUS THEOLOGICAL WORKS, *p.* 32.

Autumn Holidays of a Country Parson. Crown 8vo., 3s. 6d.

Commonplace Philosopher. Cr. 8vo., 3s. 6d.

Critical Essays of a Country Parson. Crown 8vo., 3s. 6d.

East Coast Days and Memories. Crown 8vo., 3s. 6d.

Landscapes, Churches, and Moralities. Crown 8vo., 3s. 6d.

Leisure Hours in Town. Crown 8vo., 3s. 6d.

Boyd (A. K. H.) ('A.K.H.B.').—*continued.*

Lessons of Middle Age. Crown 8vo., 3s. 6d.

Our Little Life. Two Series. Crown 8vo., 3s. 6d. each.

Our Homely Comedy: and Tragedy. Crown 8vo., 3s. 6d.

Recreations of a Country Parson. Three Series. Crown 8vo., 3s. 6d. each. Also First Series. Popular Edition. 8vo., 6d. Sewed.

Butler (Samuel).

Erewhon. Crown 8vo., 5s.

The Fair Haven. A Work in Defence of the Miraculous Element in our Lord's Ministry. Cr. 8vo., 7s. 6d.

Life and Habit. An Essay after a Completer View of Evolution. Cr. 8vo., 7s. 6d.

Evolution, Old and New. Cr. 8vo., 10s. 6d.

Alps and Sanctuaries of Piedmont and Canton Ticino. Illustrated. Pott 4to., 10s. 6d.

Luck, or Cunning, as the Main Means of Organic Modification? Cr. 8vo., 7s. 6d.

Ex Voto. An Account of the Sacro Monte or New Jerusalem at Varallo-Sesia. Crown 8vo., 10s. 6d.

Miscellaneous and Critical Works—*continued.*

Gwilt.—*An Encyclopædia of Architecture.* By Joseph Gwilt, F.S.A. Illustrated with more than 1100 Engravings on Wood. Revised (1888), with Alterations and Considerable Additions by Wyatt Papworth. 8vo., £2 12s. 6d.

Hamlin.—*A Text-Book of the History of Architecture.* By A. D. F. Hamlin, A.M., Adjunct-Professor of Architecture in the School of Mines, Columbia College. With 229 Illustrations. Crown 8vo., 7s. 6d.

Haweis.—*Music and Morals.* By the Rev. H. R. Haweis. With Portrait of the Author, and numerous Illustrations, Facsimiles, and Diagrams. Crown 8vo., 7s. 6d.

Indian Ideals (No. 1).

Nârada Sûtra: an Inquiry into Love (Bhakti-Jijnâsâ). Translated from the Sanskrit, with an Independendent Commentary, by E. T. Sturdy. Crown 8vo., 2s. 6d. net.

Jefferies.—(Richard).

Field and Hedgerow: With Portrait. Crown 8vo., 3s. 6d.

The Story of My Heart: my Autobiography. With Portrait and New Preface by C. J. Longman. Crown 8vo., 3s. 6d.

Red Deer. With 17 Illustrations by J. Charlton and H. Tunaly. Crown 8vo., 3s. 6d.

The Toilers of the Field. With Portrait from the Bust in Salisbury Cathedral. Crown 8vo., 3s. 6d.

Wood Magic: a Fable. With Frontispiece and Vignette by E. V. B. Crown 8vo., 3s. 6d.

Jefferies (Richard)—*continued.*

Thoughts from the Writings of Richard Jefferies. Selected by H. S. Hoole Waylen. 16mo., 3s. 6d.

Johnson.—*The Patentee's Manual:* a Treatise on the Law and Practice of Letters Patent. By J. & J. H. Johnson, Patent Agents, &c. 8vo., 10s. 6d.

Lang (Andrew).

Letters to Dead Authors. Fcp. 8vo., 2s. 6d. net.

Books and Bookmen. With 2 Coloured Plates and 17 Illustrations. Fcp. 8vo., 2s. 6d. net.

Old Friends. Fcp. 8vo., 2s. 6d. net.

Letters on Literature. Fcp. 8vo., 2s. 6d. net.

Cock Lane and Common Sense. Crown 8vo., 3s. 6d.

Macfarren.—*Lectures on Harmony.* By Sir George A. Macfarren. 8vo., 12s.

Max Müller (F).

India: What can it Teach Us? Crown 8vo., 3s. 6d.

Chips from a German Workshop.

Vol. I. Recent Essays and Addresses. Crown 8vo., 6s. 6d. net.

Vol. II. Biographical Essays. Crown 8vo., 6s. 6d. net.

Vol. III. Essays on Language and Literature. Crown 8vo., 6s. 6d. net.

Vol. IV. Essays on Mythology and Folk Lore. Crown 8vo, 8s. 6d. net.

Milner.—*Country Pleasures:* the Chronicle of a Year chiefly in a Garden. By George Milner. Crown 8vo., 3s. 6d.

Miscellaneous and Critical Works—*continued.*

Morris (WILLIAM).

SIGNS OF CHANGE. Seven Lectures delivered on various Occasions. Post 8vo., 4s. 6d.

HOPES AND FEARS FOR ART. Five Lectures delivered in Birmingham, London, &c., in 1878-1881. Crown 8vo., 4s. 6d.

Orchard.—*THE ASTRONOMY OF 'MILTON'S PARADISE LOST'.* By THOMAS N. ORCHARD, M.D., Member of the British Astronomical Association. With 13 Illustrations. 8vo., 15s.

Poore.—*ESSAYS ON RURAL HYGIENE.* By GEORGE VIVIAN POORE, M.D., F.R.C.P. With 13 Illustrations. Crown 8vo., 6s. 6d.

Proctor.—*STRENGTH :* How to get Strong and keep Strong, with Chapters on Rowing and Swimming, Fat, Age, and the Waist. By R. A. PROCTOR. With 9 Illustrations. Crown 8vo., 2s.

Richardson.—*NATIONAL HEALTH.* A Review of the Works of Sir Edwin Chadwick, K.C.B. By Sir B. W. RICHARDSON, M.D. Crown 8vo., 4s. 6d.

Rossetti.—*A SHADOW OF DANTE :* being an Essay towards studying Himself, his World and his Pilgrimage. By MARIA FRANCESCA ROSSETTI. With Frontispiece by DANTE GABRIEL ROSSETTI. Crown 8vo., 3s. 6d.

Solovyoff.—*A MODERN PRIESTESS OF ISIS (MADAME BLAVATSKY).* Abridged and Translated on Behalf of the Society for Psychical Research from the Russian of VSEVOLOD SERGYEEVICH SOLOVYOFF. By WALTER LEAF, Litt. D. With Appendices. Crown 8vo., 6s.

Stevens.—*ON THE STOWAGE OF SHIPS AND THEIR CARGOES.* With Information regarding Freights, Charter-Parties, &c. By ROBERT WHITE STEVENS, Associate-Member of the Institute of Naval Architects. 8vo., 21s.

West.—*WILLS, AND HOW NOT TO MAKE THEM.* With a Selection of Leading Cases. By B. B. WEST, Author of "Half-Hours with the Millionaires". Fcp. 8vo., 2s. 6d.

Miscellaneous Theological Works.

*** *For Church of England and Roman Catholic Works see* MESSRS. LONGMANS & CO.'s *Special Catalogues.*

Balfour. — *THE FOUNDATIONS OF BELIEF :* being Notes Introductory to the Study of Theology. By the Right Hon. ARTHUR J. BALFOUR, M.P. 8vo., 12s. 6d.

Bird (ROBERT).

A CHILD'S RELIGION. Cr. 8vo., 2s.

JOSEPH, THE DREAMER. Crown 8vo., 5s.

JESUS, THE CARPENTER OF NAZARETH. Crown 8vo., 5s.

To be had also in Two Parts, price 2s. 6d. each.

Part I. GALILEE AND THE LAKE OF GENNESARET.

Part II. JERUSALEM AND THE PERÆA.

Boyd (A. K. H.) ('A.K.H.B.').

OCCASIONAL AND IMMEMORIAL DAYS : Discourses. Crown 8vo., 7s. 6d.

COUNSEL AND COMFORT FROM A CITY PULPIT. Crown 8vo., 3s. 6d.

SUNDAY AFTERNOONS IN THE PARISH CHURCH OF A SCOTTISH UNIVERSITY CITY. Crown 8vo., 3s. 6d.

CHANGED ASPECTS OF UNCHANGED TRUTHS. Crown 8vo., 3s. 6d.

GRAVER THOUGHTS OF A COUNTRY PARSON. Three Series. Crown 8vo., 3s. 6d. each.

PRESENT DAY THOUGHTS. Crown 8vo., 3s. 6d.

SEASIDE MUSINGS. Cr. 8vo., 3s. 6d.

'TO MEET THE DAY' through the Christian Year : being a Text of Scripture, with an Original Meditation and a Short Selection in Verse for Every Day. Crown 8vo., 4s. 6d.

Miscellaneous Theological Works—*continued*.

De la Saussaye.—*A Manual of the Science of Religion.* By Professor Chantepie de la Saussaye. Translated by Mrs. Colyer Fergusson (*née* Max Müller). Crown 8vo., 12s. 6d.

Gibson.—*The Abbé de Lamennais. and the Liberal Catholic Movement in France.* By the Hon. W. Gibson.

Kalisch (M. M., Ph.D.).

Bible Studies. Part I. Prophecies of Balaam. 8vo., 10s. 6d. Part II. The Book of Jonah. 8vo., 10s. 6d.

Commentary on the Old Testament: with a New Translation. Vol. I. Genesis. 8vo., 18s. Or adapted for the General Reader. 12s. Vol. II. Exodus. 15s. Or adapted for the General Reader. 12s. Vol. III. Leviticus, Part I. 15s. Or adapted for the General Reader. 8s. Vol. IV. Leviticus, Part II. 15s. Or adapted for the General Reader. 8s.

Macdonald (George).

Unspoken Sermons. Three Series. Crown 8vo., 3s. 6d. each.

The Miracles of our Lord. Crown 8vo., 3s. 6d.

Martineau (James).

Hours of Thought on Sacred Things: Sermons, 2 vols. Crown 8vo., 3s. 6d. each.

Endeavours after the Christian Life. Discourses. Crown 8vo., 7s. 6d.

The Seat of Authority in Religion. 8vo., 14s.

Essays, Reviews, and Addresses. 4 Vols. Crown 8vo., 7s. 6d. each.
I. Personal; Political. II. Ecclesiastical; Historical. III. Theological; Philosophical. IV. Academical; Religious.

Home Prayers, with *Two Services* for Public Worship. Crown 8vo., 3s. 6d.

10,000/9/96.

Max Müller (F.).

Hibbert Lectures on the Origin and Growth of Religion, as illustrated by the Religions of India. Cr. 8vo., 7s. 6d.

Introduction to the Science of Religion: Four Lectures delivered at the Royal Institution. Crown 8vo., 3s. 6d.

Natural Religion. The Gifford Lectures, delivered before the University of Glasgow in 1888. Crown 8vo., 10s. 6d.

Physical Religion. The Gifford Lectures, delivered before the University of Glasgow in 1890. Crown 8vo., 10s. 6d.

Anthropological Religion. The Gifford Lectures, delivered before the University of Glasgow in 1891. Cr. 8vo., 10s. 6d.

Theosophy, or Psychological Religion. The Gifford Lectures, delivered before the University of Glasgow in 1892. Crown 8vo., 10s. 6d.

Three Lectures on the Vedânta Philosophy, delivered at the Royal Institution in March, 1894. 8vo., 5s.

Phillips. — *The Teaching of the Vedas.* What Light does it Throw on the Origin and Development of Religion? By Maurice Phillips, London Mission, Madras. Crown 8vo., 6s.

Romanes.—*Thoughts on Religion.* By George J. Romanes, LL.D., F.R.S. Crown 8vo., 4s. 6d.

Supernatural Religion: an Inquiry into the Reality of Divine Revelation. 3 vols. 8vo., 36s.

Reply (A) to Dr. Lightfoot's Essays. By the Author of 'Supernatural Religion'. 8vo., 6s.

The Gospel according to St. Peter: a Study. By the Author of 'Supernatural Religion'. 8vo., 6s.

Vivekananda.—*Yoga Philosophy:* Lectures delivered in New York, Winter of 1895-96, by the Swami Vivekananda, on Raja Yoga; or, Conquering the Internal Nature; also Patanjali's Yoga Aphorisms, with Commentaries. Crown 8vo, 3s. 6d.

www.ingramcontent.com/pod-product-compliance
Lightning Source LLC
Chambersburg PA
CBHW030254240426
43673CB00040B/972